ROSALIE DU PONT;

OR,

TREASON IN THE CAMP:

A STORY

OF THE REVOLUTION.

By EMERSON BENNETT,

AUTHOR OF "PRAIRIE FLOWER," "LENI LEOTI," "FOREST ROSE," "MIKE FINK," "ELLA BARNWELL," "FAIR REBEL," "FEMALE SPY," ETC., ETC.

CINCINNATI:
PUBLISHED BY U. P. JAMES,
No. 177 RACE STREET.

The Course of Time. A Poem. By ROBERT POLLOK, A. M. With a Memoir of the Author, by Wm. Livingston Prall, Esq. A copious Index and an Analysis prefixed to each book. 32mo, cloth binding. **Price, 50 cents.**

Few modern poems exist, which at once attained such acceptance and celebrity as Pollok's Course of Time. Originally issued without a name, preface, or any other appendage, its lofty themes, exciting spirit, melodious verse, and all-powerful effects upon the reader, completely silenced criticism, and secured general and lasting popularity.

Lady of the Lake. A Poem in six cantos. By SIR WALTER SCOTT. Last revised edition, with an Introduction, Glossary, and copious Notes, by the Author. 32mo, cloth binding. **Price 50 cents.**

"There is a richness and spirit in this poem —a profusion of incident, and shifting brilliancy of coloring that reminds us of the witchery of Ariosto—and a constant elasticity and occasional energy, which seem to belong more particularly to the author now before us."—*Jeffrey.*

Paul and Virginia. From the French. By J. B. H. DE SAINT PIERRE. 32mo, cloth, gilt. **Price 35 cents.**

The Enchanted Plants. Being Fables in Verse, by MADAME MONTOLIEU, on the various Sentiments personified in the Flowers and Plants. 32mo, cloth binding. **Price 35 cents.**

The Songs of the Affections. By MRS. HEMANS. A selection of beautiful pieces from the works of this gifted writer. 32mo, cloth, gilt. **Price 35 cents.**

Pope's Essay on Man. To which is added his celebrated Universal Prayer. 32mo, bound. **Price 15 cents.**

Also, an edition of the same with Miscellaneous Poems, Epitaphs, etc. 32mo, cloth, gilt. **Price 35 cents.**

LETTER-WRITERS.

The Pocket or Popular Letter-Writer, containing a great variety of original and selected Letters on the subjects of Love, Courtship, Marriage, Friendship, Relationship, Cards of Invitation, Business, etc., etc., with a selection of Correspondence from standard authors. Also, a Dictionary of Poetical Quotations from the standard poets, alphabetically arranged. for the use of ladies and gentlemen. 32mo, **Price 35 cents;**

In making up this volume, the aim has been to present all the ordinary forms of correspondence, clothed in good language, and worded in accordance with the rules of English Grammar. The selected letters have been chosen with a view to illustrate the ease and fluency so necessary to render any correspondence pleasant; while the *Dictionary of Quotations*, a new feature in works of this class, will afford many opportunities of poetical illustrations of the writer's ideas.

The Instructive Letter-Writer, designed for the improvement of ladies and gentlemen, containing a variety of Letters on Business, Love, Courtship, Marriage, Friendship, and miscellaneous subjects; adapted to all ages and circumstances. 32mo, **Price 35 cents.**

American Fashionable Letter-Writer, original and selected, containing a variety of Letters on Business, Love, Courtship, Marriage, Relationship, Friendship, and VALENTINES, with forms of Complimentary Cards. To which are prefixed directions for Letter-Writing, and Rules for Composition. 32mo, **Price 35 cents.**

Ready Reckoner; OR, FEDERAL CALCULATOR; giving the amount in dollars and cents of any number of articles from one to one thousand, at any price from a fourth of a cent to ten dollars, and equally applicable to many other species of calculation, as is shown in the explanation. To which are added many useful tables and forms. Half bound. **Price 25 cents.**

SONG BOOKS.

The Eolian Songster. A collection of the best Sentimental, Patriotic, Naval, and Comic Songs, accompanied with Music. 16mo, **Price** paper cover **35 cents.**

United States Songster. A choice collection of the most Popular Songs. as sung by celebrated performers. 32mo, **Price 20 cents;** paper covers,

The National American Songster, containing a great variety of Popular, Patriotic, National, and Sentimental Songs. 32mo, . **Price 25 cents.**

The Negro Melodist, containing a great variety of the most Popular Airs, Songs, and Melodies, Comic, Humorous, Sentimental, and Patriotic. 32mo, **Price 25 cents.**

The New Popular Forget-Me-Not Songster, containing a choice collection of Ballad Songs. 32mo, **Price 25 cents.**

The New Negro Forget-Me-Not Songster, containing a choice collection of Negro Songs, Ballads, etc., as sung in concerts. 32mo, **Price 25 cents.**

[*For other Song Books see "DIME BOOKS."*]

Æsop's Fables, with upward of one hundred and fifty engravings. 32mo, cloth. **Price 50 cents.**

ROSALIE DU PONT;

OR,

TREASON IN THE CAMP:

A STORY OF THE REVOLUTION.

By EMERSON BENNETT,

AUTHOR OF "FAIR REBEL," "FEMALE SPY," "PRAIRIE FLOWER," "LENI LEOTI," "MIKE FINK," "FOREST ROSE," "ELLA BARNWELL," ETC., ETC.

CINCINNATI:
PUBLISHED BY U. P. JAMES,
No. 177 RACE STREET.

ROSALIE DU PONT;

OR,

TREASON IN THE CAMP.

CHAPTER I.

THE ASTROLOGER AND OUR HEROINE.

It was on a fine, pleasant morning, toward the latter part of September, 1780, that a heavy double knock resounded through the elegant mansion of Graham Percy, in Queen-street. The servant who opened the door, beheld a stranger, dressed in deep black, with a strongly-marked, deadly-pale countenance, and small, black, fiery eyes, that seemed capable of penetrating to his very soul.

"I am called Dr. Montague," said the stranger.

"Ay, yes, sir—walk in, sir," returned the servant, bowing respectfully. "My young mistress is expecting you, and has given orders to have you at once conducted to her presence."

"Lead the way," rejoined the doctor; and he followed the servant up a broad flight of stairs, to a beautiful little chamber, richly and tastefully furnished.

In one corner of this chamber stood a high-post mahogany bedstead, surrounded by silk curtains, and on a bed of down reposed the patient. A table stood near, covered with vials, pill-boxes, and the etceteras of a sick-room; and the very air had that peculiar medicinal smell, with which almost every one has, sometime in the course of his life, been made familiar.

As the physician entered the room, the silk curtain at the head of the bed was thrust aside by the patient, and at the same moment a silvery voice said to the servant:

"You may retire, and let no one intrude, as I wish to see the Doctor alone."

"How does your ladyship find yourself this morning?" inquired the physician, when the servant had withdrawn.

"Better, much better, I thank you," replied the same silvery voice. "But, Signor Carlini, you must not forget to address me as Miss Du Pont—for none of the domestics know the secret of my rank, and might be surprised should they overhear you."

"I will remember, Miss Du Pont," replied the astrologer; "and for the same reason you must not forget that I am Dr. Montague."

"Ah, true, Doctor—we have both made a mistake, and must be careful in future. You find me much altered since you saw me last."

"Some thinner, my lady—ah! Miss Du Pont, I mean—but not so much as I had counted on, from the length of your sickness."

Rosalie Du Pont was much thinner and paler than we first described her to the reader in the "Female Spy;" but still she was very, very beautiful, and her dark eyes seemed already to have regained their original lustre and vivacity. For two weeks had she been confined to her bed by fever, and much of the time had she been delirious; but she was now convalescent, and rapidly regaining her strength. Three days previous to the time we now bring her again before the reader, she had made her first effort to sit up during her sickness; and though it was only for a few minutes then yet so rapidly had she since gained strength, that she could now indulge three hours in succession in a sitting posture.

"I suppose," pursued Rosalie, "you feel somewhat curious to know why I sent for you?" and she raised herself in bed; "but the truth is, Doctor, I am eager for news, and my friends are too kind here to tell me any thing. I knew you would, if I could get you here, and therefore I sent you a note by my mute, and gave directions to all the servants, that should one Dr. Montague call, to conduct him hither without delay."

"And have you then been kept ignorant of all the important events that have taken place?" inquired Carlini, with an air of surprise.

"Of every thing, sir—I have been treated like a child."

"But did not your mute—"

"Munee has been absent for several days," interrupted Rosalie, "and only came back this morning, when I immediately sent him for you. The poor lad (the astrologer was ignorant of the sex of Munee) took on so about me, that my aunt, on her return, made some excuse to send him out of town, for fear he might excite, and so do me harm. I am even ignorant whether Sir Henry's plot succeeded or not."

"It was on the point of succeeding, when Andre was taken prisoner."

"Major Andre a prisoner?" cried Rosalie, with a start of surprise.

"Ay, and the stars proclaim his doom."

"When was he taken? and where?"

"On the twenty-third, near Tarrytown. General Arnold, who escaped, and arrived in the Vulture this morning, brought the sad intelligence to General Clinton."

"Then the traitor has escaped, and poor Andre will have to suffer?"

"Ay and not he only, I fear," said Carlini, sadly

"What do you mean?"

"Our messenger!"

"Well, what of him?"

"Heavens! and have you not heard of that even? He was taken attempting to pass the British lines."

"Well? well?"

"He swallowed the ball, as I instructed him to do; but the sentry saw him, informed his commander, an emetic was administered, the ball thrown up, broke open, and the paper I had prepared was found inside."

"Oh! this is sad news!—and what was done with the poor lad?"

"He was taken before Clinton and examined, and a pardon offered him if he would reveal his accomplices—for Clinton rightly conjectures he is not a principal in the affair."

"Well, well, what said he?"

"At first he peremptorily refused; but on being informed that, unless he revealed his dangerous secret he should be led forth to immediate execution, he begged for time to consider the matter; and Sir Henry, hoping his fears might overcome his scruples, ordered him to be closely confined in the jail dungeon, and questioned every day, until the whole truth should be elicited."

"Then he is still alive?"

"Yes, but will not be long, unless liberated, for the General limited his time to ten days, and that expires to-morrow morning."

"And the poor youth has revealed nothing?"

"Not a word; though he has cunningly led his captors to believe he would, and thus has prolonged his life almost to its utmost limit."

"And you think he will reveal nothing?"

"I am certain of it."

"Then what will become of him?"

"Unless freed to-night, he will swing to-morrow."

"Oh, heaven! this must not be!" said Rosalie, shuddering.

"No, it must not, shall not be!" returned the astrologer, firmly, compressing his lips.

"Ha! can you save him?"

"I must."

"How?"

"He must be liberated to-night, by one means or another."

"Surely you do not mean—"

"That he shall *not* die on the gibbet while Carlo Carlini lives," interrupted the astrologer, speaking in a low, determined tone.

"Oh, heaven! I am ruined!"

"How so, lady?"

"You will make a rash attempt to save the youth, will fail, and thus shall I be exposed."

"But how then, my lady?" returned the astrologer, in a cold, offended tone, drawing himself up proudly. "Dost think me a base born churl, that will betray thee?"

"O, no, no—I meant not that," replied Rosalie, quickly and earnestly; "but should you be taken, Doctor, your place will be searched, and I am fearful something may transpire to fasten suspicion upon me."

"Be not alarmed, Miss Rosalie," rejoined Carlini, in an altered tone. "I have taken care to destroy every proof that I have a single confederate. Every scrap of writing that has been sent me, by any one leagued in our cause, has been copied, without name or date, and the original destroyed."

"Ah, Doctor, you relieve my mind of much uneasiness. But you are sure, Doctor, that *all* have been destroyed?"

"I am."

"And now tell me what you propose in regard to this youth—how will you proceed to save him!"

Carlini drew close to the bed, and for a few minutes spoke rapidly, in a tone barely audible.

"Ah! I fear it will not succeed," replied Rosalie—"but I will pray for your success."

"If I fail," returned the other, impressively, "Rosalie Du Pont and Carlo Carlini have met for the last time. I have consulted the stars, and found life and death, as it were, in an equal balance, so that my mind is made up for the worst."

"Ha!" exclaimed Rosalie, a new thought striking her—"I can save this youth without any risk: strange I have not thought of it before!"

"How? how?" cried Carlini.

"That ring—behold that ring!" and Rosalie extended her white beautiful hand, and pointed to one which lay on the table. "It was presented to me by Sir Henry Clinton, through the unfortunate Major Andre, who informed me at the time, that any favor the bearer of it might demand of the General, should not be refused. Take it, and save the youth."

"No, no," said Carlini. "It would not do—for such a proceeding would be certain to expose you."

"How so?"

"Why, Clinton would seek to know what interest you have in a miserable spy; and depend upon it, suspicion would be excited, and the consequences thereof it is impossible to foresee."

"Then there is no other way but the one you propose?"

"I know of none."

"But could I not pretend that this youth once saved my life, and that out of gratitude I seek to save his?"

"Nay," said Carlini, shaking his head, "the risk is too great. No, I must try my own plan. But give yourself no unnecessary alarm—something tells me I shall succeed."

"Oh, pray heaven you may, without getting yourself into difficulty!"

After some further conversation, Carlini rose to depart, when Rosalie detained him by a few more questions.

"Have you seen Arnold?" she inquired.

"I have not," replied the other.

"Nor do you know, I suppose, where he will be located?"

"No—at present he is a guest of Sir Henry,"

"The wretch! Oh that he had been captured instead of Andre!"

"So wish both friends and foes, Miss Du Pont," answered the astrologer, a dark frown gathering on his brow. "But if heaven favors our cause, he may yet be made to suffer for his infamous treachery."

"What mean you?"

"That if I succeed in freeing this youth, without discovery, my next step will be to devise a plan to rid the earth of a monster. But I have talked too long, I fear, and so now I will take my leave, wishing you a speedy recovery."

"But should your plan succeed, you will see me again soon?"

"Ay, I will call to-morrow: if not, a last farewell;" and he extended his hand to the fair invalid.

"Farewell!" returned Rosalie, in a voice of deep emotion. "Be cautious in all you do, my friend, and may God prosper your undertaking."

The astrologer now took his leave; but scarcely had Rosalie been left to herself, when a servant entered and handed her a letter. At once breaking the seal, she read as follows:

"I have not heard from you for many days, and I feel uneasy at your long silence. God grant that no harm has befallen you! Were any thing serious to happen to my kind benefactress, Heaven only knows what its effect would be upon me. You, and the cause I serve, alone occupy my thoughts. Oh, that I could see you, if only for a few minutes, to fill your ear with the language of my heart! Oh, tell me you are well, for I am desponding. I write in haste, and know not whether this scrawl will ever reach you. I am well. Major Andre has been taken as a spy, which news you will probably hear ere this reaches you. What his fate will be, I leave you to imagine. *He and John Anderson are one.*

"I close, with a heartfelt prayer for your welfare. E. M."

This letter bore no date, and as we have shown, was worded with great caution, for there was no certainty of its reaching the destination for which it was intended. Rosalie read it twice, and pressed it to her lips a dozen times, murmuring:

"Oh, that we could meet again!"

She then sank back on her pillow, and became lost in a solemn reverie.

CHAPTER II.

THE PRISONER AND HIS VISITORS.

In the vicinity of Wall, and an intersecting street, at the time of which we write, was an old stone building, nearly square, of an antiquated appearance, having massive doors, small grated windows, and which, on three of its sides, was shut in by a high wall of masonry. It needed but a single glance at this gloomy structure, to convince the most casual observer that it was one of those *necessities* of *civilized* society, known as a prison.

The front doors opened into the keeper's office, in the rear of which was another door, strongly guarded with bolts and locks, which barred the entrance to the prison itself. There were two stories of cells above ground, with some four or five dungeons below ground. The only ventilation afforded these latter, was by means of an iron grate, set horizontally in the ceiling, and communicating with a narrow corridor which ran along between the right and left walls of the first story. This corridor, having no outlet, save through the keeper's office, was so dark as to require an artificial light to enable a person to see his way at noonday; and as the subterranean cells received their only light through a small double-grate in its solid floor, the reader can easily imagine the profound gloom in which they were buried, and the little chance a prisoner had of making his escape therefrom.

It was in the afternoon following Carlini's visit to Rosalie, that a private carriage stopped before the prison, and two personages, enveloped in overcoats, and well muffled up about the throat and lower part of the face, alighted, and ascended the steps to the front entrance of the building.

One of these gentlemen was short and stout, and the other tall and well proportioned. Both were immediately admitted into the keeper's office, when the stout personage spoke a few words aside with the jailor.

"Certainly, your excellency," replied the latter, with an obsequious bow; and he immediately hastened to procure a lantern, which he lighted; and then taking down a large bunch of keys, added, with another humble bow: "This way, your excellency—this way, gentlemen."

"Let nothing occur to reveal my name or rank," said the stout gentleman, as with his companion he entered the corridor already mentioned.

Here, having carefully secured the doors behind him, the jailor advanced a few steps, and stooping down, applied one of his keys to a lock set horizontally in the floor. Presently he raised a heavy iron door, and turning an upright iron bolt, gently lowered, by means of an iron chain, a wooden ladder, which had been fastened to the ceiling of the subterranean cells. This done, he carefully descended himself to the damp, cold ground below, and then held the light so as to guide the steps of his visitors. When they had safely reached the bottom, the keeper ascended the ladder, locked the iron trap above him, and then rejoined the others.

"You have every security against the escape of any one plunged into this gloomy abode," said the personage who had before addressed the jailor.

"Yes, your excellency—"

"Hold!" interrupted the other: "did I not forbid you to address me in this manner!"

"I beg pardon, sir! I will remember in future."

"Well, lead the way to the cell, and then enter and inform the prisoner two persons wish to speak with him."

The jailor now advanced along a narrow, gloomy passage, with a heavy stone wall on either hand, till he came to an iron door on the right, which he proceeded to unlock. Throwing this open, he disclosed a sort of vestibule, just the size of the door, and about two feet deep, with another iron door directly before him. Unlocking this, he entered the cell with his lantern, leaving his visitors without, to await the termination of his interview with the prisoner. The cell he entered was close and damp. Its size was four feet by eight, and the only air admitted into it, when the door was closed, was through the double grate in the ceiling, which, as before remarked, formed the ground floor of the corridor above. The dim rays of the lantern revealed, with a gloomy indistinctness, four damp walls, a stone floor, littered with dirty straw, a deal table, (on which was a cup of water and a small piece of stale, coarse bread,) and a pale, handsome youth, heavily ironed, and half reclining on his hard, filthy bed. Surely, unnecessary precaution had been adopted to retain in durance vile one who really seemed devoid of the strength which usually belongs to persons of his sex and age.

He was apparently about eighteen, of slender but graceful build. Though as beardless almost as one of the other sex, there was something noble, lofty, and commanding in his countenance. His forehead was high, broad, and smooth, surmounted by nut-brown, curly hair. His eye was large, dark, bright hazel; and its glances, quick and piercing, combined with an expression of active intelligence, made it very fascinating to the beholder. His nose was just sufficiently aquiline to give character to his noble countenance; and his thin lips, beautiful mouth, and well-turned chin, also denoted a quick decision and unshaken resolve.

He had been lying down upon the straw; but as the jailor entered his noisome abode, he raised himself upon his elbow, and fixing his dark eyes full on the countenance of that functionary, said, in a low, melodious, but firm tone of voice:

"Well, sir, has my time come?"

"That's more than I can say, my lad," returned the keeper of the prison, kindly, for in his heart he sympathized with the poor boy: "that's more than I can say—but there are two persons without who wish to speak with you."

"Well, show them in, sir."

The jailor went out, taking his lantern with him, which, according to the direction of the spokesman of his visitors, he placed in what, by way of convenience, we shall term the vestibule, so that its feeble rays would enable the new-comers to see their way into the cell, without allowing their countenances to be visible to the prisoner. Bidding the jailor close the outer door, and await their pleasure outside, he, who seemed to be highest in authority, advanced to the cell, followed by his companion, and thus addressed the chained tenant of the dungeon:

"Young man, I have called to request you to give me a short history of your life."

The prisoner looked up in surprise at the singularity of this request, and then, in a firm, bold tone, demanded:

"Who are you, sir, that wish to make yourself familiar with my history?"

"A friend."

"How am I to know that?"

"Will you not take my word for it?"

"First tell me your name, and what object you have in your inquiry."

"As to the name, that is of no consequence—my object of inquiry is to render you a service—to save your life if possible."

"And what has my history to do with the saving of my life?"

"More, perhaps, than you are aware of."

"Certainly more, if any thing at all."

"Will you comply with my request?"

"Yes, I will humor you, for the sake of getting at the solution of this mystery. Will you have the outline, or the detail?"

"The outline is sufficient for my purpose."

"Then I will begin by informing you that I was born in London, on the 29th of September, 1762."

"And are therefore just eighteen years of age," interrupted the other.

"I shall be in a day or two, sir," answered the youth—"that is to say," he added, in a tone slightly faltering, "should I live so long."

He paused a moment, as if in contemplation of the doom impending, and then continued:

"I am the sole survivor of six children, five of whom died in infancy. At the age of six years my beloved mother followed her offspring to the tomb. My father, overpowered with the weight of his affliction, for he loved my mother dearly, was incapacitated for business by her loss. At that time he was a thriving shopkeeper, and had amassed a handsome competence; but immediately after, he sold out, and amply providing for my education with a distant relative, made a trip to the continent. For several years I heard from him regularly, about once in six months; but he never returned again, though every letter intimated he had thoughts of doing so.

"The last letter received, was about six years ago, and in that he positively declared he should set out for England in a month. I was overjoyed at this intelligence, and longed—oh! sir, you know not how ardently—for the time to come when I could again throw my arms around his neck, and pillow my head upon his breast. Every vessel that arrived from France was then chronicled by the press, with the names of the passengers; and these lists I scanned eagerly, with a wildly-beating heart, in the hope of finding among them the endeared appellation of my beloved father.

"A month rolled away, and my anxiety became painful. This was the time my father had set for returning, and I grew feverish with impatience to behold him once more. But he came not. Another week of soul-harrowing anxiety passed, and then came the frightful intelligence of the loss of the packet-ship Alpine, with the names of those who had found a watery grave. Oh, heaven! who can describe my feelings, when I found among these latter, George Nugent, the name of my father!"

The youth paused, buried his face in his hands, and gave vent to choking sobs. In a few moments he recovered himself, by a great effort, and again resumed:

"My father perished with the unfortunate Alpine. I have never seen him since—never shall behold him again this side of the grave. For weeks after the sad news, I was confined to my bed with a brain fever. My life was for a long time despaired of—but God saw proper to restore me to reason and health. But I could not go on with my studies, and I longed for a change of scene. My guardian, a cousin of my father, consented to let me visit America, and promised to take charge of my property in my absence. I embraced the opportunity, and was soon bowling over the broad Atlantic. I landed in Boston, and becoming short of funds, wrote to my guardian for more. Six months passed away, and having received no answer, I wrote again. Still no answer came. Several times have I written since, with the same result. From some cause, to me unknown, no letter from my guardian has ever reached me, nor do I know whether he is living or dead.

"I was soon reduced to penury, and obliged to seek some means for support. Without friends, I found this no easy matter to accomplish. But at last I fell in with a kind hearted gentleman, who gave me employment as a clerk in a store. I remained with him a year, during which time the war broke out. My employer immediately took part in the struggle, and finally sold out his effects, and, I believe, placed the greater portion of his property at the disposal of his country, to assist in carrying on the war. He is now a Colonel in the American army, and, I have recently heard, stands fair for a higher promotion.

"He made overtures to me, and all in his employ, to join him. All accepted but myself. I did not wish to take part in the struggle on either side; and receiving, some time after, an offer from an Englishman in this city, to act in the capacity of a clerk for him, I gladly embraced this peaceable mode of earning my living. I came to New York nearly three years ago, and have been here ever since, in the employ of Mr. Harding. I say ever since—I mean till the occurrence of this affair, in which I have become involved, and which, I suppose, will terminate my earthly career."

"But why," said the personage, who had all along been the spokesman of the two visitors—"why, since, as you say, you did not wish to take part in the struggle on either side—why did you allow yourself to be persuaded into an act which makes your life a forfeit?"

"That is a question, sir, I choose not to answer," replied the youth, firmly. "I know my fate," he added, with something like a sigh, "and am prepared to meet it. I shall leave no kin to mourn me when I am gone."

"You know not that, sir," rejoined the other, quickly; "you know not that. Suppose I tell you your father is living?"

"Living!" cried young Nugent, with a spasmodic start. "Living! Oh! no, no—do not mock me in this terrible manner! Tell me sir, oh! tell me that it is false! and though you show me my death-warrant the next moment, on my knees, I will bless you!"

"How, sir! how, young man!" pursued the other, sternly—"would you rejoice to be confirmed in your belief of your father's death?"

"Alas! yes, since I must die myself."

"You are unfeeling, then."

"Oh! no! no!" cried the youth, a deep flush mantling his pale features: "no, no, sir—do not say that!"

"How then am I to account for the strange hope that your father is dead?"

"Because the knowledge that he is living would unman me—for then I know he will sooner or later hear of my ignominious death, and the news will break his heart."

"Well, young man, painful as the intelligence may be to you, I must tell you your father is living," rejoined the other.

"Oh, God!" groaned the youth, covering his face with his hands.

"And what is more," pursued the strange visitor, "he is now in this city."

"Merciful heaven! you are not mocking me?" exclaimed young Nugent, wildly, withdrawing his hands from his face, and looking up at the other with an agonized expression, his dark eyes gleaming as with fire.

"No, on the honor of a gentleman I am not mocking you; and unless you stand in your own light, you shall be free to clasp him in your arms."

"On what conditions?" fairly gasped the prisoner.

"That you reveal who are your accomplices."

"I thought so," cried the youth, in a tone of stern indignation, his features again flushing, but this time with a very different feeling than before. "I thought it would come to this." And then drawing himself up proudly, all traces of a tender emotion having vanished, he continued: "No, sir, I would not accept the terms of release, though I saw my father breaking his heart beside me; and that would be the strongest trial I could possibly undergo—the torture of the rack would be nothing to it. You have mistaken me, sir; and as I wish to hold malice against no one, I pardon you the error. What I refused to his excellency, Sir Henry Clinton, you may rest assured I will not grant to a stranger. Even were all you tell me true—and, pardon me, if I now suspect some artifice, to wring from me an honorable secret—even were my father now by my side, I do not believe he would counsel me to this foul dishonor, though it be the only means by which I can prolong my life."

"We shall see," returned the other; "you will soon know, for here your father stands."

"My father!" shrieked the youth, turning wildly to the other figure; "you my father!" and he sprang to his feet, like a madman, making his heavy chains clank and rattle dismally.

"Alas! my poor boy, I am indeed your father," answered the other stranger, who now spoke for the first time since entering the cell; and he threw his arms around the neck of the bewildered youth, and sobbed aloud.

"Oh God!" groaned young Nugent, fondly embracing his parent: "Oh God! that I could have been spared this heart-rending trial!—but thy will, oh God! be done."

"Now, will you not accept the proposal I have made?" asked the other visitor.

Like lightning the youth started from his father's embrace, and thundered forth:

"No! I tell you once for all, *no!* even with my father's entreaties joined to yours."

"Alas!" said the other, "then your doom is sealed."

"Pray, sir, let me speak a few words with my son in private," now pleaded the anxious parent.

"Very well, sir; I grant you five minutes' conversation," replied he in authority; and he immediately quitted the cell.

"Noble boy! you are indeed worthy to be my son," said the father, in a low tone, as the heavy iron door banged behind the one who had just gone out. "Oh, come once more to my arms, that I may again embrace you!"

"But are you indeed my father?" queried the youth, doubtingly, endeavoring to get a view of the other's features.

"You shall see, George, and judge for yourself;" and the other proceeded to get the light, which still remained where the jailor had placed it. Returning to the youth, he held it up before his own face, and added: "Do you now recognize me, George?"

The latter scrutinized the features of his supposed father, long and earnestly, and then said, with a sigh:

"No, I can not recognize you. My father's hair was dark—yours is red; my father's beard was black—yours is sandy. It seems impossible you can be the same; though there is something in the general shape of the features, like what my memory retains of my beloved parent. But I was very young when last I saw my father; and perhaps you can account for the difference in your complexion, and the color of your hair."

"George," returned the other, speaking in a low, rapid tone, "time is precious, and so we will waste no more in idle words. I came to cheer your drooping spirits, and prepare you for your release. I am in disguise, and my disguise must be perfect, since even you do not recognize your friend Carlini."

"Carlini!" ejaculated the other, with a start.

"Hush! listen, and speak not! The personage who has just left you, is Sir Henry Clinton. How I have managed to wheedle him into coming here to me, I will explain after you have effected your escape, which must be to-night. You have behaved nobly, lad, and Carlini is not one to desert his friends, more especially such as have jeopardized their lives to save him. Attend to my instructions. Here is a saw, made from the main-spring of a watch; here is a vial of oil, which will enable it to work without noise; and here is a composition of the color of the iron, wherewith to fill the crevices, should the jailor happen to approach you before your task is completed. You must work fast. Do not sever the iron entirely, but only so you can snap it at a moment's warning. Do you understand me?"

"Yes, yes," replied the other, in breathless amazement.

"Leave the rest to me. Keep a stout heart, and I will not fail you. I have two plans, but I will tell you nothing now."

Carlini then produced a composition, of the consistency of softened putty, and hastily approaching the iron doors, thrust a portion into each key-hole. By this means he had the impressions of the locks of the doors communicating with the cell of George Nugent.

Scarcely had he resumed his place beside the prisoner, when the outer door opened, and Sir Henry entered.

"Weep! weep!" whispered Carlini to George; and at the same instant he uttered a heavy moan himself, and then appeared to be sobbing convulsively, a trick the prisoner was not slow to imitate.

"Well," said Clinton, "the five minutes have expired." But neither the prisoner, nor his *soi disant* father, took any notice of the other's presence. "I say, my good sir," pursued the General, placing a hand on the shoulder of Carlini, who suddenly started, with well-affected surprise—"the time has come for you and your son to part—if, as I conjecture, he still adheres to his determination to reveal nothing."

"Alas! it is so," groaned the other. "My prayers have been of no avail. Oh George! oh

George! my son—that it should come to this!" he continued, in a heart-broken tone.

"Father, farewell!" cried George, with a fresh burst of grief, as he threw his arms wildly around Carlini's neck, and embraced him.

"Farewell!" gasped the other; and tearing himself away, he rushed from the cell, as if he feared to trust himself longer in the company of one so dear to him.

"Farewell, young man," said Clinton to the prisoner. "Unless you agree to the terms proposed, you have probably seen your father for the last time. Your doom is fixed for to-morrow at sunrise. You will thus have another night of solitude in which to reflect; and should you consent to my proposition, even at the last moment, you shall be immediately set at liberty—otherwise, no power on earth shall save you. Adieu! and think well upon your father's sorrows."

Saying this, Clinton strode out of the cell, the jailor closed and locked the massive doors, and the whole party ascended to the floor above in silence, the *soi disant* father appearing a good deal agitated.

"May I have one moment's conversation with your excellency?" said Carlini, as Clinton was about stepping into his carriage, at the door of the prison.

"Certainly, Mr. Nugent; enter, and we will talk as we ride, for my time is valuable; but I warn you not to ask for the pardon, or even reprieve, of the prisoner."

"I have a plan," said Carlini, as the carriage dashed over the rough pavement, "by which our object may yet be effected, and the accomplices of my unfortunate son be discovered."

"Speak, then, for on this point I am very anxious—as much so, perhaps, as yourself, though for a very different reason. To be frank with you, Mr. Nugent, this business troubles me more than, from a cursory glance, would seem at all needful. The case is just this. Your son was detected in an attempt to pass our lines near Harlem. On his person was found a hollow silver ball, and in that ball a document, drawn up with great care, and evidently by a master hand, giving a correct account of the intended treachery of General Arnold, and the plan we had in view for effecting an interview between him and Andre. Now as this, at the time, was a profound secret—or at least supposed to be so—known only to myself and some three or four officers in my confidence, you may readily conceive how anxious I am to find out the traitor; for that there is a traitor near my person, I am led by this to believe. Sir, I would willingly give your son his freedom, and a thousand pounds besides, for a revelation he could make in five minutes; and if you have any plan, short of absolute dishonor to myself, by which you can get at the truth, rest assured it shall have my hearty sanction."

"I have such a plan, your excellency," returned Carlini; "and since I shall take the execution of it wholly upon myself, to save the life of my unfortunate son, no dishonor can possibly accrue to your excellency. It is this: While left alone with George, vainly urging him to confess all and save his life, he suddenly interrupted me, and begged, as a great favor, that I would send him a confessor of the Romish Church, and that to him, as a spiritual adviser, and to no one else, would he unbosom himself. I was greatly shocked at this, as your excellency will readily perceive, when I inform you that I am a strict Protestant myself, and that George was educated in the latter faith. The idea then suddenly occurred to me that this whole affair might be the work of Jesuits, banded together to overthrow the rights of our sovereign, King George, in this country, in the hope of getting the new rule in their own hands. It also occurred to me, at the same moment, that this confession might be turned to advantage, by substituting a false priest for a real one."

"By heavens! a capital idea!" exclaimed Sir Henry, joyfully. "But the whole affair must be adroitly managed, or your son will detect the plot, and thus blast our hopes."

"If your excellency will be kind enough to intrust the whole management of it to me, rest assured a father's fears will adopt all necessary precautions to insure its success."

"Be it so; but you must be active; for should your plan fail, your son dies to-morrow at sunrise."

"Trust me, your excellency, there shall be

no unnecessary delay. But I must request your excellency to give me a written permit, that will admit the *priest* to the prisoner at any hour during the night."

"Ah, yes, certainly," returned Sir Henry; and then a new idea seeming to strike him, he added, quickly: "But suppose I give the jailor all necessary instructions—will that not answer as well?"

Carlini instantly perceived that the other had some slight suspicion of his double-dealing—but he answered promptly, and apparently well pleased:

"O, yes, your excellency, just as well: in fact, now I think of it, I believe it would be the better way—only I trust your excellency, in the multiplicity of business, will not overlook it."

"I will not overlook it, Mr. Nugent, but will dispatch a messenger to the jailor immediately." At this moment the carriage stopped, and the door was thrown open by a servant in livery. "Ah! here is my residence—will you step in, Mr. Nugent?" pursued Clinton, as he alighted.

"I thank your excellency," answered Carlini—"but I must set about the business we were speaking of, as the day is fast wearing away."

"Well, Heaven prosper your undertaking!" rejoined Clinton, as he turned away to enter his dwelling.

"Amen!" said Carlini, moving quickly up Broadway—but ere he was out of hearing, he heard the servant say to Clinton:

"General Arnold is anxiously awaiting your excellency's return."

"The vile traitor!" muttered Carlini, his eyes gleaming fiercely; and then he added, with a triumphant expression: "So far my plot works to a charm, and I have even made the proud and sagacious Sir Henry Clinton my dupe."

CHAPTER III.

A BOLD STRATAGEM AND ITS RESULT.

It was about ten o'clock on the evening following the events recorded in the foregoing chapters, that the keeper of the prison, wherein George Nugent was confined, being seated in his office, and in a comfortable doze, was suddenly aroused by a heavy double-knock on the outer door.

"Well," muttered the jailor, yawning, and rubbing his eyes, "I suppose he's come at last;" and he proceeded to unbolt and throw open the door, disclosing a stranger in the garb of a Roman Catholic priest. "I thought it was you—come to see George Nugent, I suppose?" pursued the keeper, addressing the new-comer.

"You have divined my purpose, sir," replied the other, in that precise tone, and with that air of religious sanctity and austerity, which so many ministers of the Gospel, of every sect, see proper to display, perhaps with a view to impress the sacredness of their calling and their own superiority upon the minds of the vulgar. "You have divined my purpose, sir; I, indeed, have come to behold that poor unfortunate youth, and, in his last hour, minister to him the holy consolations of the true faith. Will you be so kind as straightway to conduct me to his abode?"

The speaker was a tall, well-formed personage, between forty and fifty years of age. His skin was as dark almost as that of a mulatto; large, bushy, iron-gray whiskers, and mustaches, in a great measure concealed his features. His hair was of the same color as his beard, and, being short and bushy, made his head seem much larger than it really was. His eyes were black and piercing, and the general expression of his countenance was severely austere.

The jailor, in compliance with the other's request, immediately lighted his lantern, and proceeded into the interior of the prison.

"This way," he said, and led the priest down into the dungeon, and to the cell of George Nugent. "What time shall I come for you?" he inquired, while he busied himself in unlocking the two doors.

"I can not say," answered the priest, "when I shall have finished the sacred duty enjoined upon me—it depends much upon the state of mind in which I find the penitent—but if you could make it convenient to call in half an hour, I think that, if not ready to depart then, I shall be able to specify the exact time."

"Well, your reverence, I will call in half an hour," returned the jailor; and throwing open the cell door, he motioned the other to enter, adding: "Do you wish a light?"

"Of course, sir," replied the priest, with an air of surprise—"how else am I to see?"

"Well then, take this—I think I shall be able to find my way back in the dark;" and handing the lantern to the priest, the jailor withdrew, locking the doors after him.

As soon as he found himself alone with the prisoner, the priest turned to the former, who was reclining upon his straw, eagerly watching every motion, and, in a solemn tone, said:

"My son, I am truly sorry to find one so young, and apparently intelligent as yourself, incarcerated in so gloomy and loathsome a place."

"Who are you, sir? and what is your business here?" demanded the young man, assuming a sitting posture.

"I, my son, am a priest of the true faith, come to confess you, and prepare you for your long journey."

"Who sent you?"

"Sir Henry Clinton bade me come, saying you were anxious to confer with a priest of your own faith."

"But, sir, I am not a Roman Catholic."

"Indeed!" exclaimed the priest, with a start: "then there has been a mistake somewhere."

"So it would seem," replied the other, drily.

"But since I am here, will you not make a clean breast of all your errors, and so prepare yourself for true repentance and Divine mercy?"

"You evidently mistake my character," returned George Nugent, looking keenly and scrutinizingly at the other. "If you are only here in the spiritual capacity of a priest, you have made a journey in vain."

"And in what capacity, save that of a spiritual adviser and confessor, did you suppose, my son, I would come to you?"

"I did not say I supposed you would come in any capacity—for the truth is, I did not suppose you would come at all—having never seen or heard of you before."

"Well, my son, I cannot return the compliment in the same words, for I *have* heard of you before, and that it is your deliberate intention to escape from your prison to-night, assisted by a certain Signor Carlini, somewhat known as an astrologer, which is synonymous with imposter, swindler, cheat, etc."

"Good heavens!" cried the youth, turning deadly pale, completely thrown off his guard—"how learned you this?"

"Then I am right," rejoined the priest, quickly, with a triumphant smile. "Come, young man, acknowledge you are caught at last."

"I will acknowledge nothing, but that you are a low, base-born scoundrel!" cried the other, indignantly.

"Rail on, young sir—but already your friend is safely lodged within these walls, and you and he must leave them together. Do you understand?"

"Alas! and so my noble benefactor is a prisoner, and must die to-morrow? On what charge was he arrested?"

"On what charge should he be arrested, but that of being a spy in the British camp?"

"Alas! then we are doomed!" groaned the youth.

"You, at least, may escape," said the priest.

"How?"

"By confessing all you know."

"Villain, begone! or I shall be tempted to strike you with my chains!" again cried the young man, growing furious.

"But your silence will not avail your friend, since he, like yourself, is already in a dungeon."

"Then why are you so anxious for my confession?"

"Suppose I tell you Sir Henry has taken a fancy to you, and is desirous of some excuse to pardon you!"

"I am obliged to Sir Henry: but he shall never have the excuse that I turned traitor to my friend, even though it be proved, to my satisfaction, that I could do him no injury thereby."

"Well, enough of this mummery," returned the priest, with great animation. "George Nugent, you have been sorely tried, and found in every respect worthy to live, and become one of a little band secretly fighting for liberty."

"What mean you?" asked the other, in amazement.

"That in the person before you, you behold no priest, but Carlo Carlini himself."

"Gracious heavens! you?"

"Ay, I am again disguised. My face and hands are colored, and my hair and beard are false."

"Is it possible! Ah, now I perceive you are indeed my friend. How strange!"

"But the chains, lad! the chains!"

"See here!" and as the youth spoke, he snapped them in twain, and stood before the other, free of any incumbrance.

"Heaven be praised! so far my plot works well. Should kind fortune still continue propitious, in a few minutes you will be at liberty. Now let me tell you the rest of my plan;" and Carlini, for a short time, spoke to the other in a low, hurried tone.

When, at the expiration of the half hour, the jailor returned to the door, Carlini bade him enter. The moment he stood within the cell, he was seized, gagged, and bound, ere he had time to cry out for help, or make any effectual resistance. Depositing him on the straw, and seizing his keys, Carlini now bade the young prisoner follow him; and taking up the lantern, both went out, carefully locking the doors behind them. Having ascended to the corridor above, and secured the trap, Carlini whispered to his young companion to remain where he was, till he should go forward to the keeper's room, and ascertain if the coast were clear. Carefully unlocking the iron door, he peered in, and, to his surprise and dismay, beheld a large, athletic, rough-looking fellow, seated in the jailor's chair, evidently awaiting his return. Who he was, he did not know—but thought it probable he was either a turnkey, or one of the night watch. But how he was to get past him, with the prisoner, was a matter for the most serious consideration. Carlini was fertile of invention in a difficult emergency, as we have already shown; and he now thought rapidly, running a dozen plans through his mind in almost as many seconds.

"Well, Governor, is any thing the matter?" inquired the fellow, in a gruff voice, supposing he was addressing the jailor.

Carlini made a rapid signal for his young companion to step behind the door; then throwing it partly open, he entered the keeper's room, with a smile, and in a bland tone, said:

"I think, sir, the Governor, as you term him, finds some difficulty in securing the door leading to the dungeon. There appears to be something the matter with one of the bolts—perhaps you had better step in and assist him."

"O, yes, certainly;" and the brawny fellow arose from his seat, and advanced to the door opening into the corridor.

As he crossed the threshold, Carlini, who stood by the door, struck him a violent blow with his fist, on the back of his head, which stumbled him forward, and nearly stunned him. At the same instant, and before the fellow could recover himself, George Nugent sprang into the keeper's office, with the lantern, and the astrologer instantly closed and locked the door. By the time this was completed, the entrapped turnkey comprehended the trick that had been played upon him, and began to curse and rave in a way that bade fair to alarm the prison, if not the town.

"Quick! quick!" said Carlini, in a low hurried tone: "be ready here to take advantage of our so far remarkable success;" and he proceeded to unlock the door leading to the street. "There is a sentinel without here," he added, "and unless we can entrap him, we are not safe even now."

He threw open the door as he spoke, and called out, in an alarmed tone:

"Quick, sentry—this way—hasten—there is a prisoner loose, and I fear he will escape."

There was a patter of feet on the pavement, and the next moment the sentry, with his musket, sprang into the room, crying:

"Where? where? what is the trouble?"

"There!" answered Carlini, hurriedly; "do you not hear him?" as the cries of the entrapped turnkey resounded in the corridor.

"Stand by that door while I open it;" and as the soldier, not suspecting a trick, darted forward to it, Carlini and Nugent bounded into the street, the former jerking the door to after him, and locking it, as he had done the others.

Scarcely was the bolt turned, when the sentry, perceiving too late that he had been duped, discharged his musket. There was a mighty uproar now in the prison, and as the noise could be distinctly heard outside, our friends well knew there was no time to be lost.

"We must fly, George, we must fly!" said Carlini, in a startling whisper, grasping the arm of his companion; and the next moment both were speeding down the street, but running so as to make as little noise as possible.

Fortune still favored them; for the heavens, which but an hour before were brilliantly studded with stars, were now overcast by black clouds, rendering the night extremely dark; and as the streets were not lighted save by an occasional gleam from the upper window of some dwelling, and as the fugitives took good care to keep in the deep shadow of the buildings, there seemed little danger of their being successfully followed, save by the sound of their footsteps. But though they at first ran swiftly, yet instinctively, as it were, both ran on the balls of their feet, and thus greatly lessened the danger in respect to sound. And danger there was in every quarter; for the night-patrols were on duty, and it would require the utmost circumspection to elude their vigilance. For some fifty yards, the progress of our friends was rapid; and then Carlini suddenly grasped his young companion by the arm, and with a low "Hist," drew him close up against an old building, where both came to a dead halt, and held their breath in fearful suspense.

The cause of this new movement was the quick steps of a sentry heard approaching them; and a minute after, a dusky figure was seen gliding quickly forward. He passed them, without looking either to the right or left: and immediately the fugitives again darted away. The noise at the prison still continued, and presently a voice was heard shouting:

"The spy has escaped! the spy has escaped!"

As may readily be imagined, this startling cry did not tend to slacken the pace of the fugitives, who, making as little noise as possible, soon turned out of the main street into a dark alley, up which they sped with all their might. The cry, that the spy had escaped, was taken up by others; persons were heard running in various directions; and it now become painfully evident to the fugitives, that unless they soon found a hiding-place, they would be captured. Every nerve was strained, and every sense kept keenly alive to the danger that menaced them. In ten minutes from leaving the prison, they had entered the street, unobserved, where Carlini resided. If now they could reach his dwelling unseen, both felt that they would be comparatively safe. At this moment a sentinel suddenly sprang out from the deep shadow of a building, and presenting his musket to the breast of Carlini, cried:

"Stand! and give the countersign!"

Knowing that delay would be fatal, the astrologer and his companion bounded aside, and attempted to pass without speaking. The sentry pulled the trigger, and the musket went off, but fortunately doing no other harm to our friends than creating a new alarm. With the fierceness of the tiger, the speed of lightning, and the power of a giant, Carlini sprang upon the soldier, wrenched the weapon from his grasp, and, clubbing it, struck the poor fellow on the head, who fell like an ox, with a single groan, apparently lifeless. Darting away again, Carlini and his young friend reached the private door of his dwelling, just as the roll of a drum was heard sounding a fresh alarm. In every direction windows were now raised, and many a head, white with a night-cap, was seen protruding, to learn the cause of the tumult; and more than one female voice was heard to shriek forth her fears, that the enemy had besieged the town, and that all were about to be massacred by the hateful French and the barbarous rebels. But most fortunately for our friends, no one of the many on the lookout observed them, owing to the darkness; and with a private key Carlini unlocked the door, and, almost breathless, glided into the house with his young friend. Then, for the first time since setting out on his perilous mission, the astrologer breathed freely; and sinking down upon his knees, he ejaculated:

"Almighty God be praised! we are saved at last."

The commotion without increased, rather than subsided, and persons were heard running in various directions—perhaps in search of the fugitives—perhaps to learn the cause of the alarm.

"Come, my lad," said Carlini, "let me conduct you to a safe retreat."

He then led the way up stairs, followed by his young companion, and entered the black Chamber of Fate, which we described in the first portion of this true history. Crossing this to the black hangings farthest from the door, he lifted the dark curtain, and feeling about on the wall, at length touched a spring, when a small door opened, and disclosed a neat little room, containing a bed, and other necessary articles for a comfortable lodging apartment.

"Here, George," he said, "must be your abode for the present—or, in fact, till I can find a way to get you out of the city. You perceive you have only changed one prison for another, though I trust you will not find the change to your disadvantage, nor me a harsh jailor."

"God bless you!" cried the young man, grasping the hand of the other, and pressing it to his lips. "God bless you! I owe you more than ever I can repay, even with the sacrifice of my life, since I have but one life to offer, and that you have twice saved."

"Well, well, I trust even that sacrifice will not be needed now, my friend," replied Carlini. "I consider the obligation, if any there were, more than canceled, by the noble manner in which you have conducted yourself during your perilous and fearful trials. Adieu, for to-night; I will see you again to-morrow;" and with this he drew the door to its place, and the spring instantly secured it.

"Now let the hirelings of King George search to their heart's content," he muttered to himself. "As they have been foiled now, so shall they ever be; and nothing shall triumph in this glorious land, but that liberty for which we have periled our all, and for which all true hearts are ready to suffer, even to the death."

And now, taking a short leave of Carlini and his friends let us turn to another scene.

CHAPTER IV.

ONE OF THE SPIES.

On quitting the presence of General Washington, on the night before the execution of Major Andre, Major Lee at once repaired to his quarters, and sent for Sergeant Champe, at the same time issuing imperative orders that no one should be allowed to interrupt their interview. In a few minutes Champe was with the Major, who, without circumlocution, thus addressed him:

"Within the hour, Sergeant, I have been closeted with our commander-in-chief, on an affair of great importance. He wishes to find a brave heart, who will embark on a perilous but inglorious enterprise, to serve the common cause. I named you—was I wrong?"

"I freely devote my life to the cause of liberty and my country," answered Champe, proudly, "and I thank you for bringing me so favorably to the notice of our noble commander."

"And you are ready to set out this night—ay, within the hour—on an enterprise full of peril, with even the chances of ever returning against you, and without so much as saying farewell to a single comrade?"

"Major Lee," answered the noble fellow, "there are no sacrifices I would not make, in an honorable venture, to serve my country. I am a man of few words, and mean what I say—therefore proceed with your instruction."

"Well, then, to be brief, it will be necessary, in the first instance, for you to desert and go over to the enemy."

"Desert!" cried Champe, in astonishment, while a heavy frown gathered on his brow. "Desert, Major Lee? do I hear aright?"

"You do, Sergeant; for only by desertion can you accomplish the plan we have in view. Listen! It is the wish and design of Washington to seize upon that vile traitor, Arnold, and bring him to justice. This of course can only be done by some one, or more than one, deserting our ranks and joining the British. There are at present a number of real deserters from our side, and these no doubt will be placed under the traitor's command. By joining them, you will thus be near the person of Arnold, and can watch all his movements, and peradventure find an opportunity to seize him, and take him to the river, where a boat must be in waiting to convey him across to Hoboken, and thence he shall be escorted to head-quarters. You will not be alone in this business—there are others already among the enemy, with whom you must communicate, and who will render you what assistance they can. This paper contains the instructions of General Washington himself, in regard to your proceedings, and it only now remains for you to say whether you will attempt the hazardous enterprise or not."

"Major Lee," returned Champe, after a few moments' reflection, "I believe not even my most bitter enemy would accuse me of physical cowardice."

"I would venture to say not," returned Lee, not a little puzzled as to what could be the drift of the Sergeant's remarks; "certainly not, if he knew you and had any regard for truth. I do not wish to flatter you; but I must honestly say, I consider you one of the very bravest men of my corps, and that is saying no little."

"Then it must be *moral* courage I lack, Major," rejoined Champe, reflectingly.

"How so?"

"Why, for the very reason that I do not wish to undertake this mission. I fear not the personal risk I should be obliged to run—and Heaven knows the adventure would be none of the safest—but to me the idea of desertion seems terrible. I am ready to peril my life in my country's cause—but the thought of periling my honor appals me. And that I should peril the latter, as well as the former, even you, Major Lee, can not gainsay. To succeed in this business, I must indeed desert, and leave my comrades to believe me a treacherous villain; and were I to fall, I should fall ignobly, and they would glory in my death; and my name, that now stands fair with them, would become a by-word of reproach. No, no, Major, do not urge this business upon me—for, believe me, I would a hundred times rather suffer death than disgrace."

"But consider, my dear sir," pursued Lee, "what valuable service you would be rendering your country, in bringing this villainous general to justice; and remember, too, that though there are many who might for a time look upon you as a deserter, yet there are those, high in power, who will regard your noble sacrifices aright, and who, should you fall, which Heaven forefend! will take care to place your character in its true light; and then those who may have been loudest in their denunciations, will be loudest in your praise. And should you succeed, what honor would redound to you for such a glorious achievement, together with a name and fame immortal. Consider well all these things, and that, though you may suffer a temporary disgrace, yet the time may soon come when you will be able to wipe away all dishonor, and stand forth to the world a noble example of what a true heart may dare to do in the cause of freedom and his country. Unless you undertake this business, I fear me I shall not be able to find another so every way competent; and I shall the more deeply regret it, that I have almost pledged myself to General Washington on your behalf, and already he counts on you to push the hazardous undertaking to a successful issue. If you refuse, I fear the scheme will fail—for honestly I know of no other so well capacitated to carry it out. You are a man of tried courage, cool, steady, persevering, shrewd, full of resources, and inflexible."

"I fear you overrate my abilities," replied the Sergeant, modestly; "but since your heart is so strongly set upon the matter; and since, as you say, from your representation, the commander-in-chief looks upon me as engaged in the enterprise; and since I shall be doing my country some service, I will agree to go, on one condition."

"Name it," said Lee.

"That should it unfortunately happen I do not live to return, you now solemnly pledge yourself to vindicate my honor—for that is dearer to me than life."

"On my honor, as a gentleman and a soldier, I sacredly pledge myself to the terms proposed," answered Lee, emphatically.

"Enough! Where are my instructions?"

"In this paper, in the handwriting of Washington himself;" and Lee handed the Sergeant the document, which, not an hour before, had been placed in his hands by the commander-in-chief. "It will be your safest plan," he continued, "to commit the instructions to memory—otherwise the paper might fall into the hands of the British, which would be proof sufficient to condemn you as a spy."

Champe immediately drew near a table, in the center of the tent, on which stood a light, and twice read the paper carefully through. This done, he held it to the flame, and in a moment it was reduced to ashes.

"Have you not been too hasty?" asked Lee.

"No, Major, it is here, where it will never be effaced save with life," returned the Sergeant, tapping his forehead with his finger. "I know the whole plan, I approve of it, and, to the best of my poor abilities, I will endeavor to execute it. In the arrangement of every part, I perceive the wisdom of our great chief. Well, the die is cast. I go soon. Farewell, Major Lee—it may be we shall never meet again."

"Farewell," returned the other, grasping the extended hand of the noble Sergeant. "Farewell, my friend, but I hope only for a season. Bear with you the remembrance, that you leave two warm friends behind, who can appreciate you as you deserve—General Washington and my humble self."

"Thank you; I desire none better;" and with a hasty step, Sergeant Champe quitted the tent of his commanding officer.

The night was dark and cloudy, which so far favored the design of the Sergeant; but unfortunately there were signs of rain, which, if it fell, would be certain to make the road soft, and leave palpable traces of the course he had taken. But nothing daunted, now that he had settled upon his course, Champe moved stealthily forward to his quarters; and getting his valise, and such other articles as he most needed, he proceeded to the picket, at no great distance, withdrew his horse, bridled and saddled him, mounted, and dashed away upon the run.

He had not gone above a hundred yards, when he was challenged by a sentinel. Without reply, he buried his rowels in the horse's flanks, and, with an angry snort, the animal bounded away with increased speed. The sentry fired, the ball whizzed through the air, close to the sergeant's head, but fortunately missed both him and his beast, and the next moment he was out of sight.

Soon after Champe quitted the tent of Lee, the latter, being somewhat fatigued, for the day had been a busy one with him, lay down upon his rude couch, and endeavored to compose himself to sleep. But he felt feverish and restless, and could not avoid thinking of Champe, and speculating on what might be the result of his daring adventure. In Champe personally he took a deep interest, aside from his official capacity as his own orderly, and he felt great solicitude for his success, both on the score of friendship and as it concerned the welfare of the country. If the Sergeant could only get a few hours' start, before being missed, he reasoned, he would be comparatively safe; and he listened eagerly for any sound that might be taken as evidence to the contrary. The report of the sentry's gun he did not hear; and when some three quarters of an hour had elapsed, since Champe departed from his tent, he began to congratulate himself that all had gone well; but just at this moment he heard his name spoken aloud, and Captain Carnes, the officer of the day, entered his marquee in haste.

"Well?" demanded Lee, partly rising from his couch.

"Pardon me, Major, for so rudely disturbing you," answered the new-comer; "but the fact is, a dragoon of our corps has just made his escape, and I have come for your written orders to pursue him."

"What proof have you, Captain, that any one has fled?"

"Why, he passed the patrol on horseback, at a full run, and refused to answer when challenged. The sentry fired, but missed him, and then hastened to inform me what had occurred. I immediately ordered a party to get ready for pursuit, and, as I said before, have come hither for your written orders."

"Poh! poh!" said Lee, anxious to create as much delay as possible: "the sentry has been drinking, doubtless, and mistaken some frightened countryman for a dragoon."

"No, sir, the man was sober, for I questioned him closely, and know by his answers, which were brief and straight forward."

"And who do you suspect has fled?"

"I do not know, of course—but I can soon ascertain."

"Well, find out; and if it is really as you report, you shall have my orders with as little delay as possible. But it will all turn out a bug-bear story, depend upon it—although, if otherwise, you can let me know. Heigh ho! I feel very much fatigued, and I was just getting into a doze as you came in."

"But duty, you know, Major Lee"——

"Certainly, sir," interrupted the other—"certainly, I understand all that, and of course you are excused, and, if the matter turns out as you suspect, deserve much credit for your promptness and vigilance. There, go, and ascertain the truth as soon as you please."

Captain Carnes departed; and the moment he was alone, Lee muttered:

"Poor fellow! I fear for his safety now—though I will delay the pursuit as long as I can without exciting suspicion."

Some half an hour elapsed, and Captain Carnes returned in haste.

"I am sorry to say," he said, speaking rapidly, "that my suspicions were well founded. Since I left you, I have assembled my command, and, much to my regret and astonishment, find Sergeant Champe missing."

"Sergeant Champe!" repeated Lee, in well-affected surprise: "my orderly sergeant missing?—impossible!"

"True, upon my honor! Strange though it seem, in one who apparently had the good of his country so much at heart. I doubt not the fellow has all along played the hypocrite, and has now fled to the British to join that scoundrel Arnold. But if you will be kind enough to hasten with your written instructions, we may yet overtake him. It has just begun to rain, and that is in our favor; for if we can once get upon his track, we can keep it, as the shoes of his horse, like those of all the rest of our corps, have a private mark, by which we can distinguish them from all others, and in the soft, moist ground the mark will of course be conspicuous."

Lee, finding no excuse for longer delaying the pursuit, arose, in apparent haste, but managed to make even his haste prevent a quick completion of what he was about to do; for in arranging his writing materials, he accidentally, as it seemed, upset the ink, and the captain was obliged to go for his own. At last, however, the order was written out, and delivered to the captain. It was to the effect, that Champe should be taken alive, and brought directly to the Major's quarters—though, in the event of his making a stout resistance, or attempting to escape after being captured, the party in pursuit were duly authorized to use extreme measures.

As soon as this document was placed in the hands of Captain Carnes, that officer hastened to the party in waiting, and handed it to Lieutenant Middleton, who was deputed the leader of the pursuing detachment—the Captain repeating the contents, that no further delay might be occasioned by stopping to peruse it. The word was then given, and away dashed the dragoons, taking the direction of the deserter, as reported by the patrol.

That night was one of painful anxiety and feverish restlessness to Major Lee. He could not sleep; and for hours he paced the earthen floor of his tent, in no enviable frame of mind. Morning came, but brought no intelligence of either the pursuers or the pursued. They day wore slowly away, and about three o'clock in the afternoon, as the Major was sitting in his tent alone, he heard a loud, long, triumphant shout, amid which he could distinguish the words, uttered in bitter tones:

"The scoundrel is killed! the scoundrel is killed!"

"My God!" groaned Lee, in terrible agony of mind: "have I then been the means of dooming this brave, generous, and noble fel low toan ignominious death! Oh! Heaven help me! I shall never forgive myself."

He buried his face in his hands, and for a

few moments fairly sobbed aloud. Then rising, he tottered, rather than walked, to the door of his marquee, expecting to find his worst fears confirmed. He beheld Captain Carnes and Lieutenant Middleton approaching him, the latter leading a horse and bearing on his arm a cloak, both of which he instantly recognized as belonging to Champe.

"Alas! alas!" groaned Lee, mentally: "the Sergeant is dead, sure enough, and they come to bring me the supposed joyful tidings. Oh! if they could but see my poor heart in this trying moment! Well? well?" he hastily added aloud, as the officers came up, both of whom observed that his features were very pale, and that he seemed much agitated.

"We pursued the villain closely, as these trophies bear evidence," said Middleton; "but the scoundrel escaped us for all that."

"Thank God!" ejaculated Lee, catching his breath; and then, bethinking him what he had said, he added, quickly—"that he did not get off scot free."

"It was a race of life and death," returned Middleton—"but the fellow had too much the start of us; though, I'm thinking, he will remember the pursuit to the latest day of his life."

"Doubtless," rejoined the Major, turning back into his tent to conceal the joy he felt at hearing this intelligence. "Come in, gentlemen; come in, and tell me all about it. Seats, gentlemen. There, proceed."

"We had little difficulty in getting on his trail," pursued Middleton, "though unfortunately he had an hour the start."

"Ay, very unfortunate that," chimed in Lee, "and all owing to myself, too, I believe. Well, you found his trail!"

"Yes, the rain made it conspicuous; but at every place where the road forked, or another crossed it, we were obliged to halt and examine the ground, to be sure we did not miss his route. This of course delayed us considerably—so that, notwithstanding we rode hard all night, we did not get in sight of the fugitive till just after daylight. At this time we ascended a steep hill, and, to our great delight, espied the scoundrel on the brow of another, about half a mile ahead of us. As luck would have it, he saw us at the same moment, and spurred on with all his might. We pressed forward, and the race became terrific—he seeking life, we revenge.

"So certain were we now of overtaking him, and also that he would continue straight on, that we no longer thought of examining the road; but when we reached the spot where we had first seen him, we dashed forward in reckless confusion, not doubting that when we turned an angle in the road, about a quarter of a mile ahead, he would again be in sight. We soon turned the angle, but were much disappointed to behold the road straight before us for nearly a mile, but no Champe. I now looked down for the prints of his horse's feet, and judge of my vexation and chagrin, when I perceived that no horse had passed along there since the rain.

"I now ordered a halt, and sent a part of the men back to take his trail, while the rest of us kept on, hoping to find a way soon to turn off to the river and head him, for I rightly conjectured he had taken that direction. About an hour after, the party sent back joined me at a cross road, a little above Bergen, where we again came upon the tracks of the fugitive, he having reached there, apparently, by a short cut across some open fields. We again set forward together, and soon came in sight of the deserter, near the river, pushing with all his might for a British galley that lay anchored out in the stream. He saw us, and that unless he could reach the vessel, his case was hopeless, for, from some cause, his horse was very much blown, while ours seemed comparatively fresh.

"While making his last desperate effort for the river, he unlashed his valise from his saddle, and strapped it to his own back; then, as his horse drew up on the bank of the stream, he leaped over his head into the water, struck out for the vessel, and called upon the crew thereof for assistance. We were now within good musket shot, and I ordered the men to unsling their carbines, and, the moment we halted, to give him a volley. Soon after we fired a round, but unfortunately missed him. Meantime boats had put out to his assistance, and the galley opened a fire upon us to cover them. The result of the adventure is, that we captured his horse and cloak, but had the mortification to see him get safely on board the enemy's vessel."

"Well, you did well, Lieutenant," replied Lee, "and I shall take care to report you in the same light to our commander-in-chief."

"I thank you, Major," rejoined Middleton, "and assure you I sincerely regret that you will be obliged to report our failure also."

"Well, let him go," said the Major—"let him go. True, I would have liked to have made an example of him—but otherwise I feel all traitors can well be spared."

Shortly after this, the two officers took their leave, and, with a heartfelt prayer of thanksgiving, for the safety of the noble sergeant, Major Lee set out for head-quarters, to communicate the result of Champe's perilous adventure to the American chief.

CHAPTER V.

THE LOVERS.

Two days after the events recorded in the last chapter, and some five or six since the opening of this "second series," Rosalie Du Pont—now so far convalescent as to be able to quit her bed, for the most part, during the day, though she had not yet ventured to leave her room—was seated in a large, stuffed rocking-chair, poring over a volume of that truly great and immortal poem of the heaven-inspired blind bard, Milton, called Paradise Lost—a poem which, in strength of thought, powerful and graphic description, true originality, and depth of imagination, has, in our humble opinion, no equal in the English language.

The face of our beautiful heroine was yet pale, and exhibited traces of her recent illness; but still it was extremely lovely; and in its serene, languid, half-melancholy expression, was a fascination equal in power upon the beholder to any thing ever displayed there in the palmiest moments of rosy health. A loose, white linen wrapper, richly embroidered, enveloped her airy, symmetrical figure, allowing just the outlines of her person to be visible along its snowy folds, as we sometimes see a figure represented by the painter shrouded in a gossamer-like mist. From underneath this wrapper, a small, delicate foot, encased in a white satin slipper, was barely perceptible, the toe resting on the floor, and giving a slight rocking motion to the chair. One hand, with the loose sleeve pushed back, so as to display a large portion of an exquisitely moulded arm, held the book, and, for support, was gracefully resting on the cushioned arm of the chair; while the elbow of the other arm rested on the opposite side, with the hand pressed lightly against the head, which was inclined to the right. The raven tresses had been preserved to the head, much against the will of the physician, who had ordered them to be cut close—and now fell in wanton dalliance around her lovely face, alabaster neck, and over the broad collar of the snowy wrapper. The dark eyes, languid and melting, from underneath the long, drooping brown lashes, looked steadily upon the inspired page of the great poet, and the soul of the beautiful maiden was revelling in the sweet fancies, which the great bard's description of the Garden of Eden, and its then sinless pair, never fails to excite. Altogether, the picture was complete; and he must have been fastidious indeed, who, having seen it, could have wished any thing changed for the better.

A bright fire in the chimney sent out a genial warmth; and the air of the room was perfumed just enough to please the olfactory sense, without tending to satiety. Some minutes passed, during which Rosalie remained in the position just described, with her eyes fixed upon the book, when a light tap was heard on the door.

"Come in," said the fair occupant; and she raised her eyes, and glanced to the door, which opened and admitted a servant of the mansion.

"A stranger desires to know if he can see you for a few minutes alone, ma'm'selle?" said the female, dropping a curtsey, as was the custom of the day when a dependant addressed her mistress.

"A stranger!" repeated Rosalie, in surprise; "would he not give his name?"

"No, ma'm'selle—when I asked him to de

so, that I might tell you, he said it made no difference, but just say a stranger wanted a few minutes' conversation with you."

"This is singular!—did he ask for me in particular?"

"Yes, he inquired for Miss Rosalie Du Pont; and when I mentioned that you did not receive visitors now, and probably would not till you got so you could leave your room, he started, turned pale, and asked hurriedly if you were ill. I replied you had been very sick, but were now getting well fast. Upon that, he begged me, as a great favor, that I would take his message to you, and if you refused to see him on the first representation, to say it would be to your advantage to grant him a private interview. I should judge by his looks that he has lately come into the city from the country."

"Is he old or young, Helen?" inquired Rosalie, with a fresh degree of interest.

"Young, ma'm'selle, and very handsome."

"Where is my aunt?"

"She has just gone out in her carriage."

"Show him up then."

The servant retired, and, a minute or two later, ushered the stranger into the room, the latter holding his hat in such a manner as to shade his face.

"I could wish this interview strictly private," said the unknown, in a feigned voice.

Rosalie motioned Helen to retire and close the door. The moment this was done, the unknown revealed his face to the wondering Rosalie, who uttered a suppressed shriek, and in a low, tremulous tone, said:

"Is it possible, Edgar Milford, that we thus meet again?"

"We do, dear Rosalie," returned the other, coming forward and taking her hand, which, with reverent affection, he pressed to his lips; and then, emboldened by the passiveness of the other, and apparently acting from impulse only, he quickly pressed his lips to hers; and as her beautiful features became suffused with blushes, he added: "Pardon me, fair one—it is the first time I ever ventured so far—but the temptation, and my feelings, made the action irresistible."

"Captain Milford, you are bold," said Rosalie, her dark eyes flashing, and her face still retaining its crimson hue, which now seemed the flush of virtuous indignation. "You have dared to do what no man ever did before; and yet you say, '*pardon me,*' as if it were the most trivial thing in the world."

"Oh! Rosalie, I have offended you!" and the gallant Captain, still retaining the other's hand, sank on one knee by her side. "I have offended you, which I would not have done for the world. I was rash, I admit; and if you will forgive me, I promise, on my honor, as a soldier and a gentleman, never to attempt the like again—that is," he added, a moment after, "unless I have your permission."

"On that condition, and that only, will I forgive you," replied Rosalie. "Rise, Captain Milford, and please be seated."

"Ah! you have not forgiven me," said the Captain, humbly, as he arose, and threw himself into a chair which stood near.

"Why do you think I have not forgiven you?" inquired Rosalie, in a softened tone, touched by the other's manner.

"Because you addressed me so formally. When I entered, you called me by my Christian name—now you address me by my military title."

"Well, then, I will call you Edgar once more, to show you I hold no malice."

"O, thanks, fair Rosalie—thanks!"

"But how is it I see you here, Edgar?"

"First let me ask after your health. I was told by the servant you have been sick, and I know it true by your pale and somewhat wasted features."

"Yes, I have been very ill, but am now fast regaining health and strength."

"O, this must account for your long silence. I knew something was the matter, but I dreamed not it was this."

"And did this bring you to the city?"

"Not this alone—no, not this alone, dear Rosalie. I will not be hypocrite enough to say your silence was a leading cause even; though I can conscientiously say it had a certain influence upon my mind. No, I came (and the Captain looked cautiously around the apartment, and, drawing his chair close to that of Rosalie, added, in a low, solemn tone)—*I came here to serve my country.*"

Rosalie grew deadly pale, and grasping the other's arm, almost gasped:

"I understand you—a spy!"

The Captain nodded, and replied:

"It is a hateful word."

"And terrible," added Rosalie. "The penalty attached to detection is awful. The gibbet! the gibbet! Oh, Heaven! you must not die thus!"

"Fear not, dearest, if I may be allowed to term you so. My plans are well laid."

"And so were Andre's—God be merciful to him!"

"Amen to that—for he was brave and noble, and did not deserve his death."

"You knew him then?"

"I saw him die."

Rosalie covered her face with her hands, and a cold shudder passed over her delicate frame.

"Alas!" she murmured, at length—"poor Andre! what an awful fate was thine! And you saw him die? How did he bear himself?"

"As a brave and noble-minded soldier should."

"How was he looked upon by those who witnessed his execution?"

"As a man unfortunate, not criminal—as a man more sinned against than sinning—as the innocent expiator of the offenses and crimes of a villain."

"Then his enemies pitied him?"

"Ay, as never was enemy pitied before. The coldest-hearted stoic among them shed tears like a child. It was the most solemn, imposing, and heart-rending sight I ever witnessed. No one seemed calm and collected but the unfortunate prisoner."

"Describe the scene, Edgar, for I would have it from an eye-witness."

"I fear it will shock you too much, dear Rosalie—your nerves must still be weak."

"Go on! go on! I am prepared to listen;" and Rosalie threw herself back in her chair, and placed her hands before her eyes.

"I will endeavor to be brief then," rejoined Milford, "for I like not to dwell upon so sad a scene. It was first decided by General Washington, that Andre should suffer on the evening of the 1st of October; but Sir Henry Clinton having the same day sent some commissioners to treat with the American commander concerning Andre's release, and the negociation not being concluded in time, the execution was deferred till the following day at twelve o'clock. When, on the morning of the fatal day, the guard-officer announced to Andre the time fixed for the closing of his mortal career, he received the intelligence with a true soldier's firmness, and exhibited no emotion. His servant, who chanced to be in the room, was so affected that he burst into tears; upon which the prisoner turned to him, and in a severe tone said:

"'Leave me, till you can show yourself more manly!'

"At an early hour in the day, the people from the surrounding country began to gather about the fatal spot where the rude gallows had been erected, upon which they gazed with feelings of solemn awe. There appeared to be none of that levity of feeling which which usually attends an execution. Each face had a solemn, mournful appearance, as if each individual felt he was about to witness the final departure of a friend. About ten o'clock, the muffled drum was heard giving out its funeral sound, while the rest of the musicians played a solemn accompaniment. The military now began to march upon the ground, and take up positions in two long lines, reaching from the stone house, where Andre was confined, to the hill just back of the village, where he was to suffer. A little after eleven, the escort-guards proceeded to the prison, to attend the prisoner on his last journey. The outer guard formed a hollow square, and consisted of some five hundred men, under the direction of a colonel and major—the inner guard was merely a captain's command. It was my fortune to be deputed one of the two officers to take an arm of the noble prisoner, and walk with him to the gibbet, and I therefore had a good opportunity to observe him narrowly in his last moments. When we entered the room where he was confined, and announced to him our business, he arose from his seat, and with cheerful composure, as if he were merely going on a pleasure excursion, bowed gracefully, and said, with a bland smile:

"'Gentlemen, I am ready to wait upon you.'

"As I gazed upon him—so young, so handsome, so accomplished, so worthy to live, with such a brilliant and distinguished future so recently apparently opening before him—and reflected on the awfulness of our mission—that we were about to conduct him to an ignominious death—tears involuntarily started to my eyes, and I was obliged to turn away my head to conceal my emotion; observing which, he approached me, and in a tone of deep feeling, said:

"'I must thank you, Captain Milford, for this tribute of respect; it shows your goodness of heart, and I can answer for your fidelity to your country. My case is merely one instance of the fate of war, and I yield to my destiny."

"He knew you, then?" said Rosalie, in surprise.

"Yes, we had met before, under very different circumstances; and it was, perhaps, in some degree owing to myself that he was then a prisoner."

"How so?"

"You recollect you sent your servant into the country, and that we met at the Burnsides?"

"Yes, yes, I remember it well," answered Rosalie, with an arch smile, that Milford did not comprehend. "Well?"

"Well, this lad, whom I found very shrewd and knowing—remarkably so for one in his situation—threw out some strange hints about there being treason in high places; and said he had seen a letter dropped on the floor by a British officer, who called to see you, the superscription of which was *John Anderson*, and that in that letter he had read a few lines, which showed a plan to have the person to whom it was addressed come within the American lines. Now, taking every thing into consideration, and knowing that Arnold was expecting to meet a person from New York by the name of Anderson, I at once concluded that he had written the letter, and that this Anderson was an American spy in the British camp, who had been detected by his correspondence, which had accidentally fallen into the possession of the officer who called on you. From this reasoning I naturally concluded that Anderson had been arrested, and would be severely dealt with by the British. From some expression of this nature I let fall, the lad instantly inquired if I knew this Anderson; to which I replied, evasively, that I knew him only by name. He then, to my surprise, suggested that he was a British spy, but had no proof to offer in substantiation of the charge, save his own suspicions, which of course went for nothing. He then asked me if I suspected who was the writer of the letter, and I answered in the affirmative; and he then inquired if he was a man above suspicion, which I answered in the affirmative also. He then muttered something about being mistaken, but suggested that there would be no harm in watching the movements of all parties, to which I readily assented. Subsequently I communicated the information he gave me to General Washington, but purposely avoided saying any thing about Arnold, as I then believed him a pure and high-minded man, and thought that his character had been too much traduced by his enemies already. In this reserve, as events have since turned out, I fear I was wrong—but we can not tell beforehand always what is best for us to do.

"The interview with the boy, however, made a stronger impression upon my mind than I had thought at the time; and after I had returned to my own quarters, I often caught myself seriously pondering upon his words, but as often dismissed them with a hasty 'pshaw,' as being suggestions not entitled to much consideration. However, on the whole, I resolved, if any thing strange or peculiar should come under my notice, to take due note of it, and, if possible, manage so as to unravel the mystery—for that there was mystery somewhere, had become a fixed idea, of which I could not divest myself.

"Well, it so chanced, that on the day Andre had an interview with Arnold at Smith's house—but I am presupposing you have seen the whole account in the Royal Gazette."

"I have," replied Rosalie—"go on!"

"On that day, I say," continued Milford, "it so chanced that I was sent out with a patrolling party on the very road over which Andre and his guide Smith had resolved to pass, in order that the former, not being able to get back to the Vulture, should reach New York by land. Well, on their approaching my party in the evening, one of my men stopped the travelers, and demanded the password, which Smith, the spokesman of the two, was not able to give. I presented myself, entered into conversation with Smith, and inquired whither he was going; and on his replying that his object was to reach a place some distance below during the night, I tried to discourage him from proceeding, as I knew the country to be infested with lawless bands of desperadoes, who would not scruple to take his life. But he seemed bent on continuing his journey at all hazards, and this awakened my suspicion that all was not right. On examining his passport, however, I found it to be genuine, in Arnold's own handwriting, and I therefore knew I had no right to detain him. In the course of conversation, I learned that the name of his fellow-traveler was John Anderson; and my surprise, considering what had gone before, may be readily imagined.

"I could not now divest myself of a certain amount of suspicion, that this Anderson was a British spy; and I rather magnified the danger of the journey, in order to induce the parties to lie over till morning. Smith, I fancied, saw that I was doubtful of his honest intentions; and being somewhat alarmed by my discouraging representations of the country below, and fearful, if he persisted in going forward, that he would thus attract more attention to his movements than would be agreeable, finally resolved to take my advice and lie over, and persuaded his companion to do the same. In consequence of this, the parties turned back to a farmer's house near by, where they spent the night.

"I now resolved to profit by their delay, so as to have the mystery concerning Anderson, if mystery there were, unraveled; and I accordingly dispatched a note to one John Paulding, who was at the head of a scouting party below, to the effect, that, if a traveler, giving his name as Anderson, should attempt to pass him, to make some excuse for stopping and searching him—giving at the same time, as a reason for this, that I feared he was a British spy, playing a double game—for even then I did not suspect Arnold of being concerned in a plot with him, but thought it more probable he had deceived Arnold. I also added a personal description of the man, and a hint, that if he were a British spy, he would be likely, from what he had heard me say concerning the Cow Boys being out on the Tarrytown road, to take that route in preference to the other, as being for him the safer of the two.

"Well, to conclude this long digression, my messenger found and delivered to Paulding the note that night. He acted upon my suggestion, and the result you know."

"Then Andre's capture was in some degree attributable to yourself?" said Rosalie.

"Yes, I may be said to be an indirect cause of his apprehension."

"This is something new to me, and I presume is not generally known."

"No, it is known only to some three or four persons besides yourself—nor would I, for reasons of my own, have it go any further. Neither Smith nor Andre knew any thing of it, as neither do Paulding's assistants, for I cautioned Paulding to reveal the secret to no one."

"I perceive now, that Andre had good cause for knowing you, when you again appeared to him on the day of his execution."

"Yes; but when I first saw him as John Anderson, I had no idea of his being so important a personage. But a question, while I think of it. Who was the officer with you on the day that Anderson's letter was dropped in the drawing-room?"

"Why, who should it be, but poor Major Andre himself?"

"Ha! I see it all now; but your servant refused to tell me his name." After a moment's reflection, another idea seemed to strike the gallant Captain with great force; for his features quickly flushed, and as suddenly turned pale, and, in a tone of assumed indifference, he inquired: "Was Major Andre in the habit of visiting you, Rosalie?"

"O, yes," answered our fair heroine, with what seemed intended for natural frankness; and there was a roguish twinkle in her dark eyes, as she fixed them upon the half-averted face of the other, for she had divined his thoughts, and was delighted at the opportunity of testing his feelings. "Yes," she continued, with something like a sigh, "poor Andre! he used to call often to see me, and we spent many a delightful hour in each other's company."

"Indeed!" returned Milford, in a cutting tone, his features again becoming crimson with jealous vexation. "I suppose, then, your servant had orders not to tell me what British officer was with you on that day?"

"O, no—why should I give such orders?" asked Rosalie, in a well-affected tone of simple surprise. "Why should I have given such orders, when it was well known that Major Andre called almost daily to see me! I am sure I had no reason to be ashamed of his company."

"O, of course not," replied Milford, rather bitterly, and affecting to laugh. "Major Andre was a distinguished, high-minded, honorable young man, and there is no reason why any one should have been *ashamed* to have been seen in his company. On the contrary, his attentions were an honor to *any* young lady; and had he been less unfortunate, doubtless Miss Rosalie Du Pont would soon have been still further honored with an offer of his hand, even if such offer had not been already made."

"O, no, I do not think it would have gone so far as that," answered Rosalie, with an abstracted air, as if she were considering the matter seriously, and apparently taking no notice of the Captain's coldness and uneasiness. "I do not think it would have gone so far as that; for Major Andre had met with one great disappointment in love, and he was not the person to easily forget the past—to give up an old friend for a new one."

"A young maiden's sympathy with a young man, for the loss of his first love, has a wonderful effect, sometimes, in transferring his affection from a past to a present object."

"Does it?" said Rosalie, with well-affected simplicity. "Well, I must own, I did sympathize with him from my very heart."

"Of course—I could have sworn as much," replied the Captain, biting his lips with vexation. "It is a great pity poor Andre was *hung;*" and the last word was uttered with bitter, almost malignant emphasis; for what will not jealousy do, when once it takes a firm hold of the mind, and gets the upper hand of calm reflection? Though kind-hearted and humane, and one who deeply regretted Major Andre's untimely fate, yet at that moment the Captain felt something akin to fiendish joy for his supposed rival's misfortune—so much does the "green-eyed monster" change our very natures, turning our milk of human kindness into gall.

"Poor Andre!" sighed Rosalie. "But you were going to describe to me his last moments."

"True—but I think I will defer it till some other time. I fear this interview has been too long already."

"Indeed, Captain Milford!" said Rosalie, coloring.

"Ay, indeed, Miss or Ma'm'selle Du Pont, whichever prefix you please."

"You are offended, Edgar," said Rosalie, with some uneasiness.

"I feel I have been mistaken, ma'm'selle. I was not aware you and Major Andre were on such intimate terms."

"Surely, you are not jealous of one who is no more?"

"Jealousy, in this case, is not perhaps the proper word," returned Milford, coldly. "I am still under obligations to you, fair lady, and any thing I can do to serve you in return, I will do with all my heart; but, otherwise, I think it best we do not meet again."

Rosalie was now alarmed in earnest, and her color came and went rapidly, like the fitful playing of the aurora borealis. She felt that, in trying the Captain's feelings, she had gone one step too far; and yet she was loth to acknowledge her design, though she saw no other way of regaining his confidence. After a few moments of serious reflection, she said, with a forced laugh:

"I perceive you are not partial to a joke, Edgar?"

"There are some subjects of too serious a nature to be joked upon," was the reply. "If you have attempted to make a jest of my feelings, you have done wrong, and the consequences may not in the end be as pleasant as you anticipated."

"What do you mean?"

"That my nature is not one to be trifled with. Listen! I have ever believed you a pure minded, noble-hearted maiden, above the coquettish follies of your sex in general. As such, I have loved you, with a pure affection, constant as the needle to the pole. But my love, Miss Rosalie, is not a heated passion, beyond the control of reason. Only convince me that your nature is trifling, or that I am second in your esteem, and I withdraw myself from you forever. I will not deny, that since our acquaintance began, yourself and my country have occupied my thoughts, and that I have looked forward, with glowing anticipations, to the time when I could call you mine. But it was because I believed you reciprocated my attachment, although the word love has never before passed my lips to you. If I have been mistaken, as our late conversation tends to convince me I have, then farewell to one portion of my dreams of the future, and henceforth let my country have my undivided attention. I am not one to sue for your love, or your hand. I am as proud as yourself—though, for aught I know, there may be a great disparity in our births, as the world goes. You, for aught I know, for you have never revealed your history to me, may be nobly born; but that has little weight with me, who am engaged in a cause that proclaims equality to be one of its fundamentals; and whatever you may be by the accident of birth, I shall judge of you alone by your character and principles. You are young, beautiful, accomplished, and wealthy; and if ambitious, can aspire to any distinction; and, I seriously believe, can aspire with success. As I said before, I for one shall never sue for either your love or your hand. Love comes spontaneously from the heart, and differs materially from either respect, admiration, or esteem. Love is something we can not control; we love, without knowing why; nor can we fix it upon an object where it has not fixed itself. Our will has nothing to do with it; and therefore the individual who sues for love, mistakes the nature of the thing he asks for; for it is beyond the power of any being to grant, or withhold, merely on the whim of the moment. If, then, there is aught in my person or character, or in both combined, that causes this emotion, I need not sue for it, as it is already mine; if not, then you have no power to grant it. The bestowal of your hand, of course, is at your own disposal; but without love on your part, however much I may love you, I would not accept of it: and if with love, pride, ambition, or any other passion should tempt you to withhold it, I would not ask it as a favor. Such, Miss Rosalie, are my sentiments, frankly avowed, and you must act upon them as you think proper."

"Can you forgive me, Edgar, for trifling with your feelings?" asked Rosalie, as the other concluded, hiding her face in her hands.

"Yes, I can both forgive and forget, for my nature is not one to bear malice. True, while speaking of Andre, I must admit that I was vexed—ay, even jealous, if you will—and that my feelings toward that unfortunate officer experienced a momentary revulsion; but a little reflection has convinced me I was wrong: and I feel I could now pity him all the same, even should you declare to me that you sincerely loved him. I do not pretend to say, that such an avowal would not cause me deep regret; but, as God is my judge, I would no longer hold malice in my heart."

"And should I avow that I loved him, but that, since all hope of him is over, I could now love you, what would be the result?" asked Rosalie, in a timid tone.

"The result would be," replied Milford with a sigh, "that there would be an impassable barrier between us—that you could never be mine. I must be *first and only*, in your heart, or nothing."

"Noble Edgar!" cried Rosalie, with animation, while a warm blush made her lovely features radiant, and her pure soul shone in her eyes: "noble Edgar! your manly candor, and true feeling, demand a fitting return; and I frankly acknowledge I love you, and you only, and that I never loved another."

"Bless you, sweet Rosalie!" returned the Captain, seizing her fair hand, and covering it with kisses. "Bless you, dearest, for these welcome words! You have made me the happiest of mortals."

"You may now presume more—I release you from your promise," said the fair girl, averting her crimson face.

Edgar was not slow to understand; and reverently, but with ardent affection, he pressed the seal of love upon her sweet lips.

"I have long loved you, dear Edgar," pursued Rosalie, giving full sway to her feelings; "but I did not intend to tell you so yet. Circumstances have brought the avowal to my lips, which has long been known to my heart. You must pardon me for my silly mode of testing your affection."

"I can pardon any thing," cried the other, "since I now know I am loved by the only being whose love I desire;" and again his lips sought hers, and both were happy.

At this moment there came a gentle knock on the door; and springing back to his seat, the Captain assumed a look of respect, blended with indifference; but a crimson hue remained on the lovely features of the other, in spite of her efforts to imitate his example.

CHAPTER VI.

THE INTERVIEW CONTINUED.

"Come in," said Rosalie, in a firm tone; and a servant appeared, who, approaching her mistress, whispered a few words in her ear.

"Say I am engaged; but if he will call to-morrow, I shall be happy to see him," was Rosalie's answer, aloud, to the servant. The latter retired, and our heroine added: "Come, dear Edgar, finish your description of the closing scene in the life of the unfortunate Andre, and then I have some important questions to ask you."

"I fear I shall weary you, dearest—you are not strong, remember."

"O, no, you will not weary me, believe me. It seems I could listen to you forever."

Edgar rewarded the fair maiden with a look more eloquent than words, and then resumed his touching story.

"I think I mentioned, that after entering the prisoner's apartment, to conduct him to the gibbet, I unavoidably gave way to my emotions, and also what he said to me on that occasion. I replied, that though the fate of war made it my duty to be one of his conductors to the fatal tree, yet there was no one who would more deeply sympathize with him in his misfortune than myself. He thanked me in heartfelt terms, and said he had one regret in being so soon called away, and that was, that he would never be able to show his gratitude to American officers, for their universal kindness to, and sympathy with him, during his sojourn among them.

"Andre possessed a self-sacrificing heroism seldom met with in any country or age. One remarkable trait in his character, was, that he seemed never to think of himself when there were others in the case. Even here, in his last moments, when about to set out on his solemn march to the place of execution, he apparently gave no thought to death, only so far as it would deprive him of the power of serving his friends; and while all around him were moved to tears, he alone was calm and composed.

"On that fatal morning, Andre had taken great pains with his personal appearance. But an hour or two before our entrance, he had washed, and shaved, and dressed himself with great care in the rich full uniform belonging to his distinguished rank, which his servant had brought from New York, during his confinement, for this especial purpose. His features were pale, and his look was solemn—but otherwise he might have been taken for an officer going forth to attend a review.

"Giving the other officer and myself each an arm, he quitted his prison with a firm step. On coming without, and perceiving such a concourse of military and citizens before him, with every eye fixed upon himself, and every look expressive of the deepest sympathy, a sweet, sad smile was called upon his pale countenance, and there remained during the first part of his last solemn march. I have said that the military, with the exception of that detached as a guard to the prisoner, was paraded in two long, parallel lines, reaching from the stone house to the hill on which Andre was to suffer, and that outside of these lines, on every commanding position, the citizens were assembled in vast numbers, all anxious to behold the doomed one. With the exception of General Washington and staff, all the general and field officers were present on horseback, and had taken up their positions along the lines on both sides, where, in silence, and with looks of melancholy, they awaited the approach of Andre. A solemn, mournful death-march was played, and the guard, with the prisoner in the center, began to move forward. Never shall I forget that slow, impressive procession. Save the music, a death-like stillness prevailed; for the very soldiers moved forward, apparently, without making the least sound. Pity, awe, and gloom pervaded all classes. Every eye was bent upon poor Andre, and tears flowed fast and freely on all sides, even from men unaccustomed to the melting mood. Andre alone seemed composed and firm, and his arm, resting on mine, did not tremble in the least. To use his own language, he felt buoyed above the terror of death. As his eyes glanced from right to left, he here and there recognized a recently-made acquaintance among the American officers, to whom he bowed gracefully, and with an air of noble serenity, which caused them to turn aside their faces to conceal their emotion. Oh! the annals of the world do not produce a parallel, of a man being led to execution so universally lamented by friends and foes. When I say foes, I mean those of course politically opposed to him—for I do not believe, that in that awful moment, there was a single soul who beheld Andre, that did not wish his fate were otherwise. Even Washington, it is said, shed tears when he signed his death-warrant. Of all the noble beings that have from time to time perished ignominiously, there have always been some who rejoiced in their doom—Andre alone forms an exception.

"I have said, that during the first part of our fatal march, a sweet, sad smile lingered on the pale features of the prisoner; but when we came in sight of the gallows, the smile suddenly forsook his face, he involuntarily shrunk back, and for the first time I felt his arm tremble.

"'Why this emotion, sir?' I said to him.

"'Captain Milford,' replied he, in a tone I shall never forget, it was so touchingly mournful, 'I fear not death, but I detest the mode.'

"Death itself had no terrors for Andre—but the idea of being hung appalled him. His last request to Washington was, that he might be shot; and until he beheld the awful gibbet, looming up dark and terrible from the brow of the eminence, he had entertained the hope that he would be permitted to die a soldier's death. Washington would have granted his request, had it not conflicted with imperative duty.

"At last we reached the fatal spot; the music ceased, and an awful gloom and silence prevailed. For some moments Andre had to wait at the foot of the gibbet, while things were put in complete readiness for the last part he was destined to play in this drama of life. During this momentary suspense, I observed that he was uncommonly agitated. He placed his foot upon a loose stone, and rolled it back and forth nervously, while there seemed to be a choking sensation in his throat, as if he were vainly attempting to swallow.

"Perceiving at length that all was ready, he stepped quickly into the wagon, which had been placed under the gallows. For a moment he seemed to shrink, as he contemplated the horrible engine of death, and a visible shudder passed through his frame; but instantly regaining his composure, he elevated his head, with heroic firmness, and exclaimed:

"'It will be but a momentary pang.'

"He then produced two white handkerchiefs; and taking off his hat and stock, bandaged his own eyes with one, and handed the other to the provost marshal, who loosely pinioned his arms with it. During this proceeding, the spectators, military as well as civil, literally rained tears. I did not observe a dry eye in all the crowd.

"The executioner now fastened the rope to the cross-beam of the gallows, and with a firm hand Andre adjusted the noose to his neck, without assistance. Now came the most awful moment of suspense; and nothing could be heard but here and there a long-drawn sigh, or a choking sob, from the deeply-affected spectators. The bandage was around his eyes, the rope around his neck, and all were waiting to see the victim launched into eternity, when,

"'Major Andre,' said Colonel Scammell, in a clear, distinct, but slightly tremulous tone, 'if you wish to speak, you now have an opportunity.'

The unfortunate prisoner, with a gesture of graceful dignity, slowly raised the handkerchief from his eyes, and glancing calmly around, said, in a low, firm tone, placing one hand upon his heart:

"'*I pray you bear me witness that I meet my fate like a brave man.*'

These were the last words poor Major Andre ever uttered; and as he again drew the handkerchief over his eyes, the signal was given, the cart moved from under him, and he remained suspended by the neck. His struggles were brief and slight; death soon came to his relief; and so he perished, in the noon tide of life and glory: God rest his soul in peace!"

"Amen!" returned Rosalie, from whose soft dark eyes warm tears of sympathy were gushing, at the remembrance of the noble victim.

A pause of several moments ensued, during which each seemed occupied in contemplation of the melancholy subject; and then wiping the tears from her eyes, Rosalie said, hurriedly, and with a look of great anxiety:

"And now tell me of yourself, Edgar—how is it I find you here? and have you not periled your life by coming hither?"

"Fear not, dearest," answered Milford, in a low tone, but full of assurance. "I have not ventured hither rashly. But we must speak low, while I communicate the secret; for should it get wind, my life would be the forfeit."

"Oh! Heaven be merciful, and prevent so horrible a catastrophe!" shuddered Rosalie. "Oh! Edgar, since I have told you I love you, I now freely confess, that were any evil to befall you—were you in fact to lose that life so dear to me—I do not think I should survive the blow."

"O, bless you, sweet, dearest Rosalie! this is indeed love worth living or dying for!" exclaimed the Captain; and impulsively he caught the fair girl in his arms, and strained her to his heart; while his lips were pressed to hers, with that sacred, holy feeling of intense affection which has in it more of heaven than earth. "Henceforth, dearest," he continued, "I will consider my life not my own, but thine, and will jealously guard it as a trust from thee."

"Thanks! Edgar, thanks! for in that life I live. You may think it strange, to hear me speak thus, and may perhaps think I exaggerate under the impulse of the moment; but oh! believe it not! for I speak what I know, from a calm, sober review of my inner self. I am not as others, and the world calls me eccentric; and many doubtless think my eccentricity originates in a foolish desire to attract attention—to be the observed of all observers—but they are mistaken. I act as nature prompts, with perhaps a too contemptible opinion of the so-called world, but certainly with no desire to be one of its favorites. My nature, being different from others in one particular, may, for aught I know, be so in all; but one thing is certain, I can have no lukewarm friendship nor love. Love, in fact, is a term, which, in my vocabulary, is synonymous with idolatry and adoration; and hence, if the object of my love were destroyed, all desire of life would go with it. Thus, you see, dear Edgar, to what a strange, exacting creature you have pledged your affection, and in my heart I pray you may have no cause to regret it."

"O, no! never, never!" cried the other, with passionate warmth. "Regret it? regret a happiness second only to that of heaven? O, yes, I will regret it, when the repentant sinner regrets his entrance into immortal paradise. But, dear Rosalie," added Milford, looking with a lover's look into the soft, dark, melting eyes of the lovely being before him, "though I would remain in your sweet presence forever, yet I know that my time is limited, and duty compels me to hasten our interview to a close. You are naturally anxious to know wherefore I am here—I will tell you;" and Milford drew up his chair close to that of Rosalie's, and, in a voice scarcely above a whisper, thus proceeded:

"Soon after the flight of Arnold became known to Washington, a paper was intercepted, in which the name of a certain American general was found in such a connection as leads our commander-in-chief to fear there are others, high in power, concerned in the recently-discovered plot of treason. At all events, it is important he should know whether or no he is justified in entertaining suspicions of this general's integrity; and for this purpose I am here, with his private sanction; though it is of course believed by my comrades that I have deserted."

"In other words, as I said before," whispered Rosalie, with an expression of alarm, "you are here in the capacity of an American spy!"

"Such, I must admit to you, is the truth."

"Oh! then, for heaven's sake! be prudent! oh! be very prudent, and cautious, or you will be detected; and I hardly need tell you what will be the result of detection."

"No, I know my danger, and have come prepared for the worst. Washington advised me to see you; but cautioned me not to do any thing that could possibly fasten suspicion upon you, even should my own plans be frustrated. And yet, you perceive, I scarcely arrive in the city, ere I call upon you openly, in the broad light of day. Do you not fear, dear Rosalie, I have compromised your safety?"

"I fear nothing for myself, Edgar, but every thing for you. Tell me! have you run any risk in coming hither?"

"I think not, for I came with Sir Henry Clinton's sanction."

"Indeed! you have seen Sir Henry then?"

"Yes, I was with him this morning. In fact, the guard who arrested me, immediately on my crossing the lines, gave me over to an officer, who insisted on taking me at once to head-quarters. This, by the by, was exactly what I desired. Sir Henry received me kindly, but with an air of reserve. He wished to know my object in crossing the British lines in the uniform of a rebel; and I replied by stating, that, being tired and disgusted with the rebel service, particularly since being compelled to officiate in the execution of poor Major Andre, I had deserted in my regimentals, and hoped to find a safe asylum beneath the banner of St. George. He then asked me if it were my intention to enlist in the American Legion; explaining himself by saying, that the deserters from the rebel army, of whom there were quite a number in the city, would form a select corps, and be under the immediate command of Brigadier General Arnold. I answered to this, that for the present I wished to rest and look around the city; but that it was not improbable I would enlist, should any action against the rebels be meditated.

"'Well,' he said, 'there will soon be work for all to do; and if you see proper to join us, you shall be allowed to retain your rank.'

"I thanked him for his kindness, and said I would take it into serious consideration, and would let him know my resolve in the course of a week, or ten days at the farthest. He then inquired particularly about the last hours of poor Andre, what the rebels thought of, and how they felt toward him; and during the time he was the subject of our conversation, I observed that Sir Henry was much affected, and that he was often obliged to turn aside his face to conceal his emotion. Of course I spoke in the most enthusiastic terms of Andre, and told him I did not think there was a single individual who knew him that did not regret his death.

"'Poor Andre!' he exclaimed, in a voice husky with emotion. 'Poor Andre! I loved him, sir, as I would my own son, and feel that his place can never be supplied;' and as he said this, I observed the large tears roll slowly down his cheeks, which he did not attempt to conceal.

"I was deeply affected myself, and my heart yearned toward his excellency for this pathetic tribute to the memory of the unfortunate victim of circumstances. We dropped the subject, and Sir Henry resumed his wonted composure.

"He then made several inquiries respecting the American army, its numbers, the result of Washington's visit to Count Rochambeau, and what I supposed were his present plans. I answered as best I could, and at the same time appear frank and give him as little information as possible. My answers were evidently satisfactory; for he said they tallied with those of another American officer who had deserted, and whom he had questioned a day or two previous. I inquired to whom he alluded, and he replied his name was Champe, and that he had been an orderly sergeant of Major Lee's. Now I knew of Champe's desertion before I made the attempt myself; and it is my belief that his object and mine are much the same; though I know nothing positive, for my instructions did not mention him. It was intimated in them, however, that I should find assistance where I least expected, in the development of my scheme."

But is this Champe a man of honor and strict integrity?" inquired Rosalie.

"Yes, in every sense of the word; and what is more, he and I are sworn friends."

"But you have not seen him?"

"No."

"And when do you expect to?"

"If he is one of us, to-night—or if I do not see, I shall hear from him."

"And what do you mean by one of us?"

"This question from you, Rosalie?—are not you in the secret?" asked Milford, in some surprise.

"If you mean by the secret, the little band whose watchword is '*Liberty*,' I think I understand you."

"The same—I was right."

"But you spoke of some scheme to be developed; that I do not understand; for if your business here is merely to ascertain whether a certain general be treacherous or not, I see in that no complexity."

"That is only one part of my mission here, and is easily executed; the other is more difficult."

"And pray what is that other?"

"The seizure of the traitor Arnold—no less."

"Good heavens!" cried Rosalie, in alarm; "surely you are not enlisted in so dangerous a project as that?"

"Yes, it is even so."

"But it may cost you your life!"

"I hope not; for since I have seen you, I have every wish to live."

"Oh! the thought that you may fail is terrible, and makes me tremble."

"God bless you, sweet Rosalie! I will be trebly cautious for your sake."

"Oh! you must, dear Edgar, you must; now that you know how much I love you, you can easily divine the consequence to myself, should you fail and be detected."

"There is hazard in the undertaking, I know—but God is above us all, and in him I put my trust."

"Ah! Edgar, I thank you for that consoling thought! and for that noble sentiment, I love you still more, if that such a thing be possible. Yes, we will put our trust in God, and hope for the best. That he is with us, in our glorious struggle for liberty, I believe; and if he is with us, we shall yet be triumphant. To God let us ever look, in prosperity or adversity—such is my religion."

"And such is true religion, a thousand times more acceptable in his sight than canting creeds."

"But how will you pursue your plan? and where do you expect to meet your confederates?"

"You know one Signor Carlini?"

"Yes, and now I understand all. Well, may God watch over, prosper, and protect you; but oh! dearest Edgar, as you love me, do nothing rash! Better your design should fail, than that your dear life be too much put in jeopardy."

"Should I be led to contemplate any thing rash, I will think of Rosalie du Pont, and pause to reflect," was the gallant rejoinder.

"Thanks! thanks!—but go on and finish your story. You have not yet informed me how you came hither with Sir Henry's consent."

"True. Well, as our interview was about closing, I mentioned your name.

"Do you know her?" he inquired, with a look of some surprise.

"'I have reason to know something of her, your excellency,' I said; 'for mainly to her do I owe my release, as a prisoner of war, after the taking of Charleston.'

"'Ah, yes, I remember now her intercession in behalf of an American officer. And you, then, were the person? Milford! Milford!' he added, musingly; 'yes that was the name. You are very fortunate, sir, in standing so high in her esteem. You could not have had a better intercessor; for well I recollect that, at the time, I felt as if I could refuse her nothing, knowing her as I did to be so loyal.'

"'I have to thank both your excellency and herself for that especial favor, and I assure you I am not ungrateful,' I replied.

"'Yes, you say well, it was a special favor in your behalf,' he replied; 'for in setting you free—or rather, in conniving at your escape—I acted contrary to what I then believed my duty; but, as I said before, I felt at the time I could refuse the fair petitioner nothing.'"

"Ah! that is what troubles me," sighed Rosalie. "Sir Henry Clinton has been very kind and indulgent to me, and my conscience ofttimes reproaches me for abusing his confidence. He believes me so loyal, and puts such implicit reliance on all I say or do, that I often feel guilty, self-condemned; and I am obliged to call to mind the vast importance of the cause I serve—not only to the present generations, but to generations yet unborn—more, to the world, the whole human race, —I am obliged, I say, to call to mind the superior consideration of liberty over all minor matters, to justify myself in my own eyes for my duplicity."

"Ay," returned the Captain, "I have thought and felt the same, and only console myself with the reflection, that the end must justify the means. But I must hasten my departure, for already have I overstayed my time. In reply to Sir Henry's observations concerning the wherefore of my release, I said that I hoped he had never had reason to regret his clemency on that occasion; and added that Miss Rosalie Du Pont and myself had corresponded ever since; and that I doubted not he had more than once had the benefit of intelligence conveyed in my epistles.

"'Ah, then,' he replied, 'you, I am to understand, were the source from which she obtained her information of the doings of the rebel army.'

"'I flatter myself some portion of it came through me, your excellency,' I answered.

"'Thanks," he rejoined, 'thanks, sir, for your loyalty, even while in the enemy's ranks! Do you know the address of Mis Rosalie Du Pont?' he inquired.

"'I know she resides in Queen-street, your excellency.'

"'You would do well, I think, to call on her.' He then gave me your number, adding: 'I think she is now about, so that you will have no difficulty in seeing her.'

"I knew not then to what he alluded; but now suppose he referred to your illness, of which I had heard nothing till informed by the servant. Rest assured, dear Rosalie, I gladly availed myself of Sir Henry's permission to visit you—or rather, perhaps, his intimation that I should do so—for, above all others, it was what I most desired."

Some further conversation followed, and then Milford took his leave; Rosalie charging him, with tearful eyes, as he valued her happiness, to do nothing rash, and fervently praying that guardian angels might attend his steps and keep him from a fatal failure.

CHAPTER VII.

A YANKEE PEDDLER.

On Broadway, about half-way between the Park and Battery, where at present stands that beautiful edifice of modern construction, known as Trinity Church, with its needle-shaped steeple towering to the very clouds, there was, at the time of which we write, an open space, used as a parade ground for the soldiers, and called by the British the Mall. Here, in pleasant weather, detachments of soldiers, under subalterns, were drilled and paraded daily, to the amusement of such adults and children as felt disposed to view them from the opposite side of the street; and such is the *penchant* of all classes for military display, that the Mall never lacked spectators, of all ages, sizes, and colors, but mostly of the female sex.

The afternoon of the same day on which Captain Milford had his interview with Rosalie Du Pont, as he was sauntering down Broadway, in a musing mood, he approached the Mall, and perceived a sergeant drilling some raw recruits. Mechanically he paused to look at their maneuvers, which were so extremely awkward as to cause him to smile involuntarily. While gazing at them, and wondering where so many ungainly, clumsy fellows had been picked up, he became aware of some one standing beside him; and on turning to look at the new-comer, he was surprised to find him a brother officer, who had been made prisoner at the same time as himself, namely, at the taking of Charleston, the May previous. Of these prisoners, numbering some five thousand, rank and file, many of them had been brought to New York, and the subalterns and privates had been placed aboard the prison-hulks, of which mention was made in the "Female Spy," though most, if not all, of the commissioned officers, had been allowed the range of the city on parole. Thus it was, that Captain Milford so unexpectedly came in contact with Lieutenant Harden, who was at liberty, in the heart of the British camp, though in neither the capacity of a deserter or spy.

"Why, as I live, it is Captain Milford!" exclaimed the Lieutenant, extending his hand, as a mutual recognition took place. "I am delighted to see you, Captain, though I would rather it had been in a rebel camp, as the red-coat gentry here have termed our quarterings. But where on earth have you come from, Captain? It was reported you had escaped—it is not possible you are again a prisoner?"

"What news since I saw you, Harden?" inquired Milford, evading the other's question.

"O, well, we have no news here of any consequence; and what we do get, is of course the English version. Things with us jog on much as usual. The men are dying by hundreds in the prison-ships, and we officers are gradually getting thinned every day."

"How do you mean—sickness?"

"Ay, sickness, assassination, and duels."

"Good heavens! assassination, say you?"

"Ay; you seem surprised—but we are getting used to it here. Many of our officers here are sons of gentlemen, and have money; and money, united with idleness, begets dissipation, and dissipation here leads to the most deplorable results. To American officers, the British officers are very insolent; and besides refusing to associate with them, they embrace every opportunity to insult them. The consequence is street encounters and duels; and by some strange fatality, the insolent red-dogs almost invariably come out triumphant. Then let one of us get a little intoxicated, and stray away from his companions, in the night, and the chances are ten to one that he never returns alive."

"This is horrible!" exclaimed Milford. "Can nothing be done to remedy the evil? Would not a complaint to General Robertson, the Commandant of the city—or to His Excellency, Sir Henry Clinton, Commander-in-Chief——"

"It was tried," interrupted Harden, "and the answer received, was, to the effect, that the British commanders would do what lay in their power; but that it would be impossible for them to prevent gentlemen from resenting insults—that if we did not wish to be killed in duels, we should not fight them—and that the best way to keep from being assassinated, would be to remain at our quarters; or, if we must needs go out, to go out in a body, and strictly sober."

"Well, much of it is good advice, I must admit," returned Milford.

"But you have not told me of yourself," pursued the other. "Is it true you escaped at the time it was so reported? for we did not know whether to rejoice at your liberty, or mourn for your death."

"It is true I escaped then," answered the other.

"How is it, then, I again find you here? have you been taken prisoner a second time?"

"No!" said Milford, abruptly, the color mounting to his forehead.

"Ha!" exclaimed the other, as a dark suspicion crossed his mind; "surely, I am not to be allowed to suppose you have deserted? O, no—no—that could not possibly be!"

Milford turned away his face in much confusion, and pondered rapidly on his reply. It would not do for the other to know he was there as a spy, and he had already denied he was a prisoner, there was therefore no alternative; he must admit himself to be a deserter; and he further reflected, that this admission, though humiliating to his feelings, would be beneficial to his scheme, in so much, that, being treated with coldness, and even disrespect, by his brother officers, would give an air of truth to his story of desertion, and lessen the chances of his detection. He therefore answered the other rather haughtily:

"Lieutenant Harden, what you think could not possibly happen, has happened. I am tired of rebel glory; and if I again enlist in military service, it will be in that of my liege and royal master, King George."

"Heavens have mercy! what do I hear?" cried Harden, with a mingled look of astonishment, scorn, and disgust. "Another traitor! God save my country!" and wheeling on his heel, without another word, he strode away.

The first impulse of Milford was to follow him, and explain all, for he felt cut to the quick; but remembering it was necessary to his object for Harden to believe as he did, he restrained his inclination, and allowed him to depart without a word. The reader will readily perceive how severe a trial this was to a sensitive man of honor.

"Well," muttered Milford to himself, "I am serving my country, and there is more than one who knows I am not so base as I seem, and this must satisfy my conscience, if not my feelings."

He then walked musingly away, the drill no longer affording him the slightest amusement. He had scarcely gone a dozen rods, however, when he found himself approaching a group of persons congregated around some object, which seemed to excite their risible faculties to a great degree, for they occasionally laughed loud and boisterously. In his present state of mind, Milford felt no disposition to join them, and no curiosity to learn the cause of their mirth; and he was already in the act of turning abruptly away, when a familiar voice struck on his ear, and caused him to alter his intention. With an accelerated step he now approached the crowd, to ascertain if his surmise was correct.

As he drew near, the by-standers gave another merry shout; and the moment their laughter had subsided, he heard that same familiar voice again; and this time he felt sure of the identity of the individual in question; though, so compact was the circle around him, that it was some moments ere the Captain could get a glimpse of his person. But when at last Milford did behold him, he found he had made no mistake, though how and why he was there, was a matter of surprise and wonder.

In the center of a circle, composed of some twenty or thirty persons, of both sexes, all ages and sizes, and whose numbers were fast augmenting, stood our old acquaintance, Joshua Snipe, as large as life. In one hand he held a razor, and in the other a cake of shaving soap; while at his feet was an open wooden box, displaying not only many duplicates of the articles in hand, but also various other simple "notions," such as thread, tape, needles, pins, lace, sewing silk, coarse jewelry, etc. Josh was, to use one of his own peculiar expressions, "wide awake," and was descanting in very earnest tones upon the merits of his very valuable commodities, but more especially upon those he held in his hands, which he seemed determined to sell, whether the spectators would buy or not.

"Now I tell *yeou*," he went on, "my kit is jest a leetle the putiest, and slickest, in the hull united kingdom of North America, and if you was to walk from sunrise to sundown, you couldn't find the beat on't. Come, mister," addressing a tall, sallow, cynical individual, "you want that are razor and soap, I know you dew, for you've got lots of hair on your face, that haint no business there, not a darned bit. Now, if you've got a wife, jest you buy these ere, and use 'em, and if she don't bless the day you ever seed Josh Snipe, the peddler, why, the next time I see you, I'll give you tew rows of pins, free gratis for nothing."

Here the crowd gave another shout, and the tall, cynical individual growled out—

"Better mind your own business, you —— Yankee jack-a-napes!"

"That's jest what I'm doing," returned Josh, good-humoredly, winking at others of the by-standers—"that's jest exactly what I'm doing, for this here is my business, and the only business I've got to dew, without 'tis to serve King George on all occasions, bless his reverence! But I axes pardon—for maybe I hurt your feelings, for maybe you haint got no wife, and can't git one; but jest you buy one of these here razors and soap, and lather and scrape that are hair off, and I'll bet tew to one—tew tenpenny nails agin a meeting-house—that the first gal you court 'll fall in love with ye, and have ye right straight off."

Here the crowd uttered another yell of delight, and the cynical man grumbled out something about the peddler being "A —— Yankee fool," and hurried away amid the jeers of the whole party, who seemed disposed to take sides with the one who caused them so much mirthful amusement.

"Wal," said Josh, "he's gone, and good riddage, for his face fairly set my teeth on edge, it looked so tarnal, all-fired sour-like. Come, good folks, who's the next buyer? I don't like to recommend my own notions, jest because some folks might think as how I'm interested in selling 'em, that's a fact; but I dew say, that for soap *and* razor, these here is just the slickest fixins as can be found out of Bosting, where they fit Bunker hill, and got most consumptiously licked tew."

Here a voice cried out, rather sharply:

"Who got licked?"

"Why the rebels did—darn it! didn't you know that?" returned Josh, assuming a look of superiority.

"Good! good! Bravo! bravo!" cried several voices, accompanied with laughter.

"Now this here soap and razor is them kind that does their own work, and don't have to keep no help," pursued Josh, seeming all intent on disposing of his wares. "Now mind, good folks, I don't calculate to praise any thing I've got beyond its desart—but I must say, that that are razor is worth a dozen barbers—cause when you go to sleep, you've only got to put it under your piller, with the soap along with it, and when you git up in the morning, you'll find all the hair off your face, as clean as 'twas the day you was born."

As soon as the laughter, following this speech, had subsided, one of the by-standers inquired the price of the self-shaving razor; and being duly informed by Mr. Snipe, he drew out his purse, and threw down the money, observing at the same time, that if the razor proved to be worth nothing, he thought the amusement so far afforded him would still leave him the Yankee's debtor. Snipe's next customer was an old woman, who inquired the price of a paper of pins.

"One shilling, marm, and warranted gine-*wyne*," replied the dealer in small notions. "And I dew say," he continued, "them is the greatest pins ever made. Why, marm, you jest git them ere pins attached to you, and they'll stick to you through thick and thin, as long as you live; yes, marm, they'd sooner lose their *heads* than let go of your dress in a wrong time—darned if it wouldn't, that's a fact. Them's what I call courting pins, marm."

"Why so?" asked a voice.

"Because, all a gal's got to do, is jest to put 'em in thick round her waist, and tell 'em she wants protection; and if they don't bring the courting feller up to the *scratch*, then I'll agree to measure tape with a bean-pole, or chop wood for a shilling a day in haying time."

"I'll take a paper on 'em," said the old woman, fumbling in her bosom for a shilling, which she found at last, and paid over to the peddler, who received it with a polite bow and one of his blandest smiles.

Here another female customer selected a few yards of tape, when Josh, ever ready to recommend his wares, proceeded:

"That's lacing tape, marm; and though I dew say it myself, for want of somebody else to recommend it, it's the greatest tape that ever was made. Why, you've only got to put a few yards in your corsets, and it'll naturally draw your waist up jest like a wasp."

Here the male portion of the spectators roared with laughter, the old woman grinned, and the younger females simpered, and hid their faces—while Josh, with a very grave look, continued, in a way to make the mirth convulsive:

"You needn't laugh, good folks, 'cause what I tell you's true as thunder. Why, I sold a few yards of that are tape to a fat woman once, in the country, and I didn't see her agin for three months; and when I did see her, she'd got so thin round the body, that I didn't know her. 'What's the matter with ye, mother?' says I. 'Matter enough,' says she. 'Ever since you was here I've been dreadfully troubled for breath; and I'm monstrously afeared I'm agoing to lose it altogether,' says she. 'I've got such a tightness around my waist.'

"I tuk, in a moment.

"'What did you do with the tape I sold ye?' 'That's a fact,' says she. 'I didn't think on't afore, but now I see as how it is that tarnal tape, and nothin' else—it's been squeezing me, till I'm e'en a'most dead;' and with that she got out her shears, and gin it a clip; and you oughter jest heard her bones crack, as they kim back to their places agin. It was the tape that did it, that's a fact; *she'd got in a yard tew much.*"

Josh had now several laughing customers for his lacing tape; and when all that wanted it had been supplied, he went on to dispose of his other articles, recommending each with some droll story, similar to the specimens we have given.

For a small business, his sales were quite extensive; but at last they came to an end, and Josh closed his box, preparatory to taking his departure. It was at this moment, that, glancing around the circle, his eye encountered Milford. Without showing any sign of surprise, he merely said:

"Yes, mister, I'll take them are things down for you now, I guess."

The Captain, who was not slow to take the hint, that Josh wished to speak with him alone, readily answered:

"Very well—the sooner the better."

Milford now left the crowd, and walked leisurely past the Mall, up Broadway. In a few minutes he was overtaken by Josh, with his box slung under his right arm, in true peddler fashion.

"Well, Josh," were the first words of Captain Milford, spoken in a low, guarded tone—"how is it that I find you here?"

"Why, Capting, arter you left the country, it got to be mighty lonesome up there; and hearing you'd run away to the British, I thought I'd do so too—more particularly, as I had a chance to buy a peddling-feller out to a bargain, and pay him in the scrip you'd gin me. You see, he'd got all-fired scart, for fear he'd be robbed; and so he sold out to me on my own terms; and I know'd, putty wal, if I come among the Britishers, I'd soon turn my notions into the real hard silver, and make a speck by it tew."

"But was this your sole object in coming hither?" inquired the Captain, fixing his eyes keenly upon the other—for somehow he had imbibed the idea that this itinerant occupation was merely a cloak to cover some important design—and he thought it not improbable that Josh's motives, and his own, in coming to the city, were much the same.

"Wal, afore I answer you, Capting," returned Josh, guardedly, and now in turn fixing a searching look upon the other, "I'd just like to know if you've really deserted your country, as they say you have?"

"Who says so?"

"Why everybody up in your parts. They're down mighty hard on you, Capting; and I heard more'n one feller swear he'd like to put a bullet through your head."

"Yes," said Milford, who wished to try the other, "I *have* deserted the rebels, but *not* my country, which belongs to my king, and not to a rabble party of freebooters, for they deserve no better title."

"Do you mean to say that General Washington is one of these rabbles, as you call 'em?" inquired Josh, his small black eyes assuming a fiery, snaky look.

"Of course I do, since he openly acts as their leader."

"Wal, all I've got to say is," returned Josh, in a tone of forced calmness, "that the feller who says a word agin great General Washington, is a scoundrel, and I'd like the fun of licking him like darnation."

"Mr. Snipe," returned Milford, with savage sternness, "allow me to say, that the language you have just made use of, might be construed into treason."

"Construe it into what you darn please," replied Josh, sulkily; "but, I swow to Guinea, I won't take a word on't back, for you, nor nobody else—so there."

"I suppose the next thing I shall hear, you will be boasting that this Mister Washington, this rebel adventurer, is a better man than our noble sovereign, King George?"

"Wal, I don't know's I should say so, if you hadn't put me in the way on't; but, I swow to Guinea, I'll say so now, if I die for't."

"You will, eh?"

"I will, by gosh!"

"You say that George Washington is a better man than King George?"

"Yes, a better man than ever King George dared to be—the royal old scoundrel, that wants to make slaves of everybody."

"Ha! this is the declaration I wanted—this is high treason—and for this I can cause you to swing at any moment."

"No you can't," contradicted Josh, bluntly.

"Why not?"

"'Cause, *Mister* Milford, you can't prove I said so; and I'm not darn fool enough to say it agin afore witnesses."

"Please address me by my title, sirrah."

"What? got a title a'ready?"

"Am I not a Captain?"

"You *was*, till you disgraced yourself, by turning traitor, just like old Benedict Arnold, rot his picter. I ain't wicked naturally, mister; but, by Jehosaphat, I'd jest like to tramp ten miles, afore breakfast, to see all you fellows hung—I would, I swow!"

"Come, come," said Milford, laughing, "it is time to finish this farce, and talk seriously. I perceive you are true to our cause, and that is what I wished to be certain of, before taking you into my confidence. You must know, then, that I deserted for the purpose of accomplishing a great design, and that I have my country as much at heart now as ever."

"Do you mean to say you've been fooling me all this time, and that you really and truly haint gone over body and soul to the consarned Britishers?" inquired Josh, with a look of ludicrous surprise, something between fear and delight.

"Yes, my worthy friend, I mean precisely so."

"Glory, halleluiah!" cried Josh, beginning to dance a kind of jig, actually forgetting where he was in his hilarious excitement.

"Stop! behave yourself!" said Milford, in alarm; "would you attract the notice of the town?"

"Gosh! that's a fact," returned Josh, instantly resuming his former quiet walk. "I didn't think 'beout my being 'mong the tarnal Britishers; for I was so tickled to know you wasn't a turn-coat; for though I says it myself, what shouldn't, I think lots of you, Capting. But which way be you going?"

"I was merely taking a stroll; but I have much to say to you, and so suppose you accompany me to my lodgings."

"Where abeouts?"

"In Cross Alley. But stay—I will write it down, and you can come in the course of an hour; for now I bethink me, perhaps it would be as well for us not to be seen too much together."

Captain Milford then took from his pocket a pencil and slip of paper, on which he traced a few words, and handed it to Josh, saying:

"In an hour I shall expect you."

"And I'll be there," returned the other.

The two then separated, Josh continuing up Broadway, and Milford, taking a cross-street, leading to Queen, up which he sauntered, past the mansion of Graham Percy, the residence of her he loved, to Franklin Square, when he turned off to the left, down into what was called the swamp, and finally paused at the door of the house occupied by Dame Hagold, where, it will be remembered, we once saw Rosalie Du Pont, disguised as a mulatto servant.

Rapping on the door, Milford was soon admitted by the dame herself; to whom, as soon as he entered, he gave instructions concerning the peddler; who, appearing punctual to the time, was also admitted, and the two were closeted together till after night had set in. What passed between these two individuals then and there, it is not our purpose at present to divulge.

Rather let me again shift the scene.

CHAPTER VIII.

MEETING OF THE SPIES.

It was about ten o'clock on the night following the events recorded in the last three chapters of our story, that Carlo Carlini, the astrologer, sat alone in the Chamber of Fate. As we have once or twice given our readers a description of this apartment, it will only be necessary to state, that it had undergone no alterations since then. Every thing, as then, was hung in black, and the room had the same mysterious and awe-inspiring effect. The same black drapery concealed the walls, and covered the tables and seats, and the same ponderous globe lamp, of ground glass, suspended from the ceiling, above the table, gave out its mellow light. To complete the picture, and as it were to give a true duplicate of the former one, the astrologer, dressed in plain black velvet, with his jet black hair falling in profusion down the sides of his deadly-pale face, and over his shoulders, was seated exactly as then, on the same stool, and in the same place. He was alone, and apparently in a deep reverie; for his small, dark, fiery eyes were fixed, with a vacant gaze, on the table before him, and not a sound disturbed the solemn silence of the chamber.

Minute succeeded minute, and a quarter of an hour passed away, during which the astrologer might have been taken for a statue, he was so quiet, so motionless. At the end of this time, however, he suddenly altered his position, and inclining his head one side, appeared to be listening. He evidently heard some expected sound; for he immediately placed his hand on the bell-knob projecting from the table, and gave it a jerk; and as a black servant entered the room, almost at the same instant, he said, in his own peculiar sonorous tones, which, without being loud, fell on the ear clear and distinct:

"I think one or more of my expected guests has arrived. Thou wilt be cautious in all that pertains to the signals and watchwords, and obey thy instructions to the letter. Fail, (and here the dark eyes seemed to penetrate to the very soul of the negro,) fail, and thy life is forfeit. Go."

He waived his hand, and was again alone. Through the black drapery the negro had suddenly appeared, noiseless as fate, and, at the last word, he vanished like a shadow.

Some moments now elapsed, during which the astrologer seemed to listen attentively, and then three distinct raps were heard on the door.

"Who knocks?" inquired the astrologer.

"A friend of the true cause," was the answer.

"The watchword?"

"*Liberty.*"

"Enter."

The door opened, and Sergeant Champe advanced into the room.

"Welcome, worthy friend of the true cause," said Carlini, meeting him with extended hand. "Brother, I give thee greeting—thou art the first guest to-night, though the hour appointed is at hand."

If the reader is very observant of minor things, he or she has doubtless noticed a certain lack of uniformity in the language of the astrologer, as quoted on different occasions; for instance, in the use of the personal pronouns, he sometimes confining himself wholly to the singular number, as thee and thou, and at other times using the plural in the manner most in vogue at the present day. We have only to say, in respect to this disparity of language, that we suppose the astrologer had his own reasons for his different styles of speech, and that we, as a faithful chronicler, are in duty bound to record his language as he chose to utter it, without asking any questions, or being obliged to give any particular reasons therefor. But at the same time, we may, perhaps, be permitted to surmise, that when he desired to be solemn, impressive, and formal, he used the pronouns of the singular number, as being the most effective; but on other occasions discarded them, as being too stiff, stately, and marked.

"I hope there will be no failure," said Champe, in reply to the other—"for time now is too precious to be wasted."

"I trust that all will be here soon," returned Carlini. "Hark! I think I hear another signal."

The result proved him correct; and a few moments after, another knock was heard on the door. The same interrogations and answers being gone through with, the door opened, and disclosed the person of Captain

Milford. The moment his eye fell upon Champe, he exclaimed:

"Ah, it is as I thought: my old and tried friend, you are one of us, I see;" and rushing together, the two officers greeted each other with a warm embrace.

"Yes," said Champe, "I see we both have one object here. I heard you were in the city, and I readily conjectured why. I questioned Carlini here, but he would tell me nothing."

"It is not prudent to speak all one knows on every occasion," rejoined the astrologer. "Besides, I knew you, gentlemen, if true to your promises, would soon meet, and then it would be time enough to make such explanations as you might think proper."

Here Milford and Champe held a low, hurried conversation of several minutes duration, apart from Carlini; and then the Captain, advancing to the astrologer, said:

"With your permission, Signor Carlini, I will admit a friend to our secret conference."

"Art willing to be responsible with thy life for his fidelity?" asked the other.

"Yes, since this very proceeding places my life in jeopardy, in the event of his playing us false."

"I trust thou hast been prudent, then, in the bestowing of thy confidence."

"I have, Signor, for I feel my life too valuable, at the present time, to risk it lightly or foolishly. The person I wish to admit, is true to his country."

"Well, if Sergeant Champe objects not, my permission is granted," answered Carlini.

"I have already been consulted in the matter," returned the Sergeant, "and have yielded to the request of my friend—the more readily, perhaps, that I know something of the person in question, having made his acquaintance under rather singular circumstances;" and he gave Milford an arch look, who replied, with a smile:

"Ay, it was a matter of far-seeing"

"Let the stranger be admitted, since his integrity is so well vouched for," said Carlini.

The Captain left the room; but soon returned, saying:

"Your servant, Signor, refuses to let my friend enter."

"Ah, true—I had forgotten; do not blame him; he is faithful to his instructions:" and ringing the bell, Carlini, as soon as the black made his appearance, said to him: "Obey this gentleman (pointing to Milford) as though he were myself."

Milford went out again; but presently returned, accompanied by Joshua Snipe. He at once introduced him to Carlini, who seemed to regard him with considerable suspicion—more especially, perhaps, that, true to his inquisitive disposition, he had no sooner nodded awkwardly to Carlini, than he began to peer about the room, with an air of great curiosity, and even went so far as to take hold of the black drapery, as if to examine what sort of stuff it was, and then try whether or no there was a wall behind it. Milford and Champe exchanged glances, and smiled; but Carlini seemed to view the matter in a very different light; for advancing to the innocent Mr. Snipe, he tapped him on the shoulder, and said, sternly and cuttingly:

"If thy business here is to pry into my secrets, thou hast chosen a very inappropriate time. We are met for more important matters."

Josh surveyed the astrologer, while he was speaking, with a mingled look of rustic timidity, shrinking awe, and impudent curiosity; and then said, with a ludicrous sincerity, that caused both Milford and Champe to turn aside their faces, to conceal a suppressed laugh:

"I 'spose you're the owner of these here fixens? I didn't mean no harm, mister. Gosh-all-thunder! what a curious place you have got here!"

"Is this the man you have taken into your confidence, gentlemen?" said Carlini, turning away from Josh, with an expression of disgust, and addressing the others.

"He has his rustic peculiarities," answered Milford, "but he is none the less true to our cause."

"Not a darned bit," rejoined Josh, who now felt himself insulted, and spoke rather indignantly. "I 'spose a feller can feel of a little black cloth, and not altogether play the darned scamp, for all that. I told ye I didn't mean no harm, mister," he continued, eyeing Carlini insultingly, "and if you aint a mind to take the apology, just as I meant it, you can let it alone."

"Silence, sir!" cried Milford, in a stern, commanding tone; while a flush of anger passed over the deadly pale features of Carlini, and then, retreating, seemed to leave them more ghastly pale than ever.

Milford was about to proceed with a severe reprimand, when Carlini motioned him to silence, saying:

"Leave me to deal with this fellow." Then striding up to Josh, who began to retreat in some dismay, not knowing exactly what might be the consequences of too boldly "bearding the lion in his den," Carlini exclaimed, in his peculiarly full, sonorous tones: "I command thee to stand! Young man, thou dost not know me, or never would'st thou have addressed to me the language I just now heard. Doubtless thou thinkest me like unto other men—but I will *prove* to thee I am more. Thou shalt learn to fear and respect me. Here is my first lesson! I command thee to stand, paralyzed and powerless—to become a breathing statue—a living, sentient thing, without the power of volition!" and as he spoke, he slowly raised his right fore finger to a level with his head, and fixed his black, fiery eyes, with piercing intensity upon the eyes of the other.

Josh was completely over-awed by that look; and he would have withdrawn his gaze, in confusion—but, to his surprise and dismay, he found it riveted there, as by a spell. Then he attempted to retreat—but, horror of horrors, he could not move a limb! He was indeed a "living statue," rooted to the spot, against his will; and a cold shudder passed through his frame, and he felt truly he was in the presence of a being superhuman. His respiration became quick and heavy, like one panting from fatigue; an expression of terror gradually settled on his features, and large beads of perspiration pressed through the pores of his skin. Milford and Champe silently drew nigh, and gazed upon the two with surprise and curiosity; but they were not aware it was impossible for Josh to move; and they wondered at the mere position and look of the astrologer producing so singular an effect upon the other.

"Wilt be careful of thy speech to me henceforth?' sternly demanded Carlini, at length.

"I'll do any thing you say, mister, if you'll only take them are eyes of yourn off on me," replied the Yankee, in a pleading, tremulous tone.

"Enough!" returned the astrologer, or perhaps we should say magnetizer; "we understand each other now, and thou art free. But beware!" he added, impressively—"beware what thou doest! for the same eye that is upon thee now, will watch thy secret acts—ay, thy very thoughts."

He then turned calmly away, and, walking to the table, resumed the seat he occupied when introduced at the beginning of this chapter; while Josh turned aside, every limb trembling with fear, and wiped the perspiration from his face.

"Come, gentlemen," said Carlini, "let us proceed with our business. George!"

As he pronounced this name, a slight noise was heard, as of the opening of a door on the opposite side of the room to where our friends entered, the black drapery was thrust aside, and our young hero of the prison stood revealed to the company.

"Thou mayest enter now, George," pursued Carlini, "and bring with thee three seats for our guests."

The youth retired behind the hangings; but presently returned, bringing three black stools, which he placed round the table, and then silently seated himself on the one opposite Carlini.

"Seats, gentlemen," continued Carlini, pointing to the vacant stools; and as all complied with the request, (Josh still trembling from his recent fright,) the host added: "Gentlemen, it is necessary, in the first place, that you all know each other. This youth is George Nugent, the messenger dispatched by me to General Washington, to carry news of Arnold's treason, but who was detected crossing the British lines, thrown into prison shortly after, and subsequently released, in what manner matters not. Suffice, that detection now, within the British camp, would be a momentary prelude to his execution; therefore, in intrusting you with this secret, I have not only placed his life, but mine, in your hands.

It seems needless for me to say, I fear nothing from this avowal—otherwise, it would not have been made. George Nugent, these gentlemen here present are persons who prize their country, and the cause of liberty, above all other considerations, and are at this moment periling their lives to obtain an important object—no less, if I mistake not, than the seizure of that vile traitor, who, through your seizure by the British, escaped the hands of justice. Am I right, gentlemen?"

"You are right," returned Milford, while Champe nodded, and Josh gave his head an affirmative jerk. "But pardon me, Signor Carlini," pursued Milford, rising, "if I seem to break the rules of order. I must take this youth by the hand, and, in the name of liberty, say God bless him, for his noble and daring efforts in the cause of right!" and as he spoke, the Captain shook the hand of George Nugent warmly, who, overwhelmed with modest confusion, blushed to the temples, and seemed unable to articulate a word in reply, though he evidently strove to do so.

"I thank you for the hint, Captain," said Champe, also rising. "I too must express my admiration of his noble devotion to our cause;" and he grasped the hand of the youth with a pressure that could leave no doubt of his sincerity.

The astrologer looked on in silence, but evidently more affected at this ebulition of feeling than he wished to be apparent to his colleagues. He coughed once or twice, moved restlessly on his seat, and, when the others had resumed their places, said:

"Since we all know each other, gentlemen, let us now proceed to business. As a matter of form, I would suggest that each and all of us take a solemn oath, to be true to ourselves, each other, and the cause of liberty."

"The suggestion does not seem improper," returned Milford.

"I can not object to it—though, for one, I know it will add nothing to my firmness of purpose," said Champe.

"Arise, gentlemen—I will dictate the oath," rejoined the astrologer.

And as each stood upon his feet, he continued:

"By this token, we each and all solemnly pledge our honor; and, in the presence of the most high God, our great author—to whom we must render a strict account, not only of our deeds, but our thoughts—we each and all sacredly swear, that we will be true to each other, so far as the great cause of liberty to America from English oppression blends our interests; and should either of us harbor a single thought, now or henceforth, of treachery to a comrade, or to the principles we profess to hold, may the great Author of our being snatch us away from earth, and consign us to eternal perdition! As a further token of acknowledging this oath to be our true sentiment, we herewith, each and all, place our hands upon our hearts, and say, Amen!"

"Amen!" was the solemn response of all, as each pressed his heart with his hand.

"And now," continued Carlini, as each again resumed his seat, "if either of you gentlemen have a plan to propose, I, for one, am ready to listen."

"For myself," said Milford, "I have not settled on any thing definite, and I should be pleased to hear a suggestion from my friend Champe, who has been longer in the city than I, and doubtless has a better idea of what can with safety be attempted."

"My sole object in coming hither, was the seizure of Arnold," replied the Sergeant; "and to decide on the best manner of effecting this purpose, is the business on which we are met to-night. It may not be improper here to state, that I have had a private interview with Arnold, since my arrival in New York, and that, believing me to have deserted the rebels, as he now terms his countrymen, he received me with much condescension and kindness. He is anxious I shall join the American legion, composed wholly of American deserters, and which is to be under his especial command. As yet I have not given him a decided answer, but shall do so to-morrow; whether I join or not, will depend upon the decision of this secret council to-night."

"If I am not mistaken," said Carlini, "Arnold has changed his quarters, and no longer occupies apartments at the residence of Sir

Henry Clinton, but has taken a house near, which is exclusively devoted to his use."

"Such, sir, is the fact," replied Champe; "he removed to this new abode yesterday; and, I further learn, has written for his wife and family to join him."

"Well, Champe, what advantages do you expect to result from your enlistment in the Legion?" inquired Milford.

"I do not know that any will, unless it be in gaining the confidence of the General, and in being near enough to his own person, to closely note his habits, and watch his movements."

"But will you be able to effect so much by this means? Is it not more likely that, on joining the Legion, you will be dispatched to some distant quarters, there to remain till ordered from the city?"

"I think not at present," replied Champe; "and for the simple reason, that the deserters as yet have no fixed quarters, but take up their lodgings wherever they please about the city. I accidentally heard something said about having them embarked ere long, on one of the vessels in the harbor, to prevent them changing their minds and running away; but as it is not probable this will be done for a week or two, there will, I trust, be an opportunity between this and then to effect our purpose."

"Have you any plan devised, by which the traitor can be safely kidnapped?" inquired Carlini; "for if I understand your instructions rightly, gentlemen, you are to take Arnold away without harming him, that he may be yielded up to justice."

"Such are our instructions, Signor," said Milford.

"I have not settled on any certain plan as yet, for seizing the traitor," replied Champe to Carlini's question; "nor can I, till I have further opportunity of closely noting all his habits."

"And you think enlisting into the Legion will aid you in this matter?"

"I think it will at least put no obstacles in my way. Of course, I should retain my rank; and officers of the Legion are at all times admitted to the presence of Arnold, who is at present unusually affable and condescending, doubtless with a view to get well in favor in his new quarters, before resuming his natural *hauteur* and tyranny. Taking advantage of these favorable circumstances, I can be much about his person, on one pretext and another; and I will note every thing carefully, not only himself, his habits, but also his dwelling, with a view to carrying out our design."

"But how do you propose to get him out of the city when captured?" asked Carlini.

"He must by some means be gagged, and taken to the river, where a boat must be in waiting to convey him to Hoboken, where an escort must be ready, also, to conduct him speedily to the American head-quarters. To effect all this, it will be necessary to fix on a certain time for the bold attempt, and have all parties act in concert."

"It will also be necessary, then, I suppose, to have direct communication with the American camp?" said Carlini.

"It will."

"Have you fixed on any mode of transmitting information to any person there?"

"I hope to be able to find a messenger."

"Well, when you require one, let me know. I suppose, George, thou art willing to venture again, in a case of necessity?" pursued Carlini, addressing the youth.

"You are my protector and benefactor," answered young Nugent—"my life is at your disposal—do with it as you will."

"But I will not risk thy life again, lad, if I can avoid it. Heaven knows I suffered enough before, when thou wast in the tyrant's clutches. This city, however, is no safe place for thee, boy, and at the first favorable opportunity thou must leave it, to return no more, until it be in the possession of those to whom it rightfully belongs. But of this more anon."

It is needless for us to report farther, at present, what was said and done that night, by this little band of patriots. Let it suffice, that, soon after, the party broke up, and the guests departed, with the understanding that each should keep the same object in view, and meet again on the second night following, to take further counsel of each other, in regard to their hazardous design. Each of the guests went away, separately, at different times, and in different directions, so as to avoid giving the sentinels any clue to their meeting, in the event of their being observed by these nocturnal guardians of the town.

CHAPTER IX.

THE TRAITOR IN A NEW POSITION.

On his arrival in New York, after his disgraceful desertion from the Americans, Arnold, as has already been observed, became, for the time being, the guest of Sir Henry Clinton. Here he remained for several days, and was introduced to such of the leading British officers as chanced to be in the city. His reception was different by different persons. Some met him in a friendly manner, but with a certain air of reserve; which he felt the more keenly, because, in his heart, he knew himself to be a villain; others did not scruple to show plainly, that in their eyes his conduct was detestable, and that they did not feel bound to treat him as an equal, even though he had sacrificed so much for their cause. Sir Henry was almost the only one who was studiously polite and attentive; though a close observer might have detected, that he felt himself compelled to this course by circumstances and policy, rather than that he did it through any affection, sympathy, or even respect for so base a man.

To one of Arnold's proud, arrogant, domineering spirit, these silent, *intangible* rebukes, were galling in the extreme—the more so, because they were intangible, and he could bring no counteracting force against them. A look of indifference or disgust, a smile of contempt and scorn, could insult as deeply as vituperative language, or a blow; but, unlike the latter, the former did not justify what is falsely termed an honorable retaliation—that is, a settlement by steel or lead. In other words, had they come out openly, and expressed their thoughts aloud, he might have called them to a severe account; as it was, he could do nothing but bear their ill-will in silence; and this chafed him to the quick, and rendered his position any thing but enviable. Doubtless failure in his scheme, and the loss of the amiable and accomplished Andre—a loss that was deeply felt by all—for this young officer was much beloved, and his death, in one sense, might be laid to Arnold's door—doubtless this, we say, had much to do with the feeling manifest in all parties. They felt they had made an *exchange* of officers, that would in nowise be a benefit to the British army; that they had, in fact, got a vicious man in place of a virtuous one; and though they could not bring a crime home to the traitor, that would justify punishment, yet, in their eyes, he was no less the criminal, and they would inflict the only penalty in their power, which was to make him sensible of their hatred and scorn.

All this Arnold felt deeply—oh! none know, but one so fallen, how deeply—and in silence and secret he suffered far more than did his victim, even at the foot of the gibbet. He could not but reflect on the high position he once occupied in the American army—the colleague, and, in some degree, the confidant of Washington—and on what he now was, a by-word of disgrace in the mouths of those he had once despised, or looked upon as beings far beneath him. Doubtless this, too, had much to do with his treatment of inferior officers among the deserters; he felt the galling need of sympathy; and, as far as lay in his power, determined to conciliate them, and get in their good graces; till, haply, such time as he could resume his reserve and unbending *hauteur* with impunity—without the fear of their saying to his face, with a sneer, "You are a traitor, we only deserters."

The first few days of Arnold's abode with Sir Henry Clinton, before the fate of Andre was known to be sealed beyond hope, he occupied much of his time in writing, and causing to be printed, bombastic proclamations, to be distributed among the rebels, inviting them to forsake a sinking cause, and come over to the standard of King George, the rightful sovereign of America, promising that all past offenses should be faithfully forgiven, and that they should be received, with open arms, into a service that would award pay, honor, and glory. But in allowing so base a man to promulgate so shallow a device, the British overreached themselves; for among the simple-minded, but honest American soldiery, its effect was only unmitigated disgust and derision; and instead of answering the end for which it was intended, by creating disaffection, it only seemed to bind them more strongly together. True, there were a few unworthy or timid persons, who embraced his offer; but these could well be spared from the rest, and formed no very important accession to the royal cause. We have seen in what manner the supposed desertion of Champe was received by his comrades; and this we hold up as a fair sample of the general feeling of indignation which such cowardly doings caused among those who remained behind. No! they were *men*—noble hearts, battling for right against the wrong—for liberty, not for gold—and they were ready, even while starving, to yield up life rather than honor—to be freemen, or be nothing—to moisten their own soil with their own blood, rather than live the hirelings of a foreign despot.

Arnold also wrote several bombastic letters to Washington and his generals, *demanding* the liberation of Andre, and *threatening*, in case of non-compliance with his wishes, to visit his wrath, in the most summary and terrible manner, upon all such inoffensive citizens as the fortune of ruthless war might throw into his hands. But these letters, like his proclamations, defeated the ends intended for, and created only disgust, derision, or, what was still worse for the object he had in view, determined defiance. Surely, his knowledge of the brave leaders to whom he addressed himself, must have been in the most limited degree, if he did not know that *threats*, issuing from whatsoever source, would only the firmer bind them to their sense of duty, as strokes of the hammer make more compact and durable the iron passed beneath it.

Having decided on making New York his general head-quarters, and learning from Sir Henry that in all probability he would have no active occupation for some time to come, Arnold expressed a wish to establish a residence of his own, and send for his family, who, as the reader knows, had gone to Philadelphia. Sir Henry readily lent his aid to this new proposition; and a fine mansior on Broadway, but two or three removed from the one occupied by himself, was finally procured, which Arnold ostentatiously furnished by means of the gold paid as the price of his own dishonor. He then removed to his new quarters, and wrote for his family to join him; but as the facilities of traveling in those days were very different from this age of steam, he knew that a week or two must elapse ere his wife would become mistress of his household. Meantime he procured a temporary housekeeper, two or three servants, and opened in a style of splendor that he fancied would give him a consequence in the eyes of his brother officers, and tend to do away with the feeling of disgust he too plainly perceived they felt for him. But even in this he greatly missed his calculation; though there were a few selfish spirits, of inferior rank, who sought his acquaintance, and professed their friendship, with a view of making his wine, his suppers, and other extravagances, compensate them for the association.

Oh! how fallen must be the man, whose only friends are purchased with his gold!

Here, then, we again find the traitor, after his disgraceful flight from the Americans, firmly fixed among the enemies of his country, ready to play the sycophant, or tyrant, as the case might be.

It was about nine o'clock on the morning following the secret meeting of our friends, as recorded in the preceding chapter, that Arnold, in the uniform of a British officer, issued from his mansion, and mounted a fine, spirited horse, which his groom was holding by the bit before his door. Just as he was on the point of dashing up Broadway, he was hailed by another horseman, who rode up at an easy gallop.

"Ah, Colonel Malpert," said Arnold, "I am happy to see you—how do you find yourself this morning?"

"As well as can be expected," returned the other, laughing, "after the gallon of wine you sent me home with in the mid watches. I say, General, you have the real stuff, and no mistake, and I have a natural *penchant* for the pure juice of the grape. There is a family tradition, that my mother liked it before I was born; and certainly I see no reason to disa gree with her taste in that respect. But which way, General?"

"Why, I thought I would amuse myself, by riding up to see the review."

"Well, as I am that way inclined, suppose we keep each other company?"

"Agreed," returned Arnold, and the two rode off together.

The companion of the traitor was a man about thirty-five years of age, tall, well formed, with a rather handsome countenance, or a countenance that would have been handsome, but for the unmistakable lines of loose morality, and habitual dissipation, which formed its distinguishing traits. His complexion was light, with a smooth, clear skin, and his hair was a shade lighter than light brown. His eyes were of that peculiar color, of which we can convey no better idea than by the term dissolute blue. They were capable of a very fascinating expression, and also of an expression so cold, forbidding, and revengeful, that very few would care to encounter their owner when his worst passions were in full play. It is needless to specify the rest of his features; they were all fine, regular, and only needed a different expression from that they usually wore, to have made them prepossessing in the extreme.

Colonel Malpert owed the position he held in the Britith army, to wealth and influential connections, rather than to merit. True, he was brave in battle, even to rashness; but this is not the only quality requisite to a good officer. Bravery, and even rashness, may make a good fighter; but the same reckless passions displayed in the camp, always prove injurious to their possessor; and for this reason, and others we are about to mention, Colonel Malpert had become very unpopular among his brother officers; while those immediately under his command hated him almost to a man. For some willful neglect of duty, he had been tried by a court-martial, only a few days previous to Arnold's arrival in the city, and was even now under sentence of suspension for a month.

And here we see the error of the British military system, in allowing gold to purchase rank, which should only be awarded to merit. A wealthy father has an indolent, profligate son, whom he is ambitious to have distinguished, and brought into the first society—to gain, at a leap, a position which no talent or merit of his own entitle him to—and forthwith he *purchases* him a commission, and he is at once gazetted to a station he knows nothing about, and which he is perhaps decidedly unqualified to fill. Let them laugh at our republican system, if they will, of making civil citizens high military officers in a day, to meet an emergency; we think if they would look closely at home, they would find more to condemn there than abroad; for if we make citizen officers, it is to command citizen soldiers; while they allow a perfect numskull, because he has a few dollars to spend, to take high rank in the regular army, and lord it over men who secretly pity, hate, or despise him.

As we have said, Colonel Malpert owed his position to wealth and influential connections. His colonelcy had been purchased by his father, who was a wealthy commoner and a member of parliament; and he had remained in the army on sufferance—his presence had been endured where it was least wanted—and simply because it was no easy matter to get rid of him. None who knew him thoroughly, liked him; and yet the very fewest number cared to tell him so; for he was an expert swordsman, and a dead shot, and his revenge was almost certain to follow an insult. While stationed in the Indies, he had fought three duels, and in each case his opponent had been carried from the field either dead or mortally wounded. He was profligate in every sense of the word; and wine, women, and cards were his favorite means of pastime. He was a notorious gambler, and a cheat of the lowest grade. No gentleman who knew him, could be induced to play with him; for he was sure to cheat, and, if detected and exposed, was sure to challenge his exposer, or otherwise seriously injure him.

Such was the man who had now become, as it were, the bosom companion of Benedict Arnold; and we must say, we think they were well worthy of each other's delectable society. But base as he was himself, Colonel Malpert had experienced a decided repugnance to making the acquaintance of, and placing himself on terms of intimacy with, a traitor. He had at first held himself coldly aloof from a baser man than himself; but when he found that the traitor had money, and that he was disposed to spend it freely to get into the good graces of his brother officers, all imperfections, in his selfish view, were at once removed; and he proceeded to congratulate him on the happy change in his fortune, with as much seeming heartiness as if he really felt he was a great acquisition to the British army. Nay, he even went so far as to say, that he felt himself highly honored by the acquaintance, and, he hoped, also, he was not too forward in adding, the friendship of a gentleman so highly distinguished in the field, even though that distinction had been acquired among his enemies.

Whether Arnold saw through his selfish purpose or not, we shall not pause here to determine. Being excessively vain, flattery, from any source, fell upon his ear with a soothing, delicious effect; and whether the flatterer were sincere or not, it was policy for him, in his peculiar situation, to appear to think so, and make the most of his proffered friendship, even though that friendship should cost him dear in the end. Thus both parties, with a purely selfish view on both sides, established an intimacy, and apparent friendship, which, under different circumstances, might never have taken place.

As Arnold and Malpert rode up Broadway, at an easy pace, they for a time conversed about some trifling matters, of no interest to the reader. At length a pause occurred in the conversation, which was resumed by Malpert, who spoke as one who had just recalled to mind something important.

"By-the-by," he said, "I hear that you have written for your wife, who is now in Philadelphia."

"I have," replied Arnold.

"How comes it you did not mention the matter to me? I thought you and I were confidants."

Arnold glanced furtively at his companion, and there was an almost imperceptible smile of contempt around the mouth, but he answered good-naturedly:

"I do not know—I think I did tell you at the time. I certainly made no secret of it, since you have learned it from others. But is it a matter of any importance?"

"O, no—only I understand she is young, beautiful, and accomplished."

"You have never seen her, then?"

"No, I have never had that pleasure. I was not with that division of our army which quartered in Philadelphia."

"I believe she possesses all the qualifications you have named."

"Then I shall certainly seek her acquaintance the moment she arrives."

"You can not make me jealous, Colonel," returned Arnold, laughing; though a close observer might have detected that the laugh was not natural, and that the traitor exhibited certain signs of uneasiness which seemed to belie his words.

"O, I would not make you jealous for the world," rejoined the other, laughing also; "for nothing is a greater foe to friendship than Shakspeare's green-eyed monster! But a truce to this. You play an excellent game of cards, General, for one who has had a rebel education—or else your wine works to my disadvantage—for I find, this morning, that last night's sitting has left me a hundred pounds minus."

"Which another sitting would doubtless retrieve, and leave you winner of double the amount," returned Arnold, with a self-satisfied smile.

"Well, I will hope for the best," rejoined Malpert, gayly. "'Come easy, go easy,' is my motto."

At this moment this worthy pair turned the angle of a large, old building, and came in full view of the parade-ground, which for a time arrested their attention and conversation.

CHAPTER X.

A PUBLIC INSULT.

At the time of which we write, and for many years after, the site of the present picturesque edifice, known as the City Hall, was a steep unimproved hill, up which frolicsome urchins were wont to drag their sleds in winter and slide down again, and which modern innovation has completely removed, and converted into a public promenade, denominated the Park. This hill, during the period the British occupied New York, was used as the grand encampment of such portion of the army as went into quarters here; and on every side it was thickly dotted with white tents, with occasionally the marquee of an officer looming above the rest—though a large number of the latter either had private residences of their own, or took lodgings among the citizens. The camp, owing to its elevation, was picturesque, delightful, and healthy. A tall pole on its summit, with the banner of St. George streaming in the breeze, could be seen from nearly every quarter of the city, and from the shipping in the harbour.

At a convenient distance from the camp, was a broad, level plain, of several acres in extent, which was used as a grand parade-ground for the soldiers. At the moment Arnold and his companion came in sight of this plain, it was occupied by several thousand troops, going through various evolutions. The scene was grand, beautiful, and war-like. The soldiers, clad in scarlet uniforms, with their polished muskets, bayonets, and swords glittering in the clear sunlight, and continually changing positions, as they marched and countermarched, made an imposing and attractive sight; while martial strains of excellent music, discoursed by numerous bands of musicians, filled the welkin with melodious and inspiring sounds. Officers, mounted on splendid steeds, richly caparisoned, were seen dashing hither and thither, to issue or obey some command, giving a brilliant life to the moving picture, the charm of which the very fewest number would find themselves able to resist.

In the center of the plain was a slight elevation, which commanded a view of the whole; and this was occupied by a group of distinguished officers, which Arnold and Malpert at once recognized as Sir Henry Clinton and staff. Occasionally an officer dashed up to this group, remained a moment in apparent conversation, and then dashed swiftly away again to a distant part of the field, where he seemed, by his gestures, to be conveying to the next in rank below him the orders he had just received.

On two sides of this plain, just without the prescribed limits—and which limits were preserved entire, by numerous patrols, each with his musket to his shoulder, walking slowly up and down the lines—a large crowd of citizens was collected, of all ages, sizes, and colors. Men, women, and children, black and white, were indiscriminately mixed together, and all seemed to be enjoying themselves, each in his own peculiar way. A number of sutlers, with an eye to speculation, had pitched their tents here, and appeared to be doing a thriving business, in the retailing of cakes, confectionary, and liquors. Gamblers, too, with their many devices to win a few shillings from some "luckless wight," were not wanting to complete the exciting amusement of the day; and roulette, cards, and dice, appeared to receive their full share of patronage.

As the crowd of citizens occupied the two sides of the parade-ground nearest the city, Arnold and his companion, in riding down to select a position where they could best witness the evolutions of the soldiers, necessarily came in contact with the rabble. Glancing carelessly around him, without taking particular heed of any person or object, Arnold was walking his horse, and carefully picking his way through the disordered congregation of human beings, when his ear was suddenly saluted by a coarse, rough voice, which articulated the words:

"Here comes the traitor! make way for the traitor!" and this was followed by a taunting laugh.

Instantly every kind of occupation was suspended in the immediate vicinity of Arnold, and every eye was fixed upon him, with that look of vulgar curiosity by which a monster of any kind is usually regarded. As Arnold heard these words, and found himself the cynosure of a thousand eyes, his features flushed to the very roots of his hair, and his countenance, which so recently wore a look of listless indifference, now suddenly assumed a mingled expression of mortification, confusion, and diabolical rage. Tightening his rein with a nervous jerk, he ran his black, piercing eye rapidly over the mass of up-turned faces, as if in search of the person who had dared make use of such insulting language; and then, while the crowd stood breathless with suspense, as if expecting something terrible to follow, he suddenly buried his rowels in the flanks of the fiery beast he bestrode. The noble animal, unused to such treatment, instantly reared, and plunged forward, amid a universal yell of consternation from the excited populace, most of whom rushed back upon one another in terror and confusion. All were not fortunate enough to escape injury; for a large, fleshy woman, who happened to be standing right in front of the horse, was knocked down, run over, and left bleeding upon the ground. The fall of this woman was witnessed by several of the spectators, whose cries of terror instantly changed to those of rage and execration.

"Stop him!" "Block the scoundrel's path!" "He's killed a woman!" with other like expressions, were now shouted on all sides; and instantly a dozen athletic fellows, a few yards ahead—who, on the impulse of the moment, had parted right and left, to give the horse a passage—now rushed together; and two of then seizing the animal by the bit, bore him back almost upon his haunches.

With a horrid oath, and a fiendish gleam of rage upon his countenance, Arnold tore his sword from its scabbard, and swinging it over his head, aimed a death-blow at his nearest assailant. The man, who chanced to have a heavy cudgel in his hand, anticipating the murderous intention of the traitor, parried the stroke with wonderful dexterity, shivered the sword-blade, and dealt the General a blow on his sword-arm, which completely paralyzed it for the time being. He then, in a tone of authority, ordered his comrades to fall back, and very coolly led Arnold's horse out of the crowd, saying, as a parting advice:

"You miserable scoundrel of a traitor! never do you again attempt to ride rough shod over British subjects—or, if I form one of the number, by the living mass, I will put a period to your infamous career! Go, *murderer* of Andre—go, get you hence!" and as he spoke, without waiting a reply from the confused and thunder-struck traitor, he released his hold on the bridle rein, and at the same time struck the horse a blow that caused him to bound away furiously, amid the hootings of the mob.

At first Arnold seemed disposed to turn back his beast, and rush upon the crowd, in open defiance of the threats which he knew were now being uttered against him; but a moment's reflection convinced him of the folly of such a dangerous proceeding, and he allowed his horse to take his own course.

He had gone about two hundred yards, when he was overtaken by Colonel Malpert, who, instead of following Arnold's rash movements, had ridden quietly out of the crowd, where he calmly awaited the termination of the unpleasant affair. It may perhaps appear strange to some, that Malpert, being of a nature as rash as Arnold, and keenly sensitive to an insult, did not second the man he called his friend in his attempt to ride furiously over his fellow-beings; but the truth was, Malpert's friendship was only seeming, not real, and therefore he had wisely decided not to meddle in what did not positively concern him.

As he overtook Arnold, the latter was fairly gnashing his teeth with rage, and uttering bitter curses against the whole human race.

"Hold up, my friend," said the Colonel; "you are going out of your latitude altogether. Here—this way—turn off here, and you will have a fine view of the doings on the field."

"Curse the review!" said Arnold, savagely, scarcely checking the speed of his horse. "I could fight my best friend now, out of sheer vexation."

"So it would seem, since you treat *me* so cavalierly," returned the wily, smooth-spoken Colonel. "Pshaw! some scoundrel had the ill-manners to insult you, and now you are ready to curse friends and foes. Out upon you, for more fire than judgment! Why, I did not think a trifling matter could affect you so seriously—you should have borne it as calmly as I did."

"You!" rejoined Arnold, savagely, while his lip slightly curled with a sneer. "Yes, of course *you* bore it calmly, because you were not insulted."

"Indeed I was, let me tell you."

"How so?"

"Why, am I not your friend? and is not an insult to one's friend, an insult to one's self? But check your horse, I say—or, by heavens! I will not keep you company—for see, you are running away from the review entirely."

Arnold mechanically reined in his beast, and said, in a calmer tone, with something like a sigh:

"Ah! Malpert, you know not what it is to be called a traitor."

"No, that is true, upon my honor," returned the other, laughing; "but I know what it is to be called almost every thing else. But then what matters it what a man is called, so he is conscious of his innocence? You were called a traitor—very good—but you are not a traitor, nevertheless; and words are merely words after all—mere unsubstantial sounds, that linger only while they are being spoken."

"I beg leave to differ with you there, Malpert," returned the other, seriously; "words are *not* unsubstantial things; they *do* linger long after they are spoken; they cut to the heart, as they come from the heart, and they often leave an impression there that time can not efface."

"Well, well, have it your own way," responded the other; "I am not in a mood for argument just now, and shall content myself with saying, that I think you have no cause to dwell on the mere matter of being called a traitor, doubtless by some rebel at that, since no man who faithfully serves his king and country, as I know it is your intention henceforth to do, can have such a foul epithet applied to him with any weight of truth attached. Here, let us ride down here, where we can have an excellent view of all that is going on, and be entirely to ourselves."

It was about an hour after this conversation, that Malpert, begging to be excused for a few minutes, rode away, leaving Arnold alone. At this moment two persons were seen to separate from among the distant spectators, and advance directly toward the traitor, who still remained seated on his horse, noting, with the eye of a connoisseur, the movements of troops on the field, but who, for reasons of his own, did not care to take his place among the other officers. The persons alluded to drew close to Arnold, without his perceiving them, when one of the two said, in a bland tone:

"How fares your excellency to-day?"

Arnold started, and turned quickly on his saddle, evidently under the impression that this might be a new mode of insult; but on perceiving who addressed him, his countenance changed from a severe expression to a bland smile, and he said, with a show of much cordiality:

"Ah, Sergeant Champe, I am delighted to see you—and my old friend, Captain Milford—this is really a pleasure I did not anticipate. I learned, from Sir Henry, that you were in town, Captain, and I left word with him, if he saw you again, to request you to call upon me."

As he spoke, Arnold dismounted, and shook both officers by the hand warmly. He either felt greatly pleased at meeting them at this time, or else played the hypocrite to perfection.

"I am happy to see you looking so well, General," said Milford; "and for that matter, I think our recent change agrees with all of us. I, for one, I know, never felt better in my life, both physically and mentally."

"I suppose, like myself, you have had enough of rebel glory, and false promises of pay," returned Arnold, smiling, "and now feel disposed to serve a better master."

"I believe that is the truth, in every particular," answered the Captain promptly.

"What was the state of the rebel camp when you left?"

"Not a very desirable one for its ambitious leaders, I assure you. I believe Washington and his generals are beginning to fear their own shadows. All is consternation and confusion; the men are ready to desert, and only wait a favorable opportunity. I would rather be a private here, at this time, than a general there."

"Ay, sir, and no doubt you would fare better in the end. Did any of my circulars reach there before you left?"

"A few."

"What effect did they have?"

"To convince the soldiers they are doing injustice to themselves, as well as to their rightful sovereign, by remaining where they are."

"I thought my arguments were strong," returned Arnold, with a self-satisfied smile.

"You have sowed a seed that will be certain to bear fruit."

"I am glad to hear it. Ah! little did the cursed rebels know how deep would be my revenge for all the injuries and insults heaped upon me! I suppose you will join the Legion, Captain? You will be allowed to retain your present rank, and draw the same pay as any other officer, of the same grade, in the British army."

"I think it altogether likely I shall join the Legion," replied Milford, "though I will not say positively. I told Sir Henry I would like a few days to consider the matter, and he readily granted me the favor."

"Ay, Captain, Sir Henry is a true gentleman," responded Arnold; "none of your upstart Washingtons, Greenes, Knoxes, and the deuce knows how many others of like pretense; but one of your real old English stock, and worthy of all praise. I warrant me, he knows how to grant a favor to a gentleman, and not think it sufficiently wonderful to be placarded about the town, or mentioned in his report to the War Department. Well, Champe, I suppose you are in a quandary, too, and don't know whether to enlist with us or not?"

"Why, my mind is pretty well settled now, as I was saying to the Captain here, not an hour ago."

"Well, what have you decided on?"

"Enlisting."

"Good! I am delighted to hear it; for men of your stamp are just the kind we want. Have you seen the recruiting officer?"

"Not yet."

"You will find him at the barracks, just under the hill yonder."

"I shall call on him in a day or two."

"There is bounty money of three guineas for privates, and duly proportioned for officers."

"So I have been told, your excellency."

"I am trying to persuade Sir Henry to make it ten guineas, in place of three; don't you think that would be strong temptation for men, half starved where they are, to desert?"

"I do, indeed. Only proclaim ten guineas bounty, and in one month, I will answer for it, General Washington abandons the field, for want of an army to support him."

"Yes, yes," cried Arnold, "I know it. Sir Henry must be persuaded to raise the bounty; or if he can not do it, as he says he has no power, he must get permission from over the water. It must be done. Well, gentlemen, I see my friend coming, and I must ride and meet him. Call on me as soon as convenient, and take a glass of wine, and we will talk over such matters as most interest men who love their country, and feel a pride in her victories. Adieu, gentlemen;" and waving his hand, accompanying the motion with a bland smile, Arnold turned away to remount his horse.

Milford and Champe bowed and retired, as if highly pleased with so much condescension on the part of so distinguished a general.

"They are mine," smiled Arnold, as he watched their departure, till joined by Malpert.

"The hypocritical, palavering old scoundrel!" muttered Champe, when he had gained a sufficient distance, to venture, without risk, to give his thoughts free expression. "Does he take us for fools, as well as knaves?"

"He evidently does not suspect us, and that is by far the most important to us," returned his companion.

"Come," said Malpert to Arnold, "I am tired of this—what say you to riding back, and taking a quiet game of cards?"

"Agreed," returned Arnold, readily; and the next minute these two worthies were galloping away to the city.

CHAPTER XI.

STARTLING INCIDENTS.

The reader must suppose some three or four days to have elapsed since the events of the foregoing chapter. It was about the mid hour of one of those mild days of October, which are so delightful in our northern climate, that two individuals were walking slowly along the eastern bank of the Hudson, about a mile above what was then regarded as the northern limit of the city—though, at the present day, the same spot is in the very heart of the town, and far below the imaginary line drawn by the *bon ton*, to separate themselves from the vulgar hum of business. The elder of these two persons was still a young man, of about twenty-five, and of a fine, noble, commanding appearance. He wore a military undress, and carried in his hand a pole, around which was wound a line, with a fishhook attached, the point of which was imbedded in the floatcork. His companion was, to all appearance, a negro lad of eighteen, with just enough of white blood in his veins to redeem him from thick lips, a flat nose, an impenetrable skull, and give him a look of intelligence. He carried in one hand a small dish of bait, and in the other a basket, evidently intended to hold the fish, when caught.

We have said these two individuals were walking slowly along the bank of the stream; and so they continued to walk, for several minutes, the white man going before, and carefully parting the bushes to the right and left; for strange as it may seem to the denizens of the great Emporium of this continent, at this day, there was a heavy wood, with thick undergrowth, at the time of which we write, on the very ground where thousands of human beings are now so penned in with brick and mortar as scarcely to find wholesome air to breathe.

At length he of the rod came to a large rock, which so overhung the stream as to leave quite an open space between it and the water; and clambering to the top of this, he stood up, and looked carefully around; while the other stopped at its base, and seemed to wait for his superior to speak first. This rock was so surrounded on three sides by a scrubby undergrowth, which took root below its base and on the very margin of the stream, that nowhere, save from on the water, could it be discerned at the distance of ten feet. Only a few paces from these bushes, huge trees, of perhaps many centuries' growth, reared their giant trunks high in air, and stretched their hundred limbs, heavy with foliage, far over the edge of the river, forming a leafy canopy to the rock, through which only here and there a silver ray of the meridian sun penetrated. As a natural sequence of such dense foliage, all below it was in a deep shade, resembling twilight; and no one, however cautiously he might make the attempt, could approach this spot, without first being heard and seen by those already there.

"Well, George, what think you of this place for our purpose?" at length inquired the one on the rock, who, as we do not wish to mystify the reader, we may as well state here, was none other than our veritable hero, Captain Milford; while we will also add, that the color of the black he addressed, was *not* skin deep—the latter in truth being neither more nor less than George Nugent, the noble youth whom Carlini rescued from the prison.

"I do not think a better could be found." said the pseudo-black, in reply to the question of the other. "But did I understand you to say the skiff is already here?"

"Look and see if you can find it; but be careful about beating down the bushes too much; for should any one chance to pass through here, I would have no mark to arrest attention, and perhaps excite curiosity or suspicion."

George Nugent, in compliance with the request of Milford, now made a careful search along the bank, for some ten rods, on either side of the rock, and then said:

"I can find no traces of a boat."

"Did you peer under the rock?"

"As far as I could see."

"Well, look again."

"It is useless."

"I wager, if you look long and steadily under the rock this time, you will see a skiff;" and as the youth got down on his knees, on the very verge of the bank, and bent his head almost to a level with the water, the other made two or three gathers on a small cord at his feet, and a beautiful little boat slowly made its appearance, something as a cunning fish glides out from under a bank, with its eye fixed steadily on a baited hook, that is gradually made to retreat by the angler

"Nothing could be better for our design," said George; "for no person, not in our secret, would ever think of looking here for a boat."

"You must be careful how you approach and leave it," rejoined the Captain; "for discovery might not only prove fatal to our hopes, but to ourselves."

"Rest assured, I shall not be imprudent, Captain," answered the other. "Am I to go now?"

"Yes; there are no gun-boats in this part of the river, and no sentries posted in Hoboken, so that I think, if cautious, you will run very little risk. And now for your instructions. Do you see that point of land yonder, on the opposite side, a short distance higher up, which projects into the stream and is covered with scrub-oaks?"

"I do."

"Well, passing around that point of land, you will discover a beautiful little cove, and, in the center of that cove, a rock, not dissimilar to this, where you will be enabled to secrete the skiff. Having done that, you will next look for the post-office, so that you will have no difficulty in finding it when needful. By going due west from the center of that rock, some twenty-five paces, you will come to a large oak tree, which has one dry limb projecting toward you. When you have found the tree in question, imagine a plummet suspended from the end of the dry limb, and go exactly ten paces north of that, at a right angle with your course from the river, and in the very center of a small cluster of bushes, you will find a flat stone, which covers our post-office on that side of the river. This stone you must turn up frequently—daily, if possible—and whenever you find a letter under it, bear it to its address with all haste. Should you find nothing there by the day after to-morrow, and you think you can cross the river without too much risk, you may visit this spot, as it is possible I may not be able to go over, even though the matter to communicate be important. If you do cross the river, let it be in the night, and be very guarded against a surprise. If you have any communication for me. do not put on a superscription, nor allow any thing more than the initials of the writer's name to be affixed; and also have it worded so as to be understood only by those for whom intended—this is to doubly guard against a fatal accident."

"But you have not told me where to find our post-office on this side of the river."

"True; well, suppose we have it here? I do not know of a better place. Let me see!" and Milford descended from the rock, and began to search about among the bushes. "Ah! here is a stone that will serve our purpose," he said, stooping and raising one of some fifty pounds weight. "Five paces north of the largest chestnut," he added, looking up to a huge tree, and measuring the distance with his eye, in order to fix in his mind a proper direction to the exact spot, should he have occasion to send a person to find it. "This will do," he continued; "but be careful, George, to make no mistake on either side of the river."

"Shall I enter the skiff now?" asked the other.

"I think you may as well," replied Milford. "This letter," he continued, taking one from his pocket, without superscription, "I wish you to place in the hands of his excellency, General Washington; but should any thing occur to prevent your seeing the commander-in-chief by to-morrow night—or, at the farthest, the morning after—you will seek out Major Lee, and give it to him yourself—in no case trust it to the care of a third person. This letter is loaded with lead, so that, should you drop it into the water, it will instantly sink to the bottom—a precaution you must adopt with all letters you may bring, as of course you run more or less risk of being overhauled by the water-guard. Should any thing occur, obliging you to destroy this missive, you will say to General Washington, or Major Lee, that the plot regarding Arnold is in active operation, with good prospects of complete success. Tell them the traitor suspects nothing, and is narrowly watched, day and night; and should no unforeseen event mar our plans, he will probably be in our hands in the course of three or four days. Say to Lee, that if he can hover around yonder wood, with some three or four discreet and daring fellows, so that our dispatches can have a speedy answer, it will materially forward our design, as at present we know not the precise moment for executing our project. I believe that is all of importance. Oh, you may mention that the general suspected is not guilty. Now go, and may Heaven preserve you to execute your mission. You had better take this pole with you, I think, and appear to be fishing as you slowly cross the river, so that, should you be observed, you will not be so likely to excite suspicion. I will remain here until I see you land on the other side; and should you be overhauled and questioned, remember that your name is Tom, and that you are for the present my servant: if they wish to know more, refer them to me. There, good-by, and God bless you!" and Milford shook the youth warmly by the hand.

The latter now proceeded to enter the boat, and, with a final adieu, shoved out into the stream. Following the Captain's instructions, he baited his hook, and began to fish, gradually propelling his boat to the opposite shore. So slow was his progress, that it was at least an hour before he disappeared around the point of land which Milford had pointed out to him. Disappear he did at last, in safety; and the Captain, who still kept his gaze fixed in that direction, soon had the pleasure of seeing a handkerchief flutter among the bushes, which he took to be a signal that all was right.

After watching some fifteen minutes longer, and seeing no other signal, Milford withdrew from the thicket into the body of the wood, and took a course leading directly away from the bank of the river. In this manner he proceeded leisurely, in a thoughtful mood, for some time, and gradually drew near an opening which reached down to the city.

Suddenly he was aroused from his meditations, by hearing the patter of a horse's feet; and as the sound drew nearer, he felt some curiosity to see who was the rider. For this purpose he quickened his pace toward the clearing, but had not reached a point whence he could see the galloping steed, when the latter appeared to come to a sudden halt, and he heard a female shriek for help.

This was a call that could never pass unheeded by the brave and chivalrous Captain Milford; and like the startled deer flying from the huntsman, our gallant hero bounded through the bushes to the clearing, where, at the distance of about a hundred paces, he beheld a female, seated on a horse, the bit of which had been seized by a coarse-looking ruffian, who was dragging the animal toward the thicket near by; while another ruffian had hold of the terrified lady by the wrist, and, with uplifted knife, was threatening her with instant death, if she dared to scream again, or make the least noise. But these threats were unnecessary; for while he was yet speaking, the lady fainted, and lopped over the saddle-bow, toward the neck of the horse, where she remained, steadied in this position by the ruffian at her side, who also aided his companion in urging the beast into the wood, by giving him a smart slap on the flank with his hand.

All this occurred so quickly, that to Milford it seemed but a moment, from the time he first beheld the party, till all had disappeared from his sight into the thicket. What must he do? was the question he now asked himself, as he hastily retreated into the wood, so as not to be observed, as he fortunately had not been, while standing exposed, owing to the pre-occupation of the villains. What must he do? was a question easier asked than answered by one in his situation; for he was only one against two, and his only weapon a large clasp-knife, (he having given his pistols to George,) while it was almost certain the ruffians were armed to the teeth.

The first impulse of Milford was to rush to the rescue of the female, at all hazards; but a single reflection convinced him of the folly of so rash a proceeding. Milford was no coward, neither was he fool-hardy. He feared not danger, because of danger, but merely summed up the probable consequences of acting without prudence. To plunge madly forward to assist the distressed lady, and get a bullet in his brain for his foolish daring, might be considered very heroic and all that; but Milford was one to ask himself the sober question, what good could result to the unknown female from his untimely death? Would her captors be likely to treat her more leniently, from knowing that she had such a gallant champion? to say nothing of dying himself, at this time, and in so inglorious a manner. He thought not, and he thought wisely.

But the reader must not infer, from this hesitation on the part of our hero, that he had any idea of deserting the lady—abandoning her to her fate—leaving her solely to the mercy of her captors. O, no—so base, so cowardly, a thought as that, never dawned, with the faintest glimmering, upon his mind. No! if he thought of self-preservation enough to be prudent, it was with a view to the saving his own life, that he might really be of service to her.

There are two classes of individuals, both of whom would have acted otherwise than our hero. One of these, Hotspur-like, would recklessly have darted forward to save the lady; and the other, like old fat Jack Fallstaff, would have *valiantly* run away; but which of the two, all things considered, would have rendered her the most effectual service, it is impossible for us here to decide, the trial not having been made.

But doubtless the impatient reader thinks that, while we are wasting our time and his in talking in this manner, the captured female is in most imminent danger. But he must recollect, withal, that *we* are not exactly Captain Milford; and that the safety of the fair unknown depends upon him, and not on us—otherwise we might have acted differently—that is, done more and said less.

The question, what must he do, soon found an answer in our gallant hero's quick and active mind. Who the lady was, and what object the ruffians had in capturing her, and dragging her into the thicket, were matters unknown to him; but from the fact that they did not kill her instantly, he inferred her life was only so far menaced, as to make sure of all the plunder thay could lay their hands on and escape without trouble. Acting upon this idea, which, if correct, would doubtless give him time to carry out a plan that immediately suggested itself, Milford at once darted into the wood, making as little noise as possible, with the intention of taking a slightly circuitous route, and stealing upon the villains unawares, then and there to be guided wholly by circumstances.

The lapse of time between forming his plan and putting it in execution, was very short; and Milford was so fortunate, as to get within a few feet of the party, without being observed, or without arousing suspicion of any formidable antagonist being in the vicinity. In gaining so close a proximity, he was unconsciously aided by the robbers themselves; for they had not only stopped in the middle of a dense thicket, which prevented them from seeing ten feet on either hand, but they made so much noise, in stamping about and talking loudly, that the rustling of the bushes, as Milford, on his hands and knees, cautiously worked his way through them, was unheard.

At the precise moment our hero gained a position whence he could command a view of all that was taking place in the covert, the two robbers were standing in the center of a small open space, which they had made by cutting away some of the bushes and trampling down others, and both were occupied in scrutinizing a couple of rings and a large diamond brooch, which they had already purloined from the unconscious lady, who, still in a swoon, was lying at their feet, she having been removed from the horse, which was hitched to the limb of a tree close by. The lady—for lady she evidently was—was dressed in a beautiful riding habit, of dark silk velvet, whose glossy folds, and rich, blending shades, were conspicuous, even in the gloomy light which stole in from overhead. Her features were not discernible from Milford's position, for her back was toward him, and she lay almost upon her face; but that she was young and not unlikely beautiful, he judged from the raven tresses of bright glossy hair, which floated in careless profusion over her shoulders, from underneath her velvet cap, which had partly fallen off. He caught a glimpse, too, of her neck, through the curls, and of one hand that was thrown back, and the skin of both he fancied was smooth, and fair, and clear as alabaster.

But he did not contemplate her long, for his immediate business lay with her captors—

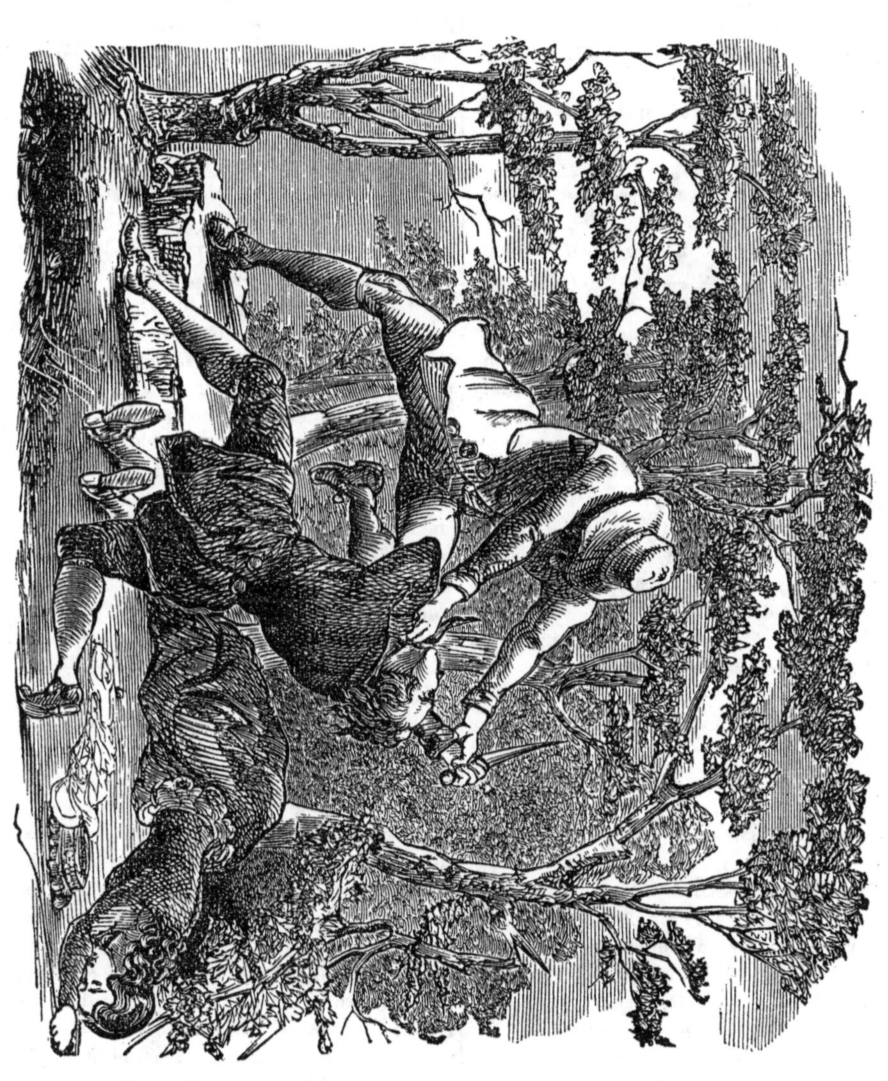

though we will not deny, that, being of a poetic temperament, what little he did see of her, made him feel strongly romantic, and brought to mind the tales he had read and heard, of how gallant knights, in olden times, were wont to rescue ladies fair from armed banditti, and bear them off in triumph, to be in turn rewarded by their hearts and hands. But then, he reasoned—that is to say, if he reasoned at all on the matter, which is so very doubtful, that we will substitute recollected—he recollected, we say, that one part of his romance could not be like those of old, insomuch as, if he proved so fortunate as to bear the lady away in safety, he could not claim her hand, nor accept it if offered, being already engaged to the only being on earth he truly loved. But notwithstanding this, he was no less compelled, by a manly sense of duty, to do all that lay in his power in her behalf. He therefore turned his whole attention to contemplating the robbers, who seemed to be in fine spirits at the success which had so far attended their operations.

Both were athletic men, with coarse villainous-looking countenances, on which only the baser passions had any play. Exposure to all kinds of weather, to all degrees of hardship, together with a total disregard of cleanliness, had given their dark complexions a begrimed, tawny hue, resembling the pictures we sometimes see displayed of old savages without their paint. A long, dirty beard, of several days' growth, and coarse, black, matted hair—which fell around their faces and over their low foreheads, down to their sullen, blood-shot eyes—did nothing to redeem their otherwise repulsive appearance.

"We've made a splendid haul, this time," said one, closely examining the rings. "If them aint real diamonds, then say that Jack Sharp's lost his peepers—eh! Jemmy Bolter?"

"The real trinkets," replied the other, holding the brooch in such a way that the diamonds threw out all the colors of the rainbow. "I knowed we'd make our expenses off from her, if nothing more. But, I say, Jack, what'll we do with the young woman? for when she comes to, there'll be more yelling. Wasn't it lucky she went off into this here nap? I hope her yell warn't heard."

"What d'ye think, we'd *best* do with her, Jem?—gag her, and let her go, or—" and he gave his companion a wicked look, and suddenly drew a hand across his throat.

"Why, yes, that there's the safest, no doubt," replied Jem; "'cause, ye see, dead folks tell no tales. But then I kind o' hate to kill her, too, Jack—for she's about the purtiest piece of human flesh I've handled for some time. If we could only carry her off now, she'd make a right nice *wife* for one on us; and when tired of her, it'ud be an easy matter to send her to heaven;" and the ruffian gave his companion a peculiar look, and closed with a brutal laugh.

"I don't exactly like that," said Jack, "'cause it's too risky; but I'll tell you what I will agree to;" and he made the other a proposition too horrible for us to chronicle.

Milford shuddered as he heard it, and he clutched firmly his knife, which he already held open in his hand, ready to strike in defence of the unfortunate lady, whenever he should see a good opportunity for making his blow effectual. The attention of the ruffians was now turned upon the female, who uttered a low moan, and was evidently about to return to consciousness. The backs of both robbers were toward Milford; and one of them stooping down, now put his rough hand upon the victim's mouth, and said to the other

"Quick, Jem!—we must gag her before she screams."

Milford thought this moment favorable to his purpose—or, at all events, that it was best to be up and doing—and scarcely had the words, just recorded, passed the villain's lips, when, like a tiger leaping upon his prey, he made a clean bound into the open space, and fairly alighting upon the back of the speaker, drove his knife into the neck of the other, before the astonished ruffian had time to know what was taking place. The stabbed villain uttered a yell of pain and rage, staggered back, laid his hand on the butt of a pistol, reeled, and finally fell to the earth, discharging the weapon in the air.

But though the Captain had disabled one, he now found himself in a very perilous situation, for the robber, on whose back he alighted, shook him off, as though he were a feathe and, springing to his feet at the same instant, threw his huge arms around him, in such a way as to pinion his own, and, gnashing his teeth with rage, and uttering a deep, horrible oath, fairly bore him to the earth. He fell heavily upon his back, and his head striking a stone, so confused and bewildered him, that for a single moment he lost consciousness. This moment, so favorable to his design, the robber improved; and jerking his hands from under the Captain, he seized the bloody clasp-knife, (still retained by the latter,) as being easier to get hold of than his own, and, throwing his right arm up, exclaimed, with an oath, between his set teeth:

"Now, —— you! take your deserts."

Milford saw the blow descending, but without power to ward it; and he instinctively closed his eyes, as he believed for the last time. At this critical instant, the arm of the robber was seized from behind, the stroke of the knife was turned aside from the heart of the Captain, the report of a pistol resounded through the wood, and a well known voice at the same time exclaimed:

"There, darn your old picter! how do you like that?"

The head of the robber dropped forward, and he rolled over on the earth, beside the Captain, without even a groan. His brain was protruding through his skull, and his soul had gone to give an account of its sinful deeds at the bar of the Most High. Milford looked up, and, to his surprise and joy, beheld the lank, ungainly figure of Josh Snipe standing quietly by his side.

"God bless you!" he rather gasped than said, with that choking sensation which is produced by either intense grief or joy.

"I hope you aint hurt, Capting," returned the other, stooping down, grasping his hand, and assisting him to rise; "though, I swow to Guinea, I don't think I was a minute tew soon in doing that chap's business."

A shrill, piercing scream, at this moment, drew the eyes of both upon the lady, who, having recovered consciousness, had just risen to a sitting posture, and was staring wildly upon the Captain.

"Merciful God! what do I see?" cried Milford, staggering back, as he caught a view of her pale, lovely features.

The reader will readily understand the reason of Milford's exclamation and emotion when he learns, that in her he had just rescued from a fate worse than death, the gallant Captain beheld the idol of his heart, the beautiful Rosalie Du Pont

CHAPTER XII.

THE LOVERS AGAIN.

Words are all too impotent to portray the emotions of the lovers, when they found themselves thus unexpectedly thrown together, under such exciting, terrible, and tragic circumstances. To rush to the side of her he loved, to kneel down, to seize her hand, and press it to his feverish, burning lips, was, with Milford, but the work of a single instant; but when he essayed to speak, he found himself completely overpowered by his feelings: his heart seemed to be in his throat; he experienced a swimming, choking sensation; and he could only gaze upon her lovely face in silence, press her soft, white hand again and again to his lips, and allow gushing tears of joy to course their way adown his manly countenance.

Rosalie herself was the first to break the silence; but it was not till after the lapse of several moments, that she could command her voice.

"O, Edgar!" she murmured at length: "O, Edgar!" and she threw her arms around his neck, and burst into tears. "Tell me," she resumed, after a pause, during which she had been giving vent to her emotions through the soft, bright gates of her soul; "tell me, dear Edgar, what has happened? There is blood upon you! Oh! Heaven, you are wounded!"

"No, no, dearest," answered the Captain, "I am unhurt; it is the blood of the vile ruffians, who have robbed, and were about to murder you. God has providentially preserved us both, by sending us a true friend in time of need;" and he nodded to Josh, who was standing by and looking on with an expression of sympathy and amazement on his plain, rustic features.

"Oh, let me thank him, then, for this noble, praiseworthy act!" rejoined Rosalie, as Milford assisted her to rise; and advancing to Josh, she took both of his hard hands in hers; and fixing her soft, bright eyes upon him, she added, in a tremulous voice: "Sir, you are a stranger to me; but for risking your life to save mine, and that of Captain Milford, you have the full gratitude of my heart. Only say what I can do for you in return, and it shall be done."

Now Josh was a brave fellow, and would have done twice as much to serve the fair being before him, and thought little of it, to say nothing of coming to the rescue of his best friend, the Captain, at any hazard; but he had never before encountered so fascinating, so beautiful, so lovely a countenance, as that of Rosalie Du Pont; and if he felt bewildered, awkward, and abashed, in being so earnestly addressed by one he regarded as little inferior to an angel, it must be attributed to his rustic education, in never having mingled in that society where such beings move the reigning stars. Therefore, if he blushed, and looked down, and scraped his feet, and felt a strange choking in his throat, as if he had suddenly swallowed all he would say and could not get it up again, he only did as nature directed, and as many another would have done under the same circumstances. At last, after several hems and coughs, and a good deal of twisting about, he managed to articulate:

"You're welcome to all I've done, gal—miss, I should say—or—a—your ladyship I mean; 'cause I didn't dew nothing but shoot that are darned scamp there; and I'd dew it agin, free gratis for nothing, if I seed him have an honest chap down, in the way he had the Capting, and jest about to stick a knife into him—consarn his old picter!"

"I shall not forget the service you have rendered me, Josh, depend upon it!" said Milford, seizing a hand of the Yankee, as Rosalie released it, and shaking it warmly. Then turning to Rosalie, he added, in a low tone: "This, dearest, is one of the gallant little band of noble spirits, in this city, who are sworn to the cause of liberty."

"But what did he mean, dear Edgar, by saying the ruffian had you down, and was about to plunge a knife into you? Were you then in such imminent peril?"

"I was," answered Edgar; "I was wholly in the power of that villain, who now lies dead, where you see; and I had closed my eyes, as I believed, for the last time;" and he briefly narrated all that had happened, from the moment when his fair listener's cries for help had first arrested his attention.

Rosalie shuddered, and unconsciously pressed closer to Milford, as she learned from his lips through what terrible perils both had passed, during the period of her unconsciousness; and when he had concluded, she slowly sank down on her knees, and, clasping her hands, and turning her sweet face heavenward, gently murmured, while two pearly tears stole into her eyes:

"To God let us render thanks for this happy preservation;" and then she prayed from her heart, in silence, while Milford and his companion stood uncovered. At length she arose, and threw herself, sobbing, upon the breast of him she loved.

"Then you did not come hither together, as I at first supposed?" she again resumed, releasing herself from the Captain's fond embrace, and drying her eyes.

"No," answered Milford; "so far as I know, our meeting here was purely accidental."

"Say providential," chided Rosalie, solemnly—"for the ways of God are in it."

"Pardon me, dearest! I meant providential, if I did not say it," returned the Captain. "But tell me, Josh, how it happened that you appeared upon the ground at such a fortunate moment? for another second's delay would have proved fatal to me."

"Why, I'll jest tell ye, Capting, how it was," answered Josh, who by this time had recovered from much of his embarrassment—though, as he was aware that the beautiful eyes of Rosalie were fixed upon him, and that she herself was an attentive listener, he did not altogether feel at his ease: "I'll jest tell ye how it was. You see, it being a right nice day for sauntering about, and I not having nothing as I cared about doing in particular, I thought I'd jest stroll round a bit, and see how I liked the look of the land near this big city, and whether it 'ud be good to farm, in case we licked the tarnal Britishers, and—"

"Hush! be careful how you make use of words that would hang you if overheard!" interrupted Milford, warningly.

"That's a fact, I swow to Guinea; I clean forgot all abeout where I was. Wal, to cut the matter short, I was jest strolling abeout in them are woods, across this ere clearing, when I seed this lady ride by a hoss-back; and she rid so putty, that I had to stop and look at her. Wal, as she was going along by these ere woods here, I seed two fellers run out and catch hold of her hoss and her, and drag 'em in here, and I heard her scream for help too. Wal, says I to myself, Josh Snipe, if you let that are gal—beg pardon! I mean your ladyship—for any body could see you was a nateral born lady, Miss—(and he nodded to Rosalie)—if you let her be taken off by them are sneaking, mean, dirty, good-for-nothing rascals, says I, and don't try to dew nothing for her, you're jest abeout as mean as they is, and a darned coward to boot. So I looked at my pistols, and seed they was all right, and off I sot, as hard as I could run, for this ere wood. Wal, I come into it a piece above here, in putty tolerable quick time, I calculate, being I's a foot, and my shoes none the best—one on 'em slips up and down at the heel like all darnation."

Here Rosalie, who had a quick sense of the ridiculous, was obliged to turn her head, to conceal a laugh; while Milford said, good humoredly:

"Well, well, Josh, never mind the shoe."

"Yes, but, Capting, I have to mind it," returned Josh, holding up one foot to exhibit it; "for it's the darndest thing to slide up and down you ever seen; and when I'm running fast, like I was then, it bothers me like all git eout—it does, I swow, that's a fact.

"Wal, as I's saying, I got to the woods at last, without being diskivered by the robbers. I knowed, too, I wasn't diskivered—for I could hear 'em talking away to themselves, abeout their own affairs—and so I crept down the edge of the bushes, along the clearing, till I got right against them; and then I dropped down on my hands and knees, and worked my way in carefully, to see if I could git a chance to do any thing for her sweet ladyship.

"Wal, jest as I'd got so I could see what was going on, up you pops, Capting, mounts that are scamp's back, and sticks t'other feller in the throat, quicker'n I could say Jack Robinson. I never was so taken 'back but once, in the hull course of my life, as I was to see you, Capting, jest rise right up there, like you'd come out of the earth; and t'other time was, when a streak o' lightning struck a tree I's under, and ripped the shoes off o' my feet, and left me sprawling on the ground, more skeered than hurt.

"Wal, afore I got over my astonishment, that are cut-throat was grappling with you; and by the time I could git to him, he was jest agoing to strike. I cotched his arm, put my pistol to his head, and keeled him over; and I'd done the same if you'd been a nigger, Capting—so I don't see what's the use of making any more talk abeout it. I happened to come in jest the right time, and I'm as glad on't as any body else can be."

"You are a noble fellow," said Rosalie, warmly; "and while I live, rest assured your gallant deed shall not be forgotten. But for the present, here is something more substantial, which I find the robbers have overlooked." She produced a well-filled purse, and held it toward Josh, adding: "Take this now, as an earnest of my sincerity—but with the understanding that my gratitude shall not cease with a recompense so paltry."

There was a look of manly pride and dignity on the sharp, shrewd, rustic features of Josh, as he drew himself up to his full height, and, with a waiving back of the hand, made answer in his own peculiar way:

"Lady, what I've done, I didn't do for hire. Your compliments make me feel proud; but your money would make me feel as mean as Sam Huskings did, when his gal cotched him robbing her mother's hen-roost. I was fetched up in the country, I know, and don't know much abeout the fashions of you city folks; but if I take pay for helping people in trouble, I hope I may be stung to death with yaller wasps!"

"Nobly said, Josh!" cried Milford, giving

the latter a hearty slap on the shoulder. "There is unpolished man enough in you to make a true gentleman. Leave him to me, Rosalie; he and I understand each other; and this day's business he shall have no cause to regret. And now tell us of yourself—how it chanced that you were riding here alone!"

"I can explain all in a very few words," answered Rosalie. "I am passionately fond of equestrian exercise; and finding myself again able to sit a horse, I ordered one to be brought, and strayed off in this direction, as being one of my favorite riding grounds. I had taken a circuit above here, and was on my return to town, when I was stopped by these ruffians. But have you looked to them, Edgar? perhaps both are not dead! and methought I just now heard a groan."

"If they are not dead, they have not got their deserts, the villains!" replied Milford; "but I will ascertain. Do not you look upon them, dear Rosalie—the sight is not fit for one of your sex and gentle nature. No, go you out to the clearing, and I will soon join you."

Rosalie complied with the request of Milford, who now proceeded to examine into the state of the robbers. The one shot by Josh, was stone dead; and he appeared to have died so suddenly, that the expression of demoniac rage and triumph on his face, at the moment he was in the act of striking the Captain, had had no time to change. It was still there—that awful look—made rigid by death; and this, together with the terrible wound in his head, from which had flowed both blood and brains, rendered him a horrible spectacle, from which the Captain, accustomed as he was to death in many a revolting form, turned away with a sickening feeling of disgust.

The ruffian stabbed by Milford was still living, but wholly unconscious. He was found lying among the bushes, much as he had fallen, with Rosalie's diamond brooch in one hand, and the discharged pistol in the other—though the nerves were so relaxed, that neither of them were retained with more than the grasp of an infant. The knife had entered the side of his neck, and cut the back part of the jugular—at least so Milford judged—and the man was bleeding to death internally.

"He is past the rope," said the Captain, sententiously, as, for a short time, he gazed upon him, and listened to his labored breathing.

"You think he'll die, Capting?" queried Josh.

"Yes, his minutes are numbered."

"Wal, what'll we do with the bodies?"

"Leave them as they are for the present. We will hasten into town, report what has happened, and let the proper authorities act in the matter as they think advisable."

"Wal, Capting, I spose there won't be no harm in taking this ere sparkling thing, that belongs to the lady?" said Josh.

"No, secure that, at all events; and that reminds me of seeing a couple of rings in the hands of the other, of which we must take possession, for fear of their being lost. If I am not mistaken, I once owned one of those rings myself."

"Ye-a-s, I see how 'tis, Capting," rejoined Josh, giving the other a sly, comical look, and jerking his thumb over his shoulder; "this ere gal—I beg pardon! I mean her ladyship—for if she aint a real lady, she oughter be——"

"Is my affianced bride," interrupted Milford, seriously. "You have seen so much, you may as well know the whole secret."

"Ye-a-s, I thought so. Wal, Capting, Josh Snipe wishes ye lots of joy; and guess you'll have it, too; for she's jest the puttiest and sweetest, and most lady critter I ever seen, in all my born days. She beats Sal Stacy clean to death—I swow, she does—and I'd die for her quicker than for any lady I ever put eyes on—that's a fact."

As Captain Milford saw no reason for disputing this assertion of his faithful and courageous follower, he merely nodded acquiescence, pointed to the brooch, and turned away to the other robber to secure the rings. In a few moments he rejoined Rosalie, and restored her her jewels, while Josh led out the horse.

"Ah! yes," said Rosalie, in a low tone to Milford, as she replaced the rings on her finger, "I was nigh losing, forever, gifts that I highly prize. This, dear Edgar," holding up the ring he had given her, "I have treasured

—O, you know not how fondly—as the remembrancer of one I loved with an undivided heart.

"Bless you!" returned her lover—"bless you, my own, dearest Rosalie!" and as the face of Josh happened at the moment to be turned from them, the Captain suddenly threw his arm around the fair girl's waist, drew her fondly to him, and imprinted a kiss of pure affection upon her charming lips.

"And this," pursued Rosalie, pointing to the other ring, as Milford released her, "was a present to me from Sir Henry Clinton, through the hands of the unfortunate Major Andre. It is a talisman, which will procure for the presenter any favor that may be asked, within the power of the donor to grant. O! Edgar, I value it so highly; for who knows, (and Rosalie dropped her voice to a whisper, and shuddered,) who knows but it may yet be required to save him I love from the fate of poor Andre!"

"Heaven forbid!" returned Milford, solemnly; "for in that event I fear its virtue would be lost. But we will talk of this as we proceed to town. Mount, dearest, and I will attend you on foot. O! my feelings are almost too great for utterance—joy at seeing you restored to health; and a thrilling, almost overpowering sensation, when I think of the awful fate you so narrowly and wonderfully escaped! Yes, as you say, dearest, the hand of God is in it; and to the day of my death, will I never cease to give thanks, for being permitted to assist in your deliverance from the hands of those highwaymen."

But we shall not pause here to repeat all that was said by the lovers on their way back to the city. One question and answer, however, we see proper to chronicle.

"Dearest Rosalie," said the Captain, in the course of a conversation which suggested the subject, "you have never told me your early history—will you not do so?"

"Yes," answered Rosalie, frankly, "I will tell you all that is necessary for you to know at present, for I feel you have a right to this knowledge. Come home with me, and you shall hear."

On reaching the city, Milford acquainted the proper authorities with the tragic occurrences of the wood: and a party of soldiers, headed by a corporal, were sent out to bring in the living ruffian—or, if he had expired, to bury him and his companion together. Josh acted as guide, and led the soldiers directly to the place of sanguinary strife; but, to the disappointment of all, neither one of the robbers, living nor dead, was to be found. A broad trail, as if made by several feet, led straight to the river, and thence all trace was lost.

CHAPTER XIII.

THE PLOT THICKENS.

The narrow escape of Rosalie Du Pont from the hands of the robbers, together with a wild, exaggerated account of the whole tragic affair, flew like lightning over the city, and, in the absence of any thing more important, caused a remarkable sensation—that is to say, remarkable for people accustomed to the thrilling events of an army life, with all its morbid details, from a single assassination up to the wholesale slaughter of hundreds in the strife of battle. Of course, all who could lay claim to the distinguished acquaintance of our fair heroine, together with many others who had never exchanged a word with her in their lives, but who thought this a capital time and pretext for forcing themselves upon her notice, now hurried to the residence of her uncle, and literally blockaded and besieged her. She had not been half an hour at home, and had scarcely finished giving her horror-struck kinswoman a recital of her terrible adventures, when carriage after carriage, containing the *elite* and *distingue* of the town, rolled up to the door, all anxious to wish her joy, and hear the particulars of the event of the day from her own lips.

Rosalie had not calculated upon this, when she invited Captain Milford to accompany her home, and listen to her history, and in consequence both were disappointed.

"I must beg you to come another day, Edgar," she said—"unless you are willing to encounter the tedium of so many fashionable calls."

"No, dearest, I thank you—I will take my leave—for in my present state of mind, it would not be agreeable for me to come in contact with so many strangers, to be stared at and questioned as the hero of your adventure. But be careful of yourself, dear Rosalie, and do not let them weary you too much—for you are not yet strong, and great excitement and fatigue might again prostrate you."

"Shall I see you again to-morrow, dear Edgar?"

"I will not promise, for I know not what a day may bring forth—but if I can, I will call."

"You must be sure and let me know when your scheme is ripe for action."

"I will endeavor to do so."

"And, oh! be very, very careful of yourself, for my sake! will you, dear Edgar?"

"Yes, dearest, yes. There, adieu;" and pressing the hand of Rosalie warmly, as he held it at parting, for the presence of others prevented a more affectionate leave-taking, the Captain took his departure.

From the mansion of Graham Percy, Captain Milford proceeded direct to the residence of the traitor Arnold. He did not enter the dwelling, however, but walking leisurely past it, turned down a narrow street, or lane, which divided it from another structure of similar proportions, that also fronted on Broadway. This lane led to an alley, which crossed it at right angles, and ran along the rear of a fine garden, which extended back from Arnold's dwelling some two hundred feet. Fronting on this rear alley—which, at the present day, is a well-paved, commodious street—was an old wooden building, in a dilapidated condition, whose heavy, gloomy, peculiar style of architecture, proclaimed it of Dutch construction, and which, for all we know to the contrary, might have been erected under the Dutch dynasty.

When Milford came in front of this old dwelling, which exhibited no signs of being inhabited, he paused, and seemed to examine it with an air of curiosity. Then looking up and down the alley, and carefully around him in all directions, and perceiving not a living soul, he glided to the rear of the crazy old structure, and rapped with his knuckles on a sagging, worm-eaten door, that, to all appearance, might have been demolished with a heavy blow of his fist.

Scarcely had the knock of our hero sounded a dull echo through the dreary apartments of the old building, when the decaying floor-boards creaked under the pressure of advancing feet, and a moment after the door stood just sufficiently ajar to admit of his entrance.

"You seem to ask no questions to-day, Mother Hagold," said the Captain, as he passed in, and closed the door behind him.

"No, cause I knowed who it was," replied the dame. "I was peeping out of one of the holes in front, and seed you when you looked up."

"Well, any news since I was here?"

"No, nothing to mention. Arnold 'pears to keep close to-day; he rode off about noon, but came back a little while ago, with the Colonel along with him."

"Doubtless the Colonel will be his best friend while his money lasts. I passed the house just now, but saw no one stirring, only the sentinel that he keeps on duty before his door."

"Guess there ain't much stirring in there but cards, money, and wine," replied the dame; "them, I reckon, keep agoing pretty regular when they two is together."

"Well, I am glad to hear he is so well occupied?"

"'Spose you'd like to see the Sargeant?"

"Yes; is he here?" returned Milford, quickly.

"He came about half an hour ago, and I got him to wait, for I thought as how you might drop in soon."

"You did right; and now I would see him at once."

Dame Hagold led the way across a large dark room, with low ceiling, and a floor that trembled under every step, to a rickety staircase, by which she ascended to the second story. Crossing another room similar to the one below, she entered a narrow corridor, where it was almost impossible to see at all; and continuing along this a few paces, she opened a door into an apartment which occupied the entire front of the house. This was the only room in the dwelling that was furnished; and this contained merely a bed in one corner, an old table, a half dozen miserable chairs, and some few household utensils, necessary to the cooking and eating department. The ceiling of this apartment was, like all in the house, very low, and the windows very small, with a few diamond-shaped panes, set in lead, but so thick, green, and dirty, that the light which struggled through them was hardly sufficient to enable one to read at noon-day. But besides these windows, of which there were two, far apart, there were several crevices in the wall next the alley; and through these you could get a much better idea of what was taking place without, than through the windows themselves. On an old chair, drawn up to one of these crannies, sat Sergeant Champe. As Milford entered, he said:

"Well, Captain, I am glad you have come. What news?"

"I have sent off our first messenger," replied the other.

"Who?"

"George."

"Has he really gone, then?"

"Yes, I saw him cross the river myself."

"I am truly glad to hear it. So much is then accomplished. But we must work fast, Captain."

"I agree with you, that delay is dangerous."

"More so, perhaps, than you are aware of."

"Ha! any thing new?"

"Yes, they talk of embarking the legion immediately."

"This is bad news, certainly. What a pity that you enlisted!"

"Had I not done so, they would have become suspicious. Even now, I fear, they think all is not right."

"This is serious, my friend; what do you think has led to it?"

"I do not know. It is possible I may be mistaken; but such is my impression."

"Do you think Arnold suspects you?"

"I hardly know how to answer. Sometimes I think he does, and at others think it only my fancy. He is not so polite and affable as he was."

"I thought he would change his manners whenever he could begin to fancy himself secure in British favor. Depend upon it, Champe, he, in his heart, only regards us as stepping-stones by which to raise himself from out the slimy depth of degradation into which his dastardly villainy plunged him. He was glad to see us, because he thought we should help to make an acquisition from the American army, that would give a shadow of truth to his infamous bombast regarding his influence to draw over to the British the best portion of the American soldiery. He was glad to talk to us, because he was isolated in his new situation, knew that he was looked upon with contempt by all honorable men, and felt the need of company and sympathy. Beyond these, he cared no more for us than he would for any tools which he found necessary to use; and, as I told you then, so I repeat, the moment he finds himself established a welcome companion of half a dozen red-coats, he will treat us with the same disdain he would a couple of sneaking dogs."

"Well, Captain, you seem to take it to heart; but what better could you expect of a vile traitor? For my part, I care not what he thinks, nor how he feels, so he does not thwart our design."

"Neither do I, Sergeant; neither do I," replied Milford, quickly. "Do not mistake me! I am not thus bitter because I feel slighted, in the remotest degree, by the withdrawal of his favor; but when I witness the proceedings of so foul a hypocrite, I can not, for the life of me, avoid becoming excited with honest indignation. But to come back to the starting point. In the present state of affairs, with a likelihood of being embarked at any moment, what do you propose, Sergeant?"

"I hardly know what to reply. I think it best we put our plan in operation as soon as possible."

"You mean, to seize him in the garden?"

"Yes."

"Well, all here is prepared for that, and yet we can not do it to-night."

"Why not?"

"Because there is no boat ready to take him across the river, and no one ready to receive him when there."

"True, true," returned Champe, musingly. "I do not like this delay; we should have worked faster."

"It is well I did not enlist when you did," said Milford.

"But if I am called away, you will be short of help."

"There is Carlini, besides my faithful follower, Josh Snipe; and doubtless, in a strait, we could depend upon Mother Hagold, here; eh, good dame?"

"Yes, yes, Captain, you're right; I'll help you with right good will, if you want me; and you won't find me no trifle either, when I once get my coat and breeches on."

"What do you mean?"

"I mean I've dressed in men's clothes afore now, and done sarvice, too, when bullets warn't nothing like as scarce as hail-stones."

"Indeed! then you will really be a valuable acquisition to our party," returned Milford, smiling.

"Only put me in a way to sarve Gineral Washington and the liberty boys, and you may count on me for *one*, at any rate. I can load and fire a musket as well as the best on 'em; and if I live, I hope to see the day when I shall be able to send a couple o' bullets through the heads of Jack Sharp and Jim Bolter, the scoundrels!"

"Jack Sharp and Jim Bolter!" exclaimed Milford, in surprise, as he recalled the names of the ruffians slain in the wood, but which tragic circumstance he had not yet mentioned to either of those present. "What do you know, Dame Hagold, of those vile cut-throats!"

"What do I know on 'em!" almost screamed the other, flushing up with passion, at the remembrance of her wrongs. "What do I know on 'em, does you ax? Why, they was at the head of the Skinners, what burnt me out a while ago; and if ever I put eyes on 'em agin, with any thing dangerous in my hands, the Lord have mercy on 'em!"

"Well, I do not think you will behold them again among the living," rejoined Milford; and he proceeded to briefly narrate the terrible events already known to the reader; while the old woman and Champe listened with breathless attention.

Nothing could exceed the delight manifested by the fortune-teller, when she heard of the death of her most bitter enemies; for Milford was under the impression that both were dead by this time; and so stated he, of course, knowing nothing of the bodies having been removed—as the party of soldiers sent out, with Josh as guide, had not yet returned.

"Ah! ha! ha! ha!" cried the dame, somewhat wildly, rubbing her hands together, and fairly dancing about the room. "I told them so—I told them so. I told the wretches I'd live to dance over their graves; and now my prediction's come true. Reckon they've got to a place by this time that's a good deal hotter nor any they made on airth. Burn me out agin, will they!—they said they'd do it agin, and the next time my fat carcass should help feed the flames; wonder who feels the most flames now? Why, Captain, I could hug you to my heart, and Josh, too, for knowing you did the business to them imps of Satan. O, I hain't felt so much joy for a year. And poor Rosalie, too—the gal was nigh going for't this time, sure. Another narrow escape! Kind Providence watches over her, I believe. She's had so many perils lately—that adventur' in the country—that fever, as like to took her off—and now this here captur', that she 'scaped from so wonderfully."

"What do you mean by her adventure in the country?" inquired Milford.

"What do I mean? why, don't you know? But I remember now, you don't know nothing about it; and now I recollect, it's a secret, too; so I musn't tell you."

Milford's curiosity, as may readily be believed, was not a little excited by this reply; but he was too much of a gentleman to pry into a secret intentionally withheld from him, although he was resolved to question Rosalie concerning it the first favorable opportunity.

"You say these ruffians were Skinners," he said, changing the subject; "how, then, do you account for their being within the British lines?"

"Arter more plunder, you may depend," answered the fortune-teller. "I 'spose they've carried on sech a high hand in the country, and got off scot-free for so long, that they thought their good fortin' 'ud bear 'em out in coming here. Who knows but they'd an idea of making their threat good, of burning me out the second time, the black-hearted scoundrels! O, I'd so liked to have been there, to have helped 'em out o' this world;" and the features of the dame assumed a truly ferocious expression.

"Well, well, they have got their deserts," returned Milford; "at least one is dead, to my certain knowledge, and I doubt not the other, before this time; if not, he only remains for the rope; so let them go. I should like to know whether any of their vile companions are in this vicinity."

"Depend upon't, they didn't come alone; they was too cowardly for that," replied the dame.

"Where is Josh?" now asked Champe.

"He went to guide a party of soldiers to the fatal spot."

"Is he to call here to-day?"

"I advised him to do so if he could manage so as to be certain of not being seen. Should each of us, at different times, be seen coming here, of course suspicion would be excited, that some plot is in progress, and this might result in the frustration of our design."

"I have thought of that," returned Champe, "and I think we had better meet here no more—especially in the day-time—in the night, of course, we run less risk."

"Well, I agree with you; we are too near the citadel of the enemy; and our scheme is apparently so near success now, that to have it frustrated, would almost be like taking the traitor from our hands. Champe, as you say, delay is dangerous; and I think, upon the whole, we had better seize the traitor before something unforeseen occurs to thwart our plans."

"Shall it be to-night?"

"No, I meant not so soon—though I would it could be so."

"And what is to prevent?"

"You remember we have no boat in readiness, for one thing."

"But cannot one be procured?"

"Possibly, though it is uncertain. It is now three o'clock, at least, and night will soon set in."

"So much the better—we can work the faster and surer."

"But the rest of our party?"

"Carlini is at home, and can be easily notified; and you say Josh will be here, in all probability. Besides, if he is not, we could manage without him; and on further consideration, perhaps it would be better that we should; for although I do not doubt his fidelity, and willingness to assist, I fear his tongue might be tempted to wag at the wrong time, and a chance word might ruin all."

"I think he will be discreet; we must make him so, at all events; I should not like to attempt the seizure without his knowledge. And there is Rosalie Du Pont—I have promised to give her notice when the scheme is ripe; besides we want the co-operation of men on the other side, and they will not be there till to-morrow night, at the soonest."

"I see you are full of objections, Captain; but nevertheless, I am for making the attempt at all risks. We must trust something to luck, of course; and if we can once get Arnold on the other side, I think we are strong enough to guard him."

"But the boat—you forget that?"

"No, I forget nothing; but surely we have one skiff, which, though small, we must make answer."

"Ay, but that is on the other side; you seem to overlook the fact that young Nugent crossed in it to-day."

"Well, to do away with that objection, I will swim over and get it after dark."

"I am as anxious as yourself, Sergeant; but really, I fear we shall be too perecipitate; this should have been thought of before."

"That is true; but I could not foreknow the news I have heard to-day, of the intention to embark the Legion immediately. The more I think of it, Captain, the more I fear delay will prove fatal to our hopes; in fact, I have a presentiment that such will be the case."

"I would I knew what is best," returned Milford, uneasily. "I should never forgive myself, if we were to make a fatal mistake now, either by precipitation or delay. Come, Mother Hagold, what do you counsel?"

"Well," replied the dame, "it isn't for a woman like me to counsel such as you; but if you think the thing can possibly be done, I agree with the Sargeant, that the sooner it's done the better. As to the boat, I think I can undertake to git one—though, mind you, I won't promise for sartain. There's Giles Broach, as lives on the East river side—a clever old man, that I did a kindness for a time ago, and who'll be willing, I dare say, to do me a return—he's got jest sech a boat as you want; and I think I could git it, without suspicion being raised; but then how to git it round here to the Hudson, would be the trouble; for sentries is out all along the rivers, as well as the water-guards, and it 'ud be almost a mericle to 'scape 'em all."

"There would be less risk in swimming the river," said Champe. "I think my plan the best."

"Well, let us see what we have to do," said Milford. "In the first place, we can do nothing without a boat: hence, on the procuring of that, rests even the *possibility* of all the rest. Well, Sergeant, you say you can swim the river and get that; but you can not attempt such a thing before night sets in, and in the meantime all must remain in suspense. Well, we will suppose you are successful—that you get the skiff, and get down the river, nearly opposite here, without being discovered: then some one must stay to guard it; and as it requires a person of great caution to do so, we will premise that you remain there, while Carlini, Josh, and myself operate here."

"And why couldn't I guard the boat, as well as the Sargeant?" put in the fortune-teller.

"Perhaps you could—I did not think of that," returned the Captain. "Well, so much the better; for then Champe would be at liberty to act with us: we will consider it settled thus, for the present, at all events. Now, then, we come to the most delicate and hazardous task—that of seizing Arnold. We have watched the traitor narrowly, for the last few days, and well do we know his habits—the most favorable one for our project of which is, and on which all our hopes of success rest, that of walking up and down his garden, alone, just before retiring for the night. Now our plan of operation, to which all have assented, and which I do not think can be changed for the better, is for two of us to secrete ourselves in the garden, in some bushes near this alley, and the moment the traitor gets near enough, to justify the conclusion that we are certain of our prey, to bound forward together, place a hand over his mouth, throw him upon his back, gag him, disarm him, bind his arms, throw an ample cloak around him, press a hat over his forehead, and then, one on either side, conduct him into the alley, through the palings we have taken off, (but so replaced that a moment's work will remove them,) and thence to guard him to the boat: and furthermore, if we chance to meet a sentinel on the way, we are to represent him as a drunken soldier, whom we are taking to the lower guard-house. This, I believe, is our plan, Sergeant."

"Yes, such is our plan, Captain, as I understand it."

"Well, now to be successful in this bold undertaking, I think our party is not too strong, all told. I would have one stationed in this old building, on the lookout, who, in the event of unexpected danger, might make some signal agreed upon, to put the others on their guard. I would have another concealed by the loosened palings, ready to come to the assistance of the two in the garden, should it be necessary, or to follow them quietly, as the case may be. Now the first mentioned duty, that of watching here, I would assign to Josh; the second, that of standing guard by the palings, to Carlini; and the third, that of seizing the traitor, to ourselves. What say you to this disposition of our little force, Champe?"

"I like your arrangement well, Captain," returned Champe, "and only regret there is a possibility—I may, perhaps, say probability—of our being obliged to delay its execution till too late. Oh! would we had taken earlier measures for bringing our scheme to an immediate crisis! It is useless to repine now; but remember, withal, I solemnly urge the propriety, the necessity, of our acting in the matter to-night."

"Well, be it so, then," rejoined Milford, anxiously. "I would that Josh were here."

"By-the-by," said Champe, after a pause, "what do you think of this Signor Carlini?"

"That he is a wonderful man."

"Have you faith in his power to predict events by the science of the stars?"

"I neither believe, nor disbelieve, having never tested it—I simply do not know. He says there is truth in the science, and I know no reason why he should tell us false."

"What do you think of the peculiar influence he exercised upon our inquisitive companion?"

"I do not know what to think—that perplexes me more than all the rest. I do not understand it; it seems something super-human: yet it may be only a science, which is not generally known. I have no faith in a supernatural power being invested in a mere mortal; and yet I am obliged to acknowledge it was wonderful. I questioned Josh upon the subject, but he could give me no information, beyond the fact, that while Carlini stood looking at him, he was unable to move a limb, or take his eyes from the dark, fiery orbs of the other."

"Well," returned Champe, "I agree with you, Captain, that he is a wonderful man, and one likely to make the most skeptical believe in his wizard-like powers. When we consider the somewhat startling manner in which a stranger is introduced into his presence, (effected of course by ingenious mechanism,) the room hung in black, the man himself, and the remarkable power he does possess, to astonish beyond comprehension, and make a lasting impression upon those who come to consult him—we can not be surprised that he is regarded, by the ignorant and superstitious, as a man leagued with the devil."

Thus conversing on various matters, another half hour slipped away, when all were somewhat startled, by hearing three distinct raps on the door through which the Captain had been admitted by Dame Hagold.

"I hope we are not suspected and ferreted out!" said Milford, starting up.

"Quick!" said the dame in a low, hurried tone, as she threw open the door of the closet, disclosing a ladder which led to a floor above, close under the roof: "Quick! get in here, mount, draw the ladder up arter ye, and lay down the boards you find up there, while I go and see who it is;" and as the others followed her directions, she closed the closet door, locked it, and hastened down stairs.

CHAPTER XIV.

AN UNWELCOME VISITOR.

"I think we are frightened without a cause," said Champe, in a low tone, as he and Milford made a hasty ascent to the cock-loft, and drew the ladder up after them, preparatory to laying down the loose boards, which would effectually conceal their retreat, even should the closet itself be searched by prying eyes. "Doubtless the applicant for admission is a no more alarming personage than honest Josh himself."

"So I think, Sergeant; but it is well enough to be on our guard, for we have a great deal at stake. A bold, daring general is not always the wisest; and a prudent retreat is far better than defeat."

"That is true; so let us block ourselves in here, while we can do it without being overheard," returned the Sergeant, as he began to lay the floor with great care, feeling along the edges of the boards, to ascertain if the joints were good, for it was too dark to see, the only light admitted into the place being through two very narrow crevices just under the eaves. "By-the-by," he continued, in the same low, guarded tone, which was scarcely above a whisper, "did it never strike you, Captain, that with all our caution, our lives are already in the hands of this woman? and that, should she choose to tell what she knows, our necks would be in the halter in less than twenty-four hours?"

"Yes, we are in her power, and have been from the first; but I have no fears on that account; for if she were not to be relied upon, in any and every emergency, she would hardly be likely to be in the confidence of General Washington."

"Ah! if she is in his confidence that is

proof enough of her honesty and fidelity. I knew nothing of her. I was made acquainted with her through you; and I asked no questions; for, knowing you to be cautious and discreet, I doubted not you had good grounds for every thing you said and did."

"Yes, in my instructions received from the General himself, I was directed where to find her, and also told that I could rely upon both her discretion and integrity, should I require her assistance. Her history, what I have been able to glean from her, is briefly this: When the war broke out, she had a husband and son, both of whom joined the American army. Her husband was killed in the battle of Saratoga, and her son afterward deserted to the British, from his post of sentry on the lines. Subsequently he fell into the hands of the Americans, was tried, and condemned to be shot. Washington was with the division that took him prisoner; and the mother of the boy, for he was a mere youth then, was there, also, as a camp-follower. As a mother, of course she felt for her son; and she flew to the noble General, and plead so earnestly for his life—representing her lonely condition, the youth of her child, the gallant deeds of his father—that the heart of our humane commander melted with pity, and her prayer was granted. In return for this generous conduct, she vowed to devote her whole energies, her life, to the cause of liberty. Shortly after, she was missing from the American camp; and it was soon ascertained she had taken up her quarters with the British, where she was among the loudest in denouncing the rebels. Washington only knew why she was there. Her son went with her, but she would never tell what became of him."

"Hist!" said Champe, in a whisper. "I hear voices, and one of them is unknown to me."

"We need not regret our precautions, then," returned Milford. "Hark!"

Our friends now heard steps approaching, and immediately after the door of the room below them was thrown open, and the voice of the fortune teller was heard saying:

"Well, you see there aint nobody here—so if you please, we'll pass on to the next room."

"Stop, hold 'ooman, not so fast!" was the gruff reply; and our friends could hear a soldier-like tread across the floor, and a clinking sound, as if a musket was being shifted into different positions. They could see nothing, and consequently remained in suspense as to what was taking place below; but their feelings may readily be imagined; for they believed their plot had, by some means, been detected, and that an officer was already in pursuit of them.

"Well, be you satisfied now?" inquired the dame.

"Why, there's nobody in this hold rag of a bed, that's sartain," growled the corporal, (for such the new-comer was,) as he thrust his bayonet several times into Dame Hagold's rude pallet. "But hit don't follow that he's not in this hold shanty, for all that. Come, hold 'ooman, you'd best give him hup, while I'm civil, for I'm bound to 'ave him, d'ye see? He can't git away, for I've got half a dozen fellows below, on the watch, that wouldn't let a mouse escape, if hit was a mouse we's hafter."

"I tell you he's not here, sir," returned the dame, tartly; "but if you don't believe me, jest look till you're blind."

"Well, somebody's 'ere—who his it then?"

"I tell you nobody's here."

"'Twon't do, hold 'ooman—twon't do; I'm too hold for that. Where's that door go to?"

"That's a closet."

"Hopen it."

"What for?"

"I want to look in there."

"It's locked," said the dame, trying it, and thus purposely delaying, that her guests might have time to make all right, in case they had at first neglected her instructions.

"Well, if hits locked, I 'spose you'd better hunlock it," persisted the corporal; "and that'll save me the trouble of smashing it down—d'ye see?"

"Ah, here's the key," rejoined the dame, who had been fumbling about in her pocket for some time.

She applied it to the door, but the lock must

have been very old and in bad condition, judging from the trouble she had in forcing back the bolt. At last, after repeated trials, and much shaking of the crazy old door, a proceeding duly appreciated by our friends above, the inside of the closet was disclosed to the eager eyes of the expectant corporal.

"You satisfied now?" queried the dame, with a triumphant look, as a single glance assured her that all was right overhead.

"Don't talk so much, hold 'ooman—don't —'cause I likes silence in the ranks, d'ye see!" said the corporal, as he thrust his bayonet into the walls, and tried the floor with the breach of his musket. "Somebody might be hover'ead," he said, looking up, and even punching the loose boards with the point of his bayonet; but which, to the surprise of even Dame Hagold, remained firm in their places—our friends having taken the wise precaution to stretch themselves across them.

Had the Corporal turned suddenly upon the dame, as he made his last remark, he would have seen enough, in her changing countenance, to rouse his suspicions; but, fortunately, he was otherwise occupied; and in another moment she was sufficiently nerved to have braved, unflinchingly, unchangingly, the most piercing scrutiny of an experienced Inquisitor.

"Somebody *might* be up there," she repeated, with a taunting laugh, when she saw the boards did not move, as the Corporal tried them with the point of his bayonet. "Hadn't I best git some tools and help you rip up the ceiling? you look like as though a little work wouldn't hurt you much."

"Silence, hold 'ooman!" returned the Corporal, angrily, withdrawing rather quickly from the closet, as though he felt half ashamed of what he was doing. "Silence, I say! them's the orders, d'ye see?"

"I'll not be silent for such a contemptible scamp as you!" replied the dame, bristling up savagely, no longer having any dread of the Corporal's anger, now that she felt that her friends were safe. "Don't tell me to be silent, in my own house, you mean, contemptible, good-for-nothing, white-livered scoundrel!" she continued, striding up to him, with the look of a fury, and holding up her hands, with bent fingers, as if she were about to bury her long nails in the flesh of his face. "Don't talk to me that way, you walking automaton! or I'll leave my marks on your ugly phiz, as sure's I'm a living woman!"

"There, that'll do, hold 'ooman," rejoined the Corporal, beating a hasty retreat, and bringing his musket to a charge, to protect himself; "that'll do; let's 'old a parley. In the king's name, I command ye halt! Now attention the 'ole, till we make a treaty of peace. In the first place, let me tell you, I've got to search this 'ouse, from cellar to garret; and hif you let's me do it quietly, well and good; but hif you don't, I 'ave to call in a couple of my men and take you prisoner. Now what do you say to that, hold 'ooman?"

"As I told ye afore, sarch till you're blind —I don't care a rap; but don't go for to tell me to hold my tongue agin, you jack-a-napes!"

"Well, then, we'll sign a treaty, hon these conditions; you're to talk has much has you please, and I'm to prosecute my search, hunmolested. Now this his settled, hold 'ooman, d'ye see? So right about face—march!"

"I'll not stir from this room," said the dame, resolutely: "and if you want to sarch farther, you'll have to do it alone, or else call in some of your jack-asses from outside."

"Well, hold 'ooman, can't say I'm particular hanxious for your company: so I'll hadvance and reconoiter alone; but hif I sees any suspicious hobject, you may depend, mother Gunn, I'll charge hupon't, with the 'ole column, rank and file. Hattention, Corporal Jones! trim the line—right face—march!" and with this, the petty officer quitted the room, doing the mock-heroic with a serio-comic air, that made even Dame Hagold laugh in spite of herself, as she threw herself into a seat to await his return.

In about ten minutes or so, he reappeared, and said:

"I don't find nobody, hold 'ooman; so I shall leave you to your meditations, and 'ope you'll 'ave a nice time hov't, d'ye see!"

"Well, I 'spose you won't be afeard, now, to tell me who you've been searching for, and why you thought he was here?"

"Why, hold 'ooman, has I told ye before, I've been looking for a fellow that hought to 'ave a rope round his neck, d'ye see? Somebody told me they seen a man sneaking round 'ere, not long ago, and I thought it might be 'im, d'ye see!"

"Well, who is he? and what's he done?"

"His name's John Hageld, and——" A cry from the other interrupted the Corporal, who immediately added, "But what's the matter with you? d'ye know 'im?"

"My son!" groaned the dame, covering her face with her hands—"my son!" Then quickly starting up, she fairly gasped: "But what's he done? what's he accused of now?"

"Murder!" was the brief and appalling answer.

"Oh! heaven have mercy on me!" groaned the dame, as she staggered into her seat, and again buried her face in her hands.

For several minutes she sat rocking to and fro, and groaning with maternal anguish; then withdrawing her hands from her face, she continued:

"But tell me, sir, the whole particulars, and conceal nothing!" She waited a moment for an answer, but none came. "Do you refuse to answer a mother's questions concerning her child!" she pursued, again starting up from her seat, and turning to where she supposed the Corporal was standing. "Ha! he is gone!" and she flew out of the room, and down the stairs, to overtake and question him.

But she was too late; not a soldier remained in sight. The Corporal, wishing to avoid a scene, and having no cause for further delay, had beat a hasty retreat, but with a determination to keep a watch upon the old building, since he had discovered it to be the abode of the mother of the fugitive.

How much this circumstance affected the designs and arrangements of our little band of heroic spies, the sequel will show.

For something like half an hour, Dame Hagold sat on the stairs, sobbing with grief; and then recollecting her guests, she returned to the apartment containing the closet, and opening the door of the latter, informed them that the coast was clear. In a few moments Milford and Champe made their descent from the cock-loft. It required no explanations from the dame as to the cause of her grief, for they had overheard all that had passed between her and the Corporal.

"I sincerely condole with you in your misfortune," said Milford, in a soothing tone

"I must bear up agin it," answered the dame, wiping her eyes; "I must bear up agin it. He seems predestined to die by the halter. I've done all that I could for him; he'd never take my advice; and now he must 'bide the consequences. It's hard, gentlemen—'tis indeed—for I'm a fond mother; but I won't be more weak nor foolish than I can help. There, I'm right now—right as I can be—and your business must go on afore all others."

"Well, Champe," said Milford, turning to him, "something must be done—what shall it be? Shall we make the attempt to-night? or leave it for to-morrow night?"

"To-night, if possible," answered Champe; "for I have a presentiment, that any longer delay will be ruinous. I must go back to my quarters, however, and, on some pretense or another, manage to obtain leave of absence for the evening."

"And if it be refused?"

"Then I will take it, at the first favorable opportunity, and meet you at the oak, at the edge of yonder wood, where we have twice met before. In either case, I will meet you there, as I think it less hazardous than coming here, since it is more than likely this house will be watched. The signal shall be the same as before, the hooting of the owl. I must ascertain, too, the pass-word for the night."

"I think you are right in supposing the house will be watched; for, if I am not mistaken, the corporal will have a spy in this vicinity; therefore, I approve of your proposition. But I fear we shall run some risk in leaving it, and, therefore, be obliged to wait till night sets in."

"I dread so much delay," returned Champe, "but know of no better plan."

"The night is not far off," rejoined Milford, looking out through a crevice, "and, to all appearances now, will be favorable to our object. The sky is becoming overcast with clouds."

"I hope it will not set in to rain," said

Champe, with considerable uneasiness, as he also took a survey of the heavens; "for although such an event might favor our secret movements, it would be equally destructive to our hopes in another quarter."

"Ah! yes, I understand you: Arnold, of course, would not take his usual walk in the garden."

The conversation was here interrupted again, by another knock on the door below. Again our friends hurried into the closet, and up the ladder; and the dame, having locked them in, went down to ascertain who was the new-comer, and what his business. Presently our friends heard the voice of Josh; and descending from the cock-loft, they waited, with some impatience, for the woman to let them out.

"Well, Josh," said the Captain, "we have been expecting you some time; what news do you bring?"

"Wal, Capting, them are chaps we peppered up in the woods there, has got away, and gone clean, slick, hide and hair."

"Gone?" echoed Milford, in surprise.

"Fact, I swow to Guinea."

"How did they get away!"

"Wal, that's more'n I know; but gone they was when I got there; and the fellers that went up with me wouldn't 'a believed they'd been there at all, and that we'd lied about the hull affair, if it hadn't been for the cut away and stamped-down bushes, and the blood on the ground, and some tracks, that looked like several fellers had carried 'em off to the river. We follered them tracks to the water, but didn't find nothing o' the chaps themselves, and so we calculated they'd put out in a boat."

"This is strange!" mused Milford.

"I don't see nothing strange about it, Captain," chimed in Dame Hagold. "I told you them scoundrels was too cowardly to come here by themselves; and I 'spose their cutthroat companions warn't a great ways off; and so arter you'd gone, they somehow come upon their bodies, and took 'em away."

"What a narrow escape for Rosalie!" said Milford, thinking aloud, and fairly shuddering, as he recalled the horrid scene through which both she and himself had passed.

"Do you think any one saw you enter here, Josh?" inquired Champe.

"Guess not—I didn't see nobody looking."

"Well, as you are one of us, you will understand how necessary it is to be cautious, when I tell you this house has been searched by a British officer, and that we are now staying here to avoid detection, till night, when we contemplate setting about putting our plan into immediate execution."

"What! you mean the taking of him?" and Josh jerked his thumb over his shoulder in the direction of Arnold's residence.

Champe nodded an affirmative.

"To-night?"

"If possible."

"A new arrangement, then, I calculate."

"Yes;" and Champe proceeded to explain it, with as much brevity as the subject would admit of. "If it does not rain before midnight," he said, in conclusion, "I see no insurmountable object to the accomplishment of our design, unless it be the want of a boat; and I must venture to swim the river for one, rather than let that deter us from making the trial."

"What sort of a boat do you want?" inquired Josh.

"Any row-boat would answer, capable of containing half a dozen persons."

"Wal, as I's coming down here, along the bank of the river, I seen one, hitched by a rope to a tree, not fur up, that I guess 'll jest do the thing nicely," returned Josh.

"This is good news: we must secure it, at all hazards."

A general consultation now took place, every trivial affair was duly discussed and arranged, and, as soon as night had drawn her sable curtain, so that they could depart without being seen, our gallant little band of spies separated, to meet again at a certain place at a certain hour.

The events consequent upon that meeting will be detailed in their proper place.

CHAPTER XV.

OUR HERO AND HEROINE.

An hour or two after nightfall, Captain Milford called at the mansion of Graham

Percy, and expressed a desire to see Rosalie Du Pont.

"She's been thronged with visitors all the afternoon, sir, and she's very much fatigued," answered the domestic, in a hesitating manner.

"Nevertheless, I must see her, if only for a few moments," rejoined Milford.

He was accordingly shown into a private parlor; and presently Rosalie made her appearance, looking very pale, but, if any thing, more beautiful and interesting than ever.

"O, Edgar," she said, throwing herself upon a seat, "I am nearly worn out. So many fashionable visitors, who said so many meaningless nothings, and asked so many questions, and required so many repetitions of the horrible events through which I have passed, that, considering the excitement too under which I labored, I do think it little short of a miracle if I retain my senses."

"Well, I will not detain you long, dear Rosalie," said Milford, in reply; "and of course the history you were about to give me of yourself, must be dispensed with for the present."

"You seem serious, Edgar," returned Rosalie, with some anxiety; "has any thing new of importance occurred?"

"Yes," answered the other, in a low, guarded tone; "we have resolved to seize the traitor to-night, if possible."

"To-night!" exclaimed Rosalie; "you alarm me! Why to-night? I thought the attempt was not to be made for some days."

"So thought I, when I saw you last; but our original intentions are changed; we fear delay."

"But to-night—it is so sudden—my heart too misgives me! Oh! Edgar, I would you had not come on this perilous business! Oh! if any thing should happen to you;" and the bare thought conjured up such strong emotions in the heart of the fair maiden, that, impulsively, she started up from her seat, threw her arms around the other's neck, and wept.

"Nay, dearest Rosalie," said Milford, tenderly, fondly straining her to his beating heart. "Nay, dearest, give yourself no uneasiness; I will be very, very prudent; and I think we are guarded against any serious danger."

"*All* danger is serious, is alarming, is terrible, if it menaces you, Edgar," was the tremulous answer of the lovely Rosalie. "To-night, too!—oh, to-night!—can you not put it off another day?"

"No, dearest, our plans are settled; but why do you object to this night, more than to another?"

"I do not know; it is so sudden, Edgar—so unexpected; and then, I seem to have a strong foreboding that all will not go well—that something terrible will happen. I want delay—I know not why—but I want delay. Oh! dear, dearest Edgar, if you love me, do not make the attempt to-night! Promise me, dear Edgar—will you?"

"If it merely rested with myself, my own dear Rosalie, I would promise, I would grant you any favor; for oh! I love you dearly, devotedly, almost to madness. But, dearest, you would not counsel me to dishonor, I am sure; you would not have me desert my companions at the last moment; you would not have me now shrink, like a coward, from the task I have undertaken, and have my name a by-word of reproach among my comrades!"

"Oh! no, no; but could you not persuade your companions to delay the attempt a day or two longer?" said Rosalie, in a sort of pleading tone.

"And that very delay we fear will increase, rather than diminish, the danger of our undertaking. Besides, having consented to the arrangement for to-night, what reason should I give for putting it off to a later period? I could not tell them the truth—that your request alone had influenced me to this step."

"No, Edgar, no, that would not do, certainly," said Rosalie, hurriedly, a modest blush suffusing her lovely countenance. "Ah me!" she sighed; "what is to be done?"

"Really, dearest," returned Milford, in a tender, soothing tone, "I think you are needlessly alarmed."

"I hope so—I pray I may be!" she replied, with energy. "But I should be more heroic —I, who have been through so much, with a stout heart: I should not shrink now, like a timid school-girl, from the mere anticipation of danger; but we cannot always master our feelings, dear Edgar, and act as reason dictates; we can not always be nerved beyond a quivering fear: for every human being has a vulnerable point; and apprehension, if not for ourselves, at least for those we love, will, at certain times, as the great bard says of conscience, 'make cowards of us all.' The excitement and fatigue I have so recently undergone, have relaxed my nerves, and rendered me unfit for your communication."

"I regret, then, to have made it," returned the Captain; "but you know you made me promise——"

"Ay, and if you had not kept it," interrupted Rosalie, "I should have had my faith in your honor shaken. No, Edgar, you did right; and I hope this weakness—for weakness I know it to be—will soon pass away, so that I can show myself worthy of a brave soldier's regard."

"Ah! Rosalie, dearest," rejoined Milford, imprinting a kiss upon her tempting lips, "you are worthy the regard of the bravest of the brave; and as I ponder upon the blissful thought, that you are pledged to me, that you may one day be mine, I feel that I am blessed far beyond my deserts."

"And I have precisely the same feelings," returned Rosalie, looking up affectionately into the other's face; "and my happiness is only counterbalanced by the fear of losing you. For myself, danger rather has a charm than otherwise; but for you, I tremble."

"And you have been through other perils than those with which I am acquainted, I understand," said Milford, the words of the fortune-teller now recurring to him. "What adventure have you lately had in the country?"

"Who says I have been in the country lately?" asked Rosalie, coloring.

"Ha! it is true then, I see, by that tell-tale blush," rejoined Milford. "Ah! Rosalie, you have been unkind—O, very unkind—to keep this a secret from me. I thought I possessed your entire confidence."

"But who says I have been in the country of late?" repeated the other.

"Dame Hagold."

"Indeed! did she then tell you—"

"What?" inquired the Captain, as Rosalie suddenly paused. "Did she tell me what?"

"Ay, what did she tell you?" returned Rosalie.

"Well, she told me nothing. She seemed about to do so, but, recollecting herself, ended by declaring it a secret."

"Well, I would rather not be more explicit at present, dear Edgar; sometime, if we both get safely over our present perils, I will tell you all."

"Then I will not question you, dearest, any further," replied the Captain; "it is enough for me to know you have reasons for wishing to remain silent."

"Ah! thanks, dearest Edgar, thanks; for by this I see your confidence in me is not impaired, although I am obliged to mystify you a little."

"Dear Rosalie," returned Milford, gazing fondly upon the countenance upturned to his, "I would sooner doubt myself than you. Were all the world to accuse you of a wrong, and make the accusation strong in truth by reason of their oaths; and were you, with your dark, bright eyes, all calmly looking into mine, to declare, with your sweet lips, the accusation false; I would believe your unassisted word before all other evidence in opposition."

"Ah! this is love," cried Rosalie, with glowing animation; "this is love—the pure, the true, the lasting, holy, ever-faithful love—which, living, gives us bliss; and dying, makes us happy; for love like this is not of the 'earth, earthy;' but of that glorious region we hope to gain when we have run our race below, and death hath set on us the seal of immortality. To feel ourself so loved, by one we love in turn, creates within the mind the purest, most delicious, happiness that mortal is destined to know—though it may be as dross to gold, compared to what the good may know hereafter."

"Yes, that hereafter is a blessed prospect to such as live aright while here," returned Milford, musingly. "Were it not for that, what melancholy, gloom, and misery would surround us!—and oh! how awful would be the contemplation, that when grim death should come to sever those who love, the separation would be made eternal! Thank God! we have a hope, that rises o'er such shades of gloom, even as God's bow of promise arches o'er the storm."

"And you have hope that we shall meet again, when time has run its course?" said Rosalie, looking fondly upon her lover's noble countenance.

"I have that hope," replied Milford, "else should I be most miserable."

"Then to that hope I'll cling, even should the worst befall thee, dearest Edgar," returned the fair girl, while two bright, pearly tears stood in her lustrous eyes.

"Ay, sweet Rosalie, that hope shall be the star upon life's path, to guide and cheer us both, although portentous clouds at times rise in our horizon, and threaten us with dire destruction. But, dearest, however painful it may be to both, I must remind you now, that it is time for us to part."

"So soon, dear Edgar?"

"Ay Rosalie, for I must not keep my comrades waiting."

"And perhaps we are now to part for the last time!"

"God only knows—but I will hope not."

"Oh! if it should be, Edgar!"

"Then you must mourn me as one that died a martyr to liberty."

"Well, well—I will try to bear up. Be still, heart! be still!"

"Should I chance to fall, dearest," said Milford, in a tremulous tone, "you will see that justice is done my memory?"

"Yes—yes—dear—dear—Edgar," sobbed the fair girl; for in spite of her efforts to be stoical, to appear calm and composed, her feelings almost choked her utterance.

"And now farewell, Rosalie!" rejoined the Captain, fondly embracing the gentle, true-hearted maiden.

"But, ere you go," said the other, "tell me where you meet, and what is your plan of operation?"

Milford, in a low tone, hurriedly informed her of the whole arrangement; and then said, in conclusion;

"But an idea has just struck me, which causes me fresh anxiety."

"Speak! what is it?"

"That, should I be detected, or be successful, suspicion may fall on you as an accomplice."

"Indeed! Edgar—how so?"

"From the fact, that our intimacy is known to Sir Henry Clinton. It is all well enough so long as he believes me a deserter; but the moment it is discovered I am a spy, he will naturally become suspicious of you. A thousand recollections will then flash upon his mind, tending to strengthen this impression; and oh! I tremble at what may be the consequences to yourself!"

"And if you are taken, Edgar, I scarcely care what those consequences may be," returned Rosalie, sadly and gloomily; "and if you are successful, I shall too much rejoice to let them trouble me. But that you may not be uneasy on my account, let me assure you that nothing more serious will happen than a fashionable disgrace—loss of caste in society—the which, you may rest assured, will not trouble me beyond a passing inconvenience. I might perhaps find it to my advantage to leave the city; but even that would be pleasant than otherwise; for I could then openly mingle with those noble patriots, whose success and welfare I have so much at heart, and whose society to me is far dearer than that of their would-be oppressors."

"And you stand high, dear Rosalie, with the best and noblest of these noble men; for almost the last words of Washington to me, were words of caution, respecting the endangering of your safety."

"Ah, Edgar, believe me, I feel more pride in knowing I am, or have been, a momentary object of solicitude on the part of that great and good man, than I should at learning I had become a favorite at the court of the mightiest sovereign of Europe; so much superior to accidental royalty, in my humble opinion, is this nobleman of nature. But I am delaying you: I will do so no longer. Go, Edgar, go! and may the good God protect you! Be cautious, Edgar! be prudent! and if you are tempted to do any thing rash, think of me, pause, and reflect. There, adieu! adieu! but Heaven grant it is not forever."

"Farewell," returned Milford—"farewell, dear Rosalie--farewell! If our plan succeeds, it may be long ere we shall meet again; if it fail, it may be longer still; therefore, a last, a fond farewell—perchance the very last that we shall ever exchange on earth—and should our next meeting be in heaven, there is no parting there."

As Milford said this, he strained the weeping Rosalie to his heart, in a long, fervent, and silent embrace—pressed his lips for a moment to hers—and then, seeming to tear himself away, rushed from the room; while she, half fainting, sank upon a seat, and burying her face in her hands, gave full vent to her overcharged feelings. Suddenly she sprang to her feet, and hurrying up to her little boudoir, closed the door, and said to Munee, who sat by the table, reading:

"Quick! girl—my disguise!"

The mute looked astonished, and picking up a pen, wrote:

"What new adventure now, my dear mistress?"

"I can not explain now: quick! my disguise!"

"Unless you let me go with you, I will not assist you," wrote the other.

"Well, go—yes, you shall go—but hasten! hasten! my disguise! quick! every moment is an age;" and Rosalie became almost wild with excitement.

Ten minutes later, two figures glided through the shrubbery and garden, in the rear of Percy's mansion, and out of the gate that opened upon the bank of the river.

A stranger, to have seen them, would have pronounced them two mulatto youths.

CHAPTER XVI.

THE QUARREL AND THE ALARM.

In a small, well-arranged cabinet, on the second floor, which could be entered through a larger apartment, or by a private staircase that led down to the garden, General Arnold and Colonel Malpert were seated, a few hours subsequent to the events of the preceding chapter. A small mahogany table stood between the two, and on this lay cards, and two large piles of money. A chandelier, with numerous sconces, in which were set burning wax tapers, was suspended from the ceiling, directly over the table, and threw a strong light upon the features of our two worthies. The faces of both were flushed, as if from wine, of which there were some three or four kinds, standing on a side-board, within reaching distance. Arnold's face was not only flushed, but there was a kind of intense anxiety, of almost wild excitement, displayed in its expression, which may be frequently seen on the countenance of a desperate gambler, when fickle fortune turns against him, and he resolves to retrieve his loss or lose the last penny he has in the world. In rather striking contrast to the features of the host, were those of his companion. He did not exactly smile; but his face expressed a secret self-satisfaction, a sort of suppressed triumph, which told, as plainly as expression could tell, that he was the winner, and that he had very good reasons for believing he was likely to remain so.

For some time the game continued without a word being spoken on either side, during which the pile of money on Arnold's side of the board gradually decreased, while that of his opponent increased in the same ratio. At length, the whole of Arnold's was staked, and immediately after raked down by the Colonel, who looked up with an expression, which seemed to say, "Will you venture more to-night?"

The traitor was much excited. He looked at the board, at the cards, at the money, and then exclaimed, with an oath, as if in answer to the other's look:

"Yes, I'll try you another hundred."

He reached over for one of the bottles, filled a drinking cup of silver, and drained it at a draught. He then pushed it to the Colonel, who filled the cup in like manner, and placed it to his lips. But, unlike Arnold, he did not drain it. He watched his opportunity, and while the other was occupied in getting a hundred pound note, threw it out of the window, smacking his lips at the same time, and saying:

"Ah! that is capital wine, my dear General

—capital!—the real juice of the grape, and no mistake. I have reason to fear such wine as that, General; for I am fain to attribute some of my ill luck to that."

"You don't seem to have any ill luck lately, Colonel," returned the traitor, as he handed the other the note already referred to, and proceeded to draw a hundred sovereigns from the heap of money which still lay loose upon the table. "Five hundred pounds you were winner yesterday, three hundred the day before, and these one hundred sovereigns are all that remain of one thousand to-day."

"Yes, I have had rather good luck for a day or two, I will admit," rejoined the Colonel; "but then, my dear General, you must consider how much I lost before."

"Ay, sir, eight hundred pounds altogether, which leaves you, at this moment, nine hundred the gainer."

"Which I may lose again this very sitting. Ah, General, were it not for the ups and downs in this game, I fear there would be very little pleasure in it—it would soon become very tiresome."

"Well, give me the ups, and I care little who has the downs," said Arnold.

"I believe you, upon my honor," returned Malpert, with a smile so equivocal, that the other was at a loss whether to regard it as ironical, or as a species of pleasantry.

"Well, come, shuffle the cards, Colonel, and let us to business, for it is waxing late."

"Then you are determined to play more, eh?"

"Yes, till I win your pile, or lose mine."

"Have at you, then," returned the Colonel, shuffling the cards, and pushing them over to the other to cut. "A sovereign ante, I suppose, the same as before?"

"Yes," replied Arnold, tossing one of the gold pieces upon the center of the table, where Malpert mated it by a similar coin.

The cards being dealt, and Arnold having examined his hand, pushed up fifty sovereigns to the ante, without speaking. His opponent pushed up ninety-nine.

"Ha! I see you mean to tempt me to stake the last penny," said Arnold. "I call you," he added, pushing up his remaining forty-nine pieces.

"Three aces and two jacks," answered Malpert, throwing down his hand.

"Beat again, by ——!" cried Arnold, springing up from the table. "And I was so sure of winning!" he added, showing three kings and two tens.

"We both had powerful hands, it seems," returned Malpert, as he quietly raked down the money. "Shall we try it again, General?"

"No, no—not to-night—not to-night," replied the other quickly: "a thousand pounds is enough to lose in one day—I might almost say at one sitting."

"It is nearly twelve, too," rejoined Malpert, looking at his watch.

As he was about replacing it in his fob, Arnold suddenly moved the table from between himself and the other, and catching Malpert by the wrist, drew a card from his sleeve, and held it up before him, while his own features assumed a look of diabolical rage.

"Can you tell me what that is, sir?" he demanded, fiercely.

For a moment or two, the Colonel was taken completely aback, and looked confused and embarrassed; but he was too old a practitioner in roguery, to be long off his guard, for the single circumstance of being detected in cheating, albeit he deeply regretted its having occurred with a victim he had just fairly begun to fleece. Summoning all his coolness, impudence, and effrontery to his aid, he soon recovered his wonted composure, and looking quietly at the colored pasteboard, which Arnold, fairly trembling with suppressed rage, held before him, he replied, with the greatest *sang froid:*

"Why, that is a card, dear General, I do believe."

"Don't dear general me, sir, any more!" cried Arnold, ready to burst with passion. "You think that is a card, do you?—you are certain of it, are you?—look sharp, and be sure!—it is a card, is it?"

"It is, upon my honor," replied Malpert, as if answering some serious question of mighty import.

"Say rather upon your *cheating*, for honor you have none," rejoined Arnold, with savage sarcasm. "Well, sir, it is a card, you admit; now look again, and you will see, by what seems a rather singular coincidence, that it is an ace."

"It is, indeed," returned Malpert, gravely, looking at the card, as if it were a curiosity. "Yes, a card, and an ace," he added; "singular coincidence, truly."

"And found in your sleeve, sirrah!"

"Well, yes, I believe it was."

"And by aces you just now won a hundred pounds!"

"An indisputable fact, as I'm a gentleman."

"Well, sir, please to tell me how I came to find that card in your sleeve!"

"I do not know, I'm sure; shouldn't be surprised to learn you saw it there, as it were by accident."

"No, sir—I mean to ask you how the card came to be there?" thundered Arnold, stamping his foot violently.

"O, ah! yes—you wish to know how the card came to be there? Yes, I understand you now. Well, my dear General, I put it there."

"You did? you put it there? you admit it?" roared Arnold, almost black in the face with passion. "Sir, allow me then to pronounce you a cheating scoundrel!"

"And who says it?" quietly asked the other.

"I, sir—*I* say it! and repeat it!"

"And pray who and what are you?" pursued Malpert, in a sneering, cutting tone of irony. "If I am a cheating scoundrel, who only cheat a knave, pray what are you, that sought to betray your own countrymen for gold? who have not only cheated the gallows of its due, but let an *honest* man be hung in your place! It is highly becoming in one like you to recriminate—forgetful, while you throw stones, that you live in a glass house, of so frail a structure that one blow may demolish it."

"Colonel Malpert, this is heaping insult on insult," cried Arnold, furiously.

"It is telling a plain truth, nevertheless," returned the other, drily.

"You have robbed me, sir!"

"And you the King's treasury. I only have the double honor of stealing from a thief and a traitor."

Arnold fairly foamed with rage; and it was some time ere his worst passions, now raised to the highest pitch, would allow him to articulate a syllable in reply.

"Sir!" he said, at length—"this insolence is unbearable!—and, by ——! I will have satisfaction!"

"At any time, and in any manner you please," was the quiet rejoinder.

"Leave my house, sir!" stamped Arnold, who really did not care to meet the other under the circumstances, particularly as he knew him to be a dead shot, and one of the best swordsmen in the army.

"I shall quit your house with pleasure," replied Malpert, who, although of a rash and fiery nature, had, throughout the altercation, shown a wonderful self-command, not even allowing his voice to rise above an ordinary tone of speech.

"And never *dare* to darken my doors again!" pursued the traitor, who chafed like a tormented ox at the other's quiet indifference and *nonchalance*.

"As you please," returned Malpert, preparing to depart.

"Quick! sir—begone! ere I throw you from the window!" continued Arnold, beginning to pace up and down the room.

"Nay, if that is your game, I may as well take a hand," was the cool response of the Colonel, as he again threw himself upon a seat, keeping his eye steadily fixed upon the other.

Arnold stopped short in front of the Colonel, and for a moment or two glared upon him, his face wearing a truly ferocious expression. He fairly trembled with rage, and more than once seemed on the point of springing upon his adversary; but whether that cool blue eye of the other, which now appeared lighted by a latent fire, that made it fearful to look upon, restrained him—or whether he felt it a sort of disgrace to attack a man in his own house—are matters unnecessary for us to decide; though we feel we risk nothing for veracity in saying that the two combined exercised a controlling influence; certain it is, however, he did not attempt to put his threat in execution, but resumed his walk up and down the room in scornful silence.

Malpert sat and watched him for some five minutes; but save a rather more sinister expression than usual, which had gradually settled upon his countenance, together with a slight curl of the lips, which formed a sneering smile, a stranger would have seen nothing in his looks, to indicate the bitter, deadly hatred he felt toward the man he had so lately termed his friend. At length he slowly rose, deliberately poured out a cup of wine, drank it off, looked at his watch, and said, in a very bland tone:

"Upon my honor, it is midnight: really, I must be going. Adieu, *Brigadier*, till we meet again;" and with this sarcastic valedictory, which met with no response, he coolly walked out of the cabinet, closing the door behind him.

The moment he was alone, Arnold threw himself heavily upon the seat, placed his arms upon the table, and rested his face upon them. For the space of half an hour, he did not once change his position; and only his labored respiration, which made his chest heave and fall, was audible.

At length he arose, threw off a cup of wine, took two or three hasty turns up and down the room, and then descended to the garden, by the back staircase already mentioned.

The night was cloudy, dark, and rather raw, but it had not yet rained, and the cold breeze came with soothing power upon the traitor's feverish temples. For several minutes he paced to and fro, in that part of the garden nearest his dwelling; but at length he altered his course, and walked slowly down the central avenue, toward the rear paling, which divided his grounds from the back street or alley, as described in a previous chapter. On the inside of this paling was a dense shrubbery—it could not appropriately be termed a hedge—and as Arnold drew near to this, he suddenly paused and listened, for he fancied he heard a slight rustling of the bushes.

"It was the breeze, doubtless," he muttered to himself, and was about to resume his walk in the same direction, when he was startled by hearing a peculiar signal, and, at the same moment, a voice, in a low, guarded tone, say:

"Quick! save yourselves! you are watched, and a night-guard is secretly advancing upon you:" and as this was said, the traitor heard what sounded like the stealthy steps of more than one person gliding away down the alley.

"What, ho! guard! quick! or you will lose them!" shouted Arnold, who, knowing nothing of the parties, little dreamed how near he had been to being kidnapped—he naturally supposing them to be robbers, prowling about, perhaps with a view to break into his own premises for mere plunder.

There was a heavy trampling sound, as of men running, in answer to the call of the traitor; and presently the word "Halt," rang out clear and distinct, directly opposite him, but on the other side of the paling, in the street.

"Who hare you that called hus?" demanded the same voice, and which, had the reader been there, he would have instantly recognized as belonging to Corporal Jones.

"General Arnold," was the reply.

"Did you 'ere any body, General?" inquired the Corporal.

"Yes, and they have fled down the street; and while you stand there, like a blockhead, they are making their escape."

"*They?*" echoed the perplexed Corporal, with marked emphasis. "I don't 'alf hunderstand it; we wasn't hafter no *they;* we was hafter another scamp. We've been fooled hagin, I think; but hif they've gone, whomever *they* be, we'll hafter them. March! quick step!" and at the last words, Arnold could hear the soldiers running down the street.

"This is strange!" mused the perplexed General; and he pushed his way through the shrubbery to the paling, and endeavored to peer over the pickets into the street; but the night was so dark as to render his range of vision very limited, and he saw nothing worthy of notice.

For a few moments he could hear the trampling of human feet, gradually growing fainter and more faint, till at last the sound died away altogether, and only the soughing of a cold, damp breeze was audible. He stood a few moments longer, to let the breeze fan his feverish brow. As he was on the point of turning away, he heard the distant challenge of a sentinel; but the pass-word was doubtless given, for again all became still.

"I must inquire into this business to-morrow," he said, as he pushed his way back to the garden, and returned to the house.

The moment the door closed behind him, the shrubbery was agitated by something more than the wind; two dusky figures glided up to one corner of the paling, emerged into the street, and quickly disappeared in the darkness.

CHAPTER XVII.

THE RENDEZVOUS OF THE SPIES.

It was perhaps a quarter of an hour after the peculiar events just recorded, that a solitary individual glided into a thicket, on the outskirts of a wood, about a mile distant from the scene of the foregoing chapter. He had evidently been running very fast; for his respiration was quick and heavy, and, from his manner of sinking down upon the ground, one would have judged he was very much fatigued.

This individual had not been many minutes concealed in the thicket, when some one was heard approaching on the run. He listened attentively; but ascertaining, beyond all doubt, he heard only the foot-fall of a single person, he remained quiet. The new-comer came up panting, plunged into the thicket, paused, and drew a long breath, with a half whistle.

"Wal," he said, in a low voice, speaking to himself, "this ere's a darn putty piece of business, any how it can be fixed—it is, I swow to Guinea. Jest at the very moment when every thing was working so slick, them are soldiery scamps must come right up and spile all. Darn 'em! if I'd only had that are feller, that spoke to the Gineral, by the throat, how I would a chooked him! Gosh-all-thunder! he'd a seen stars all over his face, as thick as tick on an old sheep's back."

"Where are the rest of our friends?" inquired a clear, sonorous voice, not two feet distant from where the first speaker stood, and which proceeded from the lips of the first-comer.

"Thunder and lightning!" exclaimed Josh Snipe, (for of course the reader has recognized his voice while speaking,) "if I didn't think I was here all by myself, I'll jest gin ye leave to comb my head with a rake, and pull one o' my double-teeth with a pitch-fork—I will, by Jemima! Wal, who be you, any how?—that are voice sounds like Mister Carlini's—or Signor, as some call him."

"And thine much too loud, unless thou desirest giving our pursuers an inkling of our rendezvous," returned the other. "Thou hast rightly guessed, friend—I am Carlini; but we must speak lower, or keep silence."

"How long you been here?" inquired Josh, in a tone scarcely above a whisper.

"Perhaps five minutes—perhaps less."

"Wal, I'd like to know, now, who it was that told you the soldiers was coming; for the voice sounded like a woman's or a boy's, and different from any that I know abeout being concerned in our plan."

"The voice was from one that I little expected to find there at that time," answered Carlini; "but I can not be more explicit at present. I will only say, there were two youths, apparently, who glided away with me in the darkness, and separated from me at the first turning, they taking the left and I the right."

"Hark!" said Josh; "there's somebody else coming, I guess."

There was a sound of feet approaching, certainly; but when Josh spoke, it was so faint as to be almost inaudible. The advancing party seemed to be nearing our friends with quick, light steps, and, judging by the sound, there was more than one; but how many, or who they might prove to be, the darkness of the night, which enveloped them as in a pall, rendered it impossible to say. That they were the Captain and Sergeant, Carlini thought probable, and he ventured to give an imitation of the owl. An answer, in the same manner, satisfied him that he was correct in his surmise; and almost immediately after the new-comers gained the thicket.

"Who is here?" inquired a low voice, which our concealed friends instantly recognized as that of Captain Milford.

Carlini answered by giving his own name, and that of his companion.

"We have been most unfortunate, friends," pursued Milford, "in having been interrupted at a moment so important to our enterprise."

"It seems as if the traitor is destined to escape punishment," returned the astrologer.

"Confound that Corporal Jones!" rejoined Milford, angrily. "But for him, we should this very moment, doubtless, be bearing off our prize. Champe and I were just preparing ourselves to spring upon him, when we heard the signal of Josh, and, what really surprised us, another voice, that sounded not unfamiliar to my ear, bidding us make haste to escape. Do you know the friend that so unexpectedly warned us of danger, Signor Carlini?"

"I think I have heard the voice before," was the reply.

"Are you not at liberty to tell his name?"

"I would rather not, at present."

"Ah, then it was some one employed by yourself, without our knowledge."

"No, I was taken as much by surprise as you were, gentlemen."

"Indeed! this is strange!" said Milford, somewhat startled.

"It proves our secret is known to others," said Champe.

"That is true," returned Milford, musingly; "and the fact is not a pleasant one. Who can the person be?"

"There were two," said Carlini.

"Two! I heard but one voice."

"The other did not speak. Both fled with me along the alley, till they came to the street which crosses it, when they turned up toward Broadway, and I down toward the river. I had but a faint glimpse of their figures, it was so dark; but to all appearance they were half-grown youths."

"Ha! a thought strikes me!" returned Milford: "were they mulattoes, Signor Carlini?"

"They might have been full-blooded negroes, for all that I could see to the contrary, Captain."

"Ay, ay, sir; but I am not questioning what you *saw* of them to-night, but what you know of them from previous seeing."

"Well, I will answer to the best of my belief, Captain, by saying, I doubt not the faces of both were a few shades darker than the faces of any here."

"I have it, then! I have it!" returned Milford, somewhat excited.

"Well, out with the secret, then," said Champe.

"Why, they are Rosalie Du Pont's servants, without a doubt. I thought I had heard that voice before, and now I remember where and when. The lad that spoke is the same that came out to Burnside's, on the evening of that day you escorted me to White Plains, Sergeant."

"Ah, yes, I recollect hearing you mention it: he brought some intelligence for Washington, I think you said?"

"Yes, concerning Clinton's intentions, Anderson, and so forth. But stay! I have overlooked one very important matter," pursued the Captain, in a tone of perplexity. "It could not have been that lad, after all, for the simple reason that he is not at present in the city."

"He may have returned," suggested Champe.

"If he had, I think Rosalie would have mentioned it to me, in the course of our conversation to-day—or rather, I should say, yesterday—for I believe it is now passed midnight."

"It is more likely, after what happened to Miss Du Pont, that she would not think so trivial a matter, as the arrival of a mulatto lad, worth mentioning, even if the occurrence entered her mind at all, which is more unlikely still," said Champe.

"Well, my friend, you may be right," replied Milford; "and the more I think upon the matter, the more convinced am I that you are. At all events, we will rest the subject on this plausible belief, unless friend Carlini, who I am inclined to think knows, states the contrary."

"That I shall not of a surety, Captain," returned the astrologer for if you think the messenger you saw and conversed with in the country, and the person who gave us that timely warning to-night, are one and the same, I will only add, that I am of the same opinion."

"Well, so that our secret is in safe hands," rejoined Champe, "I care little whether the person that warned us is white or black, male or female. So, come, gentlemen, since we have all been fortunate enough to escape unharmed, let us consult on future measures, without delay. I must return to my quarters to-night; and it is already so late, that I fear suspicion may be excited that my absence has not been solely for the promotion of the interest of his Majesty. We have failed, on the very point of success: can any thing more be done?"

"Surely, you would not abandon our scheme thus readily?" queried Milford, in a tone of surprise.

"I merely asked a question, my Hotspur Captain; but expressed no intention, I believe, of being a double deserter and poltroon."

"Pardon me, Champe, if I have hurt your feelings! but your voice expressed so much of despondency—"

"Enough, my friend, enough!" interrupted the Sergeant. "Doubtless my voice did sound desponding, for it seems to me I have a presentiment of coming evil. But to the point. Since you take exceptions to my former question, I will now ask *what* you think best to be done, situated as we are?"

"Try it again to-morrow night," answered Milford; "and if we again fail, without being overthrown, try it again the next night; and so on, till we conquer or lose all."

"I am with you," said Champe, firmly, "to the very death—that is to say, if I can manage to get away from my corps without being suspected; but go on with the good cause at all events, whether I am present in person or not. I would willingly have sacrificed my right hand to have prevented that interruption to-night—but regrets are useless, and amount to nothing but loss of time. May we not hope to hear from Lee, ere the time arrives for a new trial, Captain?"

"Yes, if George has got safely through, I think we may count on an answer by to-morrow night, at the farthest."

"And Lee himself—will he not be here also, think you?"

"Doubtless, for such was my request."

"Then perhaps our failure was for the best, after all."

"We must try and console ourselves with that idea, at all events."

"But where is Dame Hagold, Captain? I fear we have overlooked her."

"True—she is doubtless with the boat, awaiting our arrival."

"I hope she has not been discovered," said Champe, uneasily.

"No fear of that, I think, gentlemen," responded Carlini; "for she is both shrewd and prudent. Nevertheless, I think it important she be informed of our failure immediately, lest something occur to get her into trouble."

"Yes, some one must go to her at once," rejoined Champe. "Will you undertake the mission, Josh?"

"Wal, yes, Sargent and gentlemen, I guess as how I will; for I don't think as how I can be of much sarvice here; and stretching my legs a leetle bit more, I guess won't hurt 'em none."

"Well, Josh, be very careful," said the Captain, "for we have good reason to be on the *qui vive*, after what has occurred to-night. When you get where you can speak to her without danger of being overheard, tell her that we were interrupted to-night, while on the eve of success, by the very Corporal Jones that visited her house during the day. Doubtless the fellow, who is in pursuit of her son, after learning, as he did, that she is his mother, set a spy on her house; and that spy, having seen some one of us lurking about the premises, so informed the Corporal, which led to the unfortunate result we all so much deplore. From his answer to Arnold, I know he did not suspect us, nor our object, and this is something we should be thankful for. It will, moreover, be cheering news to her, to learn her son is not yet detected; for however guilty he may be, he is still her son, and she a feeling mother, who deserves a better fortune. On this account, I can rejoice in the escape of the youth. Tell her she had better not return to the old house again, for fear of some accident that may ruin our scheme. If no one is seen to enter or leave it, during the remainder of the night or to-morrow, I doubt not the watch will be withdrawn, and that we shall, in consequence, be able to succeed in our enterprise to-morrow night."

"But if she goes not back to her late quarters, where will she go, so that you will know where to find her?" inquired the Sergeant.

"That is true—I did not think of it before," returned Milford; "I am glad you reminded me of it, Sergeant. Well, gentlemen, I leave it to you to say what you think best to be done under the circumstances."

"I think it best to see the woman before we separate," replied Carlini.

"You must of needs dispense with my company ere then," said Champe; "for it is all important I hasten back to my quarters. Even as it is, I shall have to rack my inventive powers for a plausible excuse, and I much fear I shall not be allowed to be with you again to-morrow night—though, if it be possible to steal away, I shall risk the consequences. I had much trouble in getting off to-night; and my commanding officer granted me leave of absence with what seemed a kind of suspicious reluctance."

"Well, Champe," replied Milford, "considering your circumstances, I think it best that you return at once. I have only to add, that if we make another trial, we shall adhere to the same arrangements that we adopted for to-night; and that you will find us here, if you seek us, at the same hour."

"And if you are not here at the same hour?" queried the Sergeant.

"Then you may be assured there is an important failure somewhere," answered Milford.

"Well, this being settled, I will leave you," rejoined Champe. "But I must shake hands before we part; for somehow, as I said before, I have a presentiment we shall not meet again soon, if ever;" and the voice of the noble fellow quivered, in spite of an apparent effort to appear firm and composed.

"Nay, my dear friend," said Milford, taking the hand of the other, while his own voice expressed strong emotion, "do not despond in this manner—you make me sad."

"Well, well," rejoined the Sergeant, "we will say no more about it. They may be foolish, fanciful prognostics that are flitting through my brain—I will hope they are. At all events, I will try to keep a stout heart, and do my duty, as becomes a man and a true son of liberty. But *should* any thing happen to prevent our meeting again, and should you be fortunate enough to escape to our friends, you will think of poor Champe sometimes, Captain Milford? for you at least know, whatever may be appearances, that my heart is in the right place."

"Should we not meet again, my dear Sergeant," responded the other, in a tone now rendered tremulous with feeling, "rest assured, that Captain Milford will mourn the loss of one of his dearest friends; and should you fall ignobly, Champe, and I escape, rest assured, it shall be my living endeavor to have justice done your memory, to clear your honest name of all dishonor, all reproach."

"It is all I would ask," rejoined the Sergeant, in a tone that expressed great relief from an oppressive weight that rested on his mind; "and now let what will happen, I will bear my fate with a stout heart. Adieu! Milford—adieu!" and the pressure of his hard hand spoke the feelings of his heart more eloquently than words. He next grasped the hand of Carlini. "Farewell!" he said—"farewell! We are all brothers in the great cause, and I part from you as from one in whom the same paternal blood courses. Good-by, Josh," he proceeded, taking his hand last. "Notwithstanding our first singular meeting, I regard you as a true friend, and feel I have reason to bless the hour when first we met—and this, for me, is saying much. Good-by; be vigilant, be prudent, be *true*, and you will have your reward. Farewell all!" and he rushed from the thicket, as if overpowered by his feelings.

For some moments after the Sergeant's departure, not a word was spoken; and then Milford said, with a sigh:

Ah me! I fear this presentiment of our

friend has too good a foundation, and bodes evil. His parting words are ominous; and though not much given to superstitious fancies, I believe that the mind is not unfrequently oppressed with coming events, which at the time lie hidden from all mortal eyes behind the veil of the great future."

"Man is a curious piece of mechanism," replied Carlini, "and is compounded of more mysteries than the wisest philosophers have yet dreamed of. Every year adds something to our knowledge of this wonderful machine —but it is still reserved for the great hereafter to reveal all."

"And yet you, Signor, seem to possess this knowledge in greater perfection than any I have ever known, or heard of," said the Captain.

"There are some things I know, Captain Milford, that are not known to mankind generally; I may say, the very fewest number are yet possessed of the secret I hold; yet do not talk to me of perfection; for so far am I removed from it, that the very knowledge I possess, seems only to serve as a mirror of the Almighty, wherein I behold nothing but my own ignorance. Nay, my friend, as the infant, who does not know one letter of the alphabet from another, is to the most learned of earth's scholars, so am I in regard to possessing even the first rudiments of God's mysteries, as manifested in the living walking machine called man. Ay, sir, I will go further, and say, that I believe the day will yet come, when the lisping child shall be taught treble what I now know; and yet the wisest men of that age shall be hardly on the threshold of the mighty, wonderful unexplored structure of human being. No, Captain Milford, eternity—eternity—that great, boundless, unknown, incomprehensible region, to which we are all hastening—can alone solve the mysteries of the Almighty, as displayed in one poor, weak, erring worm of the dust like ourselves; and even then, peradventure, it will take ages to do this, and this be only *one* of our many studies. How few, how very few, comprehend, in its widest significance, the potent words, '*Know thyself!*' When man does know himself, depend upon it, he will be as wise as the angels. But this is not a time and place to philosophise; let us return, therefore, to business!"

"One question first," said Milford, who felt a deep interest in the remarks of the other; "do you believe the mind has power over the body?"

"Yes, I believe any thing I can demonstrate; and what is more simple than this? The will is of course an attribute of the mind; and by a simple use of the will, we put the body in any position we please, consonant with its structure."

"And what is that power you exercise so wonderfully over others?"

"Merely the will, exercised in an unusual, and more powerful manner."

"Ah! I cannot understand it," returned Milford.

"No, my friend, nor can I; for it is *one* of the mysteries not yet revealed to mortal—perhaps never will be—though I doubt not we shall know all in a future state."

"Then the good will surely be blest in dying."

"Even so is my faith."

"One question more, and I will drop the subject—for, as you say, this is not a fit time and place for philosophising. Do you really think the mind has power to prognisticate evil? In other words, do you believe in presentiments?"

"I do."

"Then poor Champe's parting words may be the last he will ever utter in our presence," sighed the Captain.

"God only knows," replied Carlini, solemnly. "I hope not—but, like you, I have my fears."

"Well, let us to business, and trust the result to Providence. Come, Josh—away! away!—be speedy, and conduct Dame Hagold hither, that every thing may be arranged for the night and the morrow. Do not lag by the way, and mind you unite caution with haste."

"I'll do it, Capting," replied Josh; and he quitted the thicket. "I wish the Sargent hadn't said what he did," he muttered—"for I hain't felt so much like having a regular blubber sence dad licked me for letting Joe

Davis git the upper hand o' me in the last tussle we had together."

For some five minutes after the departure of Josh, Milford and Carlini held a low, secret consultation, which we do not deem necessary to report. At the conclusion of this, the latter said:

"Well, on the whole, Captain, I think I will take your advice, and return home. If I hear nothing from you meantime, I shall endeavor to be here, punctual to the minute, to-morrow night. *Au revoir*, Captain."

"Good night," returned Milford; and as soon as he found himself alone, he advanced to a neighboring tree, and seated himself on the ground, placing his back against the trunk.

He had scarcely settled himself into this position, when he was both surprised and startled, at hearing his name pronounced in a low, musical tone, that he fancied was not unknown to him.

CHAPTER XVIII.

THE SOI-DISANT MULATTO.

"Who are you?" demanded Milford, starting up suddenly, and grasping one of his pistols; for the thought occurred to him, that he might possibly have been betrayed by the very servant who as he believed, had given the timely warning during his concealment in Arnold's shrubbery.

"Fear nothing but loud speech," was the answer. "I am a friend to you and your cause;" and there was a rustling of the bushes near, as if the speaker were advancing.

"Stand, on your life! I am armed and desperate," was the warning rejoinder of the Captain, spoken in a low, firm, manly tone. "Ere you approach me, you must answer my question—Who are you?"

"One you have seen before. I am called Henry Pierpot."

"Ha! it is then as I suspected," returned the Captain, partly soliloquizing, partly speaking to the other. "Are you alone?"

"My dumb brother, Munee, is with me."

"Any one else?"

"No, Captain Milford, and you wrong me by your suspicions. Think you, if I were base enough to betray you, I should have waited till now, and be the first to approach you? Is it not more reasonable to suppose I should have done it at the time when my voice warned you of danger?"

"You are right, lad, and I have done you gross injustice," returned Milford. "But then," he added, as Rosalie, accompanied by the mute, advanced to where he stood, (for the reader is of course aware that Henry Pierpot and Rosalie Du Pont are one and the same person, with a difference only in costume, and a change in complexion, effected by dyeing.) "But then, Master Henry, how are you to suppose I suspected you of being the one who gave us the warning? for you seem to speak as one assured of the fact."

"Because, Captain Milford, I overheard a portion of your conversation with your friends, concerning myself."

"Ha! lad—were you listening then?" exclaimed the Captain, in a tone of surprise.

"I will be frank, and own I was."

"Good heavens! perhaps then we have had other listeners also!"

"I think not. I feared you might have, and therefore I came, that, if necessary, I might give you a second warning."

"How came you to be so considerate? and, in the second place, why did you expect to find us here?"

"I merely carried out the wishes of Ma'm'-selle Du Pont. She knew, it seems, that you and your friends would meet here to-night, at a certain hour, to hold a sort of council-of-war, regarding your perilous undertaking; and it seems only necessary to add, that I was present then, overheard all that was said, and therefore knew that if you failed and escaped, this was to be the rendezvous for re-uniting."

"Then you followed us?"

"I did, but at a distance, for I knew your point of destination, and therefore it was not necessary to keep close on your heels."

"But how came you to be aware of our danger?"

"By accident. As soon as I thought you were settled in your respective positions, I commenced strolling about in the vicinity—for two reasons—to keep myself warm, and, should I chance to learn of any danger, to be able, peradventure, to put you on your guard. Well, fortune favored me. I chanced to hear the tread of soldiers; and finding they were approaching the place where we stood—that is, Munee and I—we concealed ourselves near, and waited for them to come up. They halted within a few feet of us; and their leader gave them some directions in a tone too low for me to overhear what was said. They were evidently on a secret expedition; and I became suspicious that they had, by some means, been made acquainted with your designs, and were on their way to surprise and arrest you. And my suspicions changed to a certainty, when I found they shaped their course directly to the spot where you were concealed, and walked with stealthy steps, that made little or no noise. By taking a short circuit, Munee and I succeeded in getting in advance of them unperceived and unsuspected, and you know the rest."

"You have done nobly, lad—nobly, boy!" returned the Captain, warmly; "and rest assured, you shall have your reward."

"The happiness of Rosalie Du Pont is all the reward I seek," rejoined the *soi-disant* Henry, "and that can only be secured by the safety and happiness of Captain Milford."

"Henry," said Milford, a vague suspicion flashing across his mind, "are you not other than you seem?"

"That is a singular question, Captain Milford," answered our heroine, not a little startled, lest he had divined her secret, and anxious to gain time to ponder upon her reply. "I believe all persons are different than they seem, for it is very seldom the outer and inner man exactly correspond."

"I perceive you evade my question," rejoined Milford. "In other words, are you a mulatto servant?"

"I am not a white one, sir."

"If you are one of any kind, then have you been educated far above your station."

"I have had a good education, Captain Milford, I do not deny; and neither am I a servant by compulsion, or necessity. Munee and I were both born free, and we both have property enough of our own to render us independent of labor; but it is a pleasure for us to serve Miss Rosalie and her friends."

"She is fortunate in having two such faithful attendants. But I understand only one of you remains with her!"

"Only one of us is with her constantly—I have been out of town."

"So I understood: when did you return?"

"I have been in the city two days."

"And how long do you expect to remain here now?"

"I can not say; all depends on circumstances; it is possible I may leave to-morrow night."

"And where, and with whom do you reside when out of town?"

"I beg your pardon, Captain Milford—but that is a question I must decline answering."

"Right, my lad—only answer what you see proper, for I have no right to pry into your secrets. But, if you will permit me, I will make some further inquiries, touching different matters."

"Certainly, Captain—ask any question you please, so you grant me the same privilege in answering."

"Well, then, how long have you known Rosalie Du Pont?"

"Since she was a child."

"You know her history, then?"

"Yes, Captain."

"Were you also born in France?"

"Yes, Captain."

"How long have you been in this country?"

"As long as herself, Captain."

"And how long may that be?"

"I decline answering."

"Did you and Munee come to this country together?"

"We did, Captain."

"Are the parents of Rosalie living?"

"I decline answering any thing pertaining to her parentage or history, Captain."

"Well, I will change the subject. You have not forgotten our first meeting, I suppose?"

"I shall never forget it, Captain."

"Time has proved you right in your suspicions of there being treason in high places;

for the very man for whose honor and integrity I then vouched, has since turned traitor."

"I am aware of it, Captain, and that your object here is to seize and take him where justice will be done him. But speaking of that, reminds me of a part of my errand hither. From what I overheard, I suppose your arrangements for to-morrow night are the same as those of to-night?"

"The same."

"And where can you be found meantime, should I have occasion to deliver you a message?"

"I can not say. To-night I shall remain in the woods, for I care not to go back into the city again."

"I think your plan a wise one—but I fear you will suffer from cold."

"No; I have lain out many a night, in the dead of winter; you forget, lad, I am a soldier, inured to hardship and privation; besides, I shall not attempt to sleep to-night, and the mere loss of rest will be nothing."

"But is there no plan by which a message can reach you, if necessary?"

"Yes; have it committed to paper, and placed at the foot of this very tree, under a small stone."

"Then, ere to-morrow night, you will probably receive a message from my mistress."

"And if I do, it will not be the first from her that has reached me in a similar manner. In the course of our correspondence, we have both had occasion to make post-offices of the very stones."

"I am aware of that, Captain, having more than once been post-boy myself. But it is late; and having done my errand, I must now bid you good night. If one as humble as myself might suggest a parting caution, it would be that, when you meet your friends here again, you do not converse in a tone above a whisper. You spoke low and guardedly to-night; but notwithstanding, you are aware I overheard you; and in so perilous an undertaking as yours, you cannot be too careful of your secret."

"Be assured, Henry, we shall not be so imprudent again. Tell Rosalie I shall expect to hear from her to-morrow, and that she must not allow her spirits to be depressed by our failure. The party of soldiers that alarmed us to-night, were not searching for us, and knew nothing of us or of our designs—therefore I feel confident we shall not be interrupted at the second trial. Say to her that she is ever in my thoughts, and first and last in my prayers. Good night."

"Good night," returned Rosalie; and she and Munee forthwith departed, leaving the Captain again alone, little aware he had been conversing with the very being whose happiness he prized above his own, and to save whose life he would have shed his heart's blood.

Milford again seated himself at the foot of the tree, and became lost in reverie. It was nigh upon half an hour ere his meditations were disturbed by the return of Josh, accompanied by Dame Hagold.

"We have failed, mother," said the Captain, addressing the latter.

"So I've heerd from Josh, here. O, wasn't it provoking to be disappointed in this way, jest when you had that villain, Arnold, right in your grasp, as one may say?"

"It was very vexatious, I will not deny."

"If I had a rope round Mr. Corporal Jones' neck, and had one eend in my hand, O, wouldn't I larn him a bit of a lesson he wouldn't forgit in a hurry! the mean, low-lived varlet, to go sneaking about in that way," returned the dame, indignantly.

"Did you know any thing of the failure till Josh found you, mother?" inquired the Captain.

"No, not exactly. I thought something was the matter, and I was afeared it was woss; for a party of soldiers came clean down to the bank of the river, and arter prowling about awhile, went away agin. I was in the skiff, right behind the heap of bushes where you told me to stay, Captain, till I heerd the signal; but though they came right close up, within a few feet of me, they couldn't see me, and I didn't calculate it was best to tell 'em as how I was there. Arter they was gone, I concluded I'd wait till I heerd something from some o' ye—or at least I thought I'd stay two hours—for I knowed if you wasn't all catched, you'd send me some message afore then."

"What did you do with the boat?"

"It's on the river, jest opposite here, Capting," replied Josh. "We thought it 'ud be safer to row up stream, than to ventur on land—leastwise I heerd a sentry down near where we was, and I got a leetle scart, for fear we might kinder git in his way somehow, and so into difficulty."

"Well, I think you acted wisely; but before morning the boat must be left in the very place where we found it—that is, if we can succeed in getting the skiff back in which George Nugent crossed the river."

"Do you calculate on gitting that back to-night, Capting?"

"Yes, if possible: will you accompany me, Josh?"

"To the death, Capting. I'm bound to stick to yeou as long as the putty 'll hold good; and I guess that 'll be till one or t'other on us gits rid of breathing—that is, if yeou say so, and haint no objections, Capting."

"You won't git much chance to sleep to-night, Captain, if you're going over for that boat," put in the dame.

"I shall not sleep to-night, mother. But that reminds me of yourself; where will you take up your quarters? for I do not think it prudent for any of us to return to your late abode, as, in all probability, the old house will be watched."

"Well, well, as for me, it don't much matter," sighed the other. "If I was dead, and in my grave, I feel I should be better off than I am now," she added, gloomily.

"Nay, Mother Hagold, do not despond," returned the Captain, in a tone of sympathy. "We should not give way to despair, whatever may be our afflictions; but remember that the one God rules ever, and that whether prosperity or adversity attend us, the orders that which to him seemeth best."

"Well, well, I don't know, I don't know," sighed the other; "if my afflictions is for the best, then great good ought to come on 'em—for they're heavy, Captain Milford—they're heavy. Oh! sir, you don't know what it is to have a criminal son, and Heaven grant you never may! I could see every friend I've got in the world, sir, put under the ground, if they only died honorably, and never make no complaint; but this trouble—this—" and overcome by her feelings, the afflicted mother sobbed aloud. "But come," she said, rousing herself, after a few moments of almost heartbroken anguish—"Come, Captain, I won't be hindering you no longer. Never mind me, but go on with your business. I'll try and meet ye all here to-morrow night, if that's what you want; and for to-night, I'll find some place to sleep. Yes, I'll go back to the house where you first seen me, and stay there. So, good night, Captain."

"Our regulations for to-morrow night are the same as those of to-night," rejoined Milford; "so if you think proper to join us, you will doubtless find some of us here."

"Well, well, count on me, if I can be of any service to ye. So, good night, and may Heaven prosper ye!"

"Good night," returned the Captain, and the dame departed. "Now then, Josh," he continued, "let us set off at once."

In a few minutes our friends reached the boat; and entering it, they took the oars, which were still muffled, and pulled steadily across the stream. The skiff which George Nugent had used last, was found without difficulty, and with this in tow they rowed back. Taking the larger boat down to the place where it had been found a few hours previously, they fastened it by a rope to a tree, and then rowed up stream to the very rock whence we saw George depart the day before.

"Here," said the Captain, in a low tone, "I think we shall be safe. Lie down flat along the bottom, Josh—I will do the same—and then we will draw ourselves under this rock."

"Thunder and lightning, Capting!" exclaimed Josh, when all was fixed as they intended to pass the night: "I've slept in woss places than this, an all-fired sight."

"It is better than going into the city, at all events," replied Milford, "and I doubt not we can get a few hours sleep after all."

And our friends did sleep. The arrangement for the night proved more comfortable than the Captain had anticipated; and though the air was cold, and the wind blew chill and damp from the east; and though, ere morning, it set in to rain; yet our friends were so sheltered, that they remained perfectly dry, and felt none of the raw gusts that moaned through the woods and swept over their heads. Their bed was none of the softest, it is true, and they had no covering but the habiliments they wore; but notwithstanding all this, they slept, and so soundly, that the cares and anxieties of the time were forgotten.

CHAPTER XIX.

A GODSEND, AND WHAT FOLLOWED.

At daylight the rain poured down in torrents; but toward noon it abated, the wind changed, and by one o'clock it ceased, and the sun could occasionally be seen between the broken clouds, that now began to float off eastward. Up to this time, our friends had not ventured to leave their hiding-place; and the spirits of Milford had been greatly depressed through the fore part of the day, lest the storm should continue for the next twenty-four hours, and completely frustrate the plans laid out for the coming night.

"There, thank heaven! the sun shines once more," he exclaimed, in a tone of joy, as he beheld the bright rays strike the water, and seemingly turn it to silver. "And now that my mind is easy on this point," he continued, "another thing strikes me as being very disagreeable."

"What's that, Capting?" inquired Josh.

"Why, we have eat nothing since last night, and have nothing in prospective."

"That's a fact, Capting, I swow to Guinea! I didn't think on't afore; but I was wondering all the time what made me so holler, and all kind o' gone like down in my stomach. Jerusha! Jemima! it 'pears to me, now I think on't, I could eat a cat's hide, with all the hair on."

"It was a great oversight in me to forget to provide food for the day. I might at least have got Carlini, or Dame Hagold, to deposit some for us in a certain place in these woods. But one can not think of every thing at once; and so we must console ourselves with the reflection, that when we do get it, it will be duly appreciated."

"Wal, I guess so," rejoined Josh—"that is, if it come afore we starve clean to death."

"We can get along very well for twenty-four hours, at least. Ah, now I think of it, I must leave you for a short time."

"Where be you a-going, Capting?"

"I will soon return," replied the other, evasively. "You will remain here: do not leave the boat, on any account, till you see me again."

The Captain then drew the skiff out from under the rock, ascended the bank into the thicket, and disappeared, shaping his course directly to the spot where he had met the *soi disant* Henry during the night. He thought it possible a letter might have been left for him under the stone; though, considering it had rained all morning, he was prepared not to be disappointed should he find none. He gained the tree, and found the stone, and his heart beat quickly as he bent down to raise it; but it beat faster still, when he beheld a neat little *billet-doux* under it. Snatching it up, he pressed it to his lips, with an excited lover's extravagance, and then tore it open, in breathless haste, and read as follows:

"I have heard of your failure, dearest, and you can judge of my feelings. I am miserable on your account, and shall remain so until you are safe. Oh! be prudent—be cautious—and above all, beware of your conversation, for the very trees have ears. I approve of your plan of passing the night, but fear the storm has rendered it a horrible night to you. You must be faint for want of food; but I have provided for you as well as circumstances would permit. In the center of the thicket, you will find a basket of provision, which I send by the bearer of this. Oh! I am so anxious to hear from you! You must permit me to send Henry to-night. You can trust him with all safety. He will remain with you till all is over. I will say no more now, but trust we shall ere long meet again. May heaven bless and preserve you! is the prayer of one who would willingly lay down her life to serve you. Adieu!"

This letter was without signature or address, and, as the reader has seen, was worded so cautiously, that had it chanced to fall into wrong hands, it would have conveyed no information leading to the detection of the parties concerned.

"God bless her!" ejaculated Milford, fervently, as he refolded and thrust the letter into his bosom next to his heart. "It is well there is a heaven hereafter, for life is all too short to repay such noble devotion as hers."

He then, after looking carefully around, to be certain he was not observed, entered the thicket, and found the basket of provisions. It was covered with a white cloth; and without even raising this, to take a peep at its contents, he passed his arm through the handle, and hurried back to his companion.

"See!" he said, joyfully, as he again stepped into the boat. "See, Josh! we are provided for—there is no danger of our starving now."

"Why, where on airth did you git that are, Capting?" queried Josh, with a look of astonishment. "You haint been clean down to the city and back a' ready, Capting?"

"No, Josh, this was sent to us by an angel."

"Dew tell! you don't mean to say, Capting, it was sent from the sky?"

"No, Josh, it was a terrestrial angel that sent it, by a dark messenger."

"You speak in riddles, Capting; but never mind; let's see what it is—for I'm as hungry as one o' Pharaoh's lean kind; I am, I swow to Guinea."

The Captain now removed the cloth, and found a large quantity of cold meat, bread, butter, cheese, and a bottle of excellent wine. It is needless to add, that for the first few minutes the provisions disappeared rapidly, and the wine was not slow in passing through the neck of the bottle down necks of very different material.

"I didn't know I was so hungry," said Milford, his mouth crammed with meat and bread.

"Wal, *I* knowed I was hungry," returned Josh, choking down a quantity that would have sufficed a modern fashionable for a whole meal; "but I swow to Guinea, Capting, I never tasted victuals so good as this, afore, in all my born days, that's a fact. I want to know who sent it; for I'll never forgit to bless 'em as long's I live. And that are wine, too—it just goes right to the spot, and warms a feller up, as if he was sleeping, like I've hearn tell the Dutch do, between two feather beds."

"Well, the giver of this feast is Rosalie Du Pont," replied Milford.

"Wal, all I've got to say is, she's as good as she is putty, and she's the puttiest critter I ever laid eyes on in the hull course o' my life. And what's more, Capting Milford, she likes you harder'n ever I seen a gal like a feller afore."

"How do you know that, Josh?" inquired Milford, coloring, but looking pleased.

"How do I know it?" returned Josh, fixing his small, black cunning eyes upon the Captain, with a serio-comic look. "Gosh-all-thunder! why, any fool might know it, that ever seen you tew together a spell, as I did yesterday."

"Hist!" cried Milford, in a whisper, looking somewhat startled; "methought I heard a noise, as of some one approaching. Lie down, and let us pull the boat under the rock, for fear of accident."

This was soon accomplished, and then our friends lay and listened. They soon had cause to congratulate themselves on having returned to their hiding-place; for steps were now distinctly heard approaching, and presently some one ascended the rock above their heads. Whether the new-comer were friend or foe, it was of course impossible to tell, and it would be hazarding every thing to make the inquiry. They therefore remained silent, and did not even allow their breathing to be audible. The person on the rock, after remaining a few minutes, leaped down into the thicket, and went away.

"I would give something handsome to know who was here, and for what purpose," whispered Milford, after the stranger had gone.

"Wouldn't it do, jest to ventur' out now, and try to git a peep at him?" returned Josh, in a whisper also.

"No, the risk is too great. I feel we have been very imprudent already; and for the rest of the day we will remain where we are."

After making a hearty meal—for hungry as they were, with their long fast, there was more food than they were able to consume—and having disposed of the wine between them, our friends felt very comfortable, and their spirits rose in due proportion. The remainder of the day they lay in their skiff, under the rock, looking out upon the tranquil river, that rolled slowly past, to mingle its waters with the great Atlantic. They rarely spoke, and never above a whisper; for the incident of the stranger, they looked upon as a warning to be more prudent than they had been, and neither felt inclined to disregard it. The monotony of their view was once or twice relieved, by the passing of a couple of schooners up the river; but save these, they saw nothing during the day worth mentioning. The night set in clear, but cold. The sun set fair, the heavy clouds of the morning were all dispersed, and the great vault of heaven was soon spangled with thousands of the bright luminaries of other worlds.

As soon as it was fairly dark, our friends again drew out their skiff from under the rock, and, with muffled oars, rowed in silence across the stream. Their object in this, was to visit the post-office on the other side, and ascertain if there had been any communication left there from their friends in the army. After some little delay, occasioned by the darkness, and the necessity they felt for being very cautious, the stone was found, and raised, when lo! to their great joy and surprise, for they had anticipated a different result, a paper was discovered, which Milford eagerly seized, but could not read for want of a light. After a whispered consultation, on the best plan to pursue, our friends started back to the boat, thinking it would be safer for them to strike a light there, than in the woods; but they had not gone many paces, when suddenly a figure rose up on every side of them, and a stern voice at the same time demanded:

"Who are you?"

"If you are true men, speak! who are you?" returned Milford; "for you are the stronger party, and have nothing to fear."

"Right, sir," replied the same voice; "and I will answer, we are the friends of liberty."

"Come you from the American camp?"

"We do."

"And what do you seek?"

"That justice be done to the guilty."

"Have I the honor of addressing Major Lee?" inquired Milford.

"I am known as Major Lee, sir. And you, if I mistake not, are ——"

"Hist! not too loud!" interrupted the other. "Have you received a message from abroad, within twenty-four hours?" pursued the Captain, who was determined not to commit himself to a wrong party.

"I have, sir."

"Pray, where is the messenger?"

"He is here."

"Let me behold him that all my doubts may be removed."

"Stand forth, lad!" said the other; and immediately George Nugent advanced to the Captain.

"Do you know me?" inquired the latter, addressing the youth, for it was too dark where the parties stood to distinguish features.

"Yes, Captain Milford," replied the youth, in a low, quiet tone, "I have not forgotten you so soon."

"Give me your hand, lad; and yours, Major; for now I am satisfied that I am among friends," rejoined Milford, joyfully.

"Fall back, men!" said Lee, as he warmly pressed the hand of the Captain; "I wish some private conversation with this gentleman." And as all drew away from their commander, he continued: "These men I believe to be trusty, Captain, and I should have no fear to place my life in their hands; but still, as there are many others concerned in our project, I think it best not to make confidants of any more than is absolutely necessary. I am rejoiced to meet you so much sooner than I expected, for we have been here scarcely above an hour. And now, my dear Captain, pray put me in possession of your plan in as few words as possible."

"The best way to do that, is to tell you what has happened;" and Milford forthwith proceeded to make him acquainted with all the events of the preceding day and night.

"Ah! how unfortunate!" replied Lee, as

the other concluded. "But for that interruption, we should, doubtless, ere this, have had the traitor in our power. Ah! a thousand pities! a thousand pities! And you say the same plan holds good for to-night?"

"Yes, Major."

"But does the traitor walk the garden every night before retiring to rest?"

"For the last four or five nights he has done so; and in the whole of that time, he has not varied half an hour from twelve o'clock."

"Pray heaven he do the same to-night."

"I only fear he may not, Major; for on his doing so, hangs our whole scheme."

"Well, well, we can only trust to Providence. Go back, Captain, and carry out your plan as agreed upon. We will wait for you on this side, about half a mile below here—for I think we can venture that near the outposts of the enemy, who, suspecting nothing, will not of course be very vigilant. I have four men with me, besides George, and seven horses, and we are armed to the teeth—so you see we are prepared for either flight or fight."

After some further conversation, touching several minor matters, Captain Milford took leave of Major Lee, and calling Josh, returned to his boat. Our two friends then rowed across the stream very slowly, letting the skiff drop down with the current. It being early yet, they were in no hurry to land, and they remained on the water till past nine o'clock. They then drew in to the shore, at a point nearly opposite the rendezvous; to which, after secreting the skiff in a cluster of bushes, they repaired, and sat down under the tree, to await the arrival of their friends.

CHAPTER XX.

A MISTAKE, AND NIGHT ALARM.

PUNCTUAL to the hour of ten, Signor Carlini made his appearance; and soon after, Dame Hagold, disguised in male attire, as she had been the previous night, and accompanied by the *soi disant* Henry. The first friendly greetings over, Captain Milford said:

"We have all met again, thank heaven! but there is one absent whom I hoped to see. Ah me! I fear friend Champe's forebodings are realized—for if possible for him to be here, he would not be a minute behind the time."

"I doubt that we see him to-night," replied Carlini; "for from what I could learn through the day, there are some important changes being effected among a portion of the soldiery; and the probability is, that, on this account, he has been denied leave of absence. It seems a pity he enlisted so soon."

"I must differ with you there, Signor; for had neither he nor I enlisted, suspicion would doubtless have been excited, that we came hither with no right feeling toward the royal cause."

"Ah, true, I overlooked that."

"Well, if Champe comes not," continued the Captain, "we must pursue our plan without him. But I have neglected to impart to you some good news. Major Lee, with four true men, and seven horses, is on the opposite side of the river, awaiting the result of to-night's adventure."

"This is good news, certainly—but how do you know this, Captain?"

"I have been across the river and seen him."

"Then George got through safely?"

"Yes, and is now with him."

"Thank Heaven!" returned the other, fervently; "my mind is now more at ease, for I feared some accident might befal him."

The conversation of this little band of heroic spies was carried on in whispers; and many things were talked over, during the next half hour, unnecessary for us to detail. Suffice it to say, that before eleven o'clock they all separated. Josh accompanied Dame Hagold to the skiff, which he silently rowed down to the point agreed upon; and then, leaving it in her charge, the same as the night before, he repaired to the rear of Arnold's dwelling, whither the rest of the party had gone singly, in order not to excite suspicion, in the event of being seen and challenged by any of the sentinels. Carlini had imparted to each the countersign for the night; so that there was little risk in meeting the patrols, unless two or more should be seen together; and perhaps no danger even then; but it was judged politic not to make the trial, since it could just as well be avoided.

Long before the arrival of Josh, Milford and Carlini had ensconsed themselves in the shrubbery, leaving Rosalie, still unknown to the Captain, to watch by the palings without. Josh drew silently and cautiously to the side of the *soi disant* Henry, and in a whisper inquired:

"Is all right, lad?"

"Yes," was the reply.

No more was said, and a deep silence succeeded. For nearly an hour, Carlini and Milford remained at their post, in the shrubbery, waiting for the appearance of one who came not. At last, just as they were about to despair of seeing him that night, a door in the rear of the mansion was heard to open and shut; and though the position in which they were, rendered it impossible for them to see if any person issued without, yet, by listening, with suspended breath, a foot-fall in the garden became faintly audible.

"At last!" whispered Milford, pressing the arm of his companion in a nervous manner, that denoted the state of his feelings: "At last we have the object of our solicitude."

"Be not too sanguine," was the reply, in the same manner; "there is many a slip between the cup and lip. Be ready, be prompt, be bold, and heaven send us success!"

"Have you the rope and gag disencumbered? for this must be speedy work."

"All is prepared, and we must spring and seize him together. But silence now—he comes this way. When you feel me squeeze your hand, know that as the signal to do your duty."

Our friends now remained silent, and quiet, listening to the sound of footsteps, which were evidently nearing them. Presently they were enabled to perceive the outlines of a figure, which was rapidly gliding toward that point of the garden where they were concealed. The advancing party, all unconscious of danger, was humming a popular air, and seemed in good spirits. As he drew near to the thicket, Carlini felt the hand of his companion, which he held in his own, tremble with eager excitement; and he ventured to say, in the lowest possible whisper:

"Be calm."

Within ten feet of the thicket, the individual our friends were watching, paused, and listened, as if he heard some unusual sound; and once or twice he seemed on the point of turning back; but finally, with a half-muttered "Pshaw!" he advanced straight to the shrubbery.

Carlini now pressed the hand of his companion, and both bounded from the thicket, and the next moment the new-comer was firmly secured in their grasp; but, by some trifling blunder, the gag, prepared for his mouth, missed it, and before the error could be retrieved, he set up an agonizing scream, shouting:

"Murder! murder! fire! thieves! help! help!"

At the first sound of his voice, which was very effeminate, with a foreign accent, both Carlini and Milford released their hold of him, in astonishment and dismay; for they needed no further proof, that he was not the man they sought, and that therefore they had committed a fatal mistake.

"It is not the traitor, after all," said Milford.

"Murder! murder! thieves! robbers! help! help!" screamed the frightened varlet, fairly dancing up and down in wild excitement.

"Hold thy tongue, fool, or I will knife thee on the spot!" cried Carlini.

But heedless of consequences, the other only repeated his outcry for help.

"Take that, knave!" said Carlini, in a hissing tone of passion; and with a blow of his fist, he laid the other senseless on the earth.

By this time there was considerable of a stir in the mansion, windows were thrown up, heads protruded, and the cry of "Guard! guard!" was shouted by some half a dozen voices.

"Good heavens! I fear we are lost!" cried Milford, in dismay.

"Quick! quick!" returned Carlini; "we must save ourselves ere too late;" and as he spoke, he darted away to the point where the palings had been removed, followed by the Captain.

"Fly! fly! oh! for heaven's sake, fly!" cried an agonized voice: "to the boat! to the boat!"

It was the voice of Rosalie that now spoke, in undisguised tones of alarm and terror; and had Captain Milford not been labouring under intense excitement, he would have recognized it as the voice of her he loved; but he thought of nothing now save his own safety, and that of his friends. As he and Carlini together reached the alley, they heard the tramp of men running, some in one direction and some in another, and at the same moment a musket was fired and the alarm-cry raised—

"Turn out, guard! turn out, guard!"

"This way, friends! this way!" cried Carlini, darting down the alley, followed by Milford, Josh, and Rosalie.

But ere they reached the cross-street that led to the river, another musket was fired, and the roll of the drum was heard in three directions, arousing many a sleeper, and filling their hearts with terror. Turning down the street leading to the river, and perceiving their way clear, as far as their range of vision could extend, for there was no artificial light to aid them, the fugitives, with Carlini still on the lead, ran as fast as they could, at the same time making as little noise as possible. But they were not destined to escape without new troubles; for they had not gone a hundred yards further, when a sentry suddenly sprang before them, from behind a tree, and leveling his musket, cried:

"If ye are true men, stand."

To stop was to be lost—for their only hope was to gain the river in advance of their pursuers, whom they could now hear running behind them, though at some distance—and therefore, goaded to desperation, Carlini, who was as brave as a lion, without replying to the sentry, rushed toward him, and made a grasp at his musket. He missed his object; and the soldier, springing back two or three paces, with the quickness of lightning, brought his piece to bear full upon the other's body, and pulled the trigger. Fortunately for the astrologer, the gun missed fire; and the next moment it was wrenched from the sentry's grasp, and, with a tremendous blow from the breech, he was stretched senseless on the half-frozen muddy ground. Leaping over his prostrate body, Carlini, throwing the useless weapon aside, shouted:

"On! comrades—on!"

"Here they go—this way—we are on the right track!" the fugitives now heard shouted behind them; and the shout was taken up by another party, some distance off to the right, who were evidently running to intercept them. Our friends now strained every nerve to gain the bank of the river, which was already in sight, with only here and there a house to intercept the view in any direction, when a small party of soldiers suddenly turned the angle of the nearest building and fairly headed them.

"We are lost," cried Milford; "but I will sell my life dearly."

"Divide! divide! each man for himself, and God for us all!" shouted Carlini.

Acting upon this suggestion, without a moment's consideration, Carlini, Milford, and Josh, each took a different direction, there being no houses here, as we said before, to prevent. As for poor Rosalie, unable to keep up with the others, she had fallen far behind; and providentially, too, as the sequel will show. At the moment the spies separated, they heard the voice of the leader of the soldiers in front of them, commanding them to halt and surrender; and as they, heeding not his order, only fled the faster, they heard the words:

"Fire and pursue them!"

Scarcely was this last command given, when the report of half a dozen muskets rang out, on the still frosty air, and as many bullets sped whizzing away in the darkness, but fortunately leaving unharmed those for whom they were intended. As our friends were now fairly separated, and running fast, it was necessary for the soldiers to divide also, and give chase, or lose them altogether. This was accordingly done; and each fugitive now had at least two men in direct and close pursuit of him, but also the satisfaction of knowing that their muskets were empty, and consequently that they could do him little or no harm before coming to close quarters. But as we can follow only one of our gallant spies at the same time, we shall proceed to chronicle the adventures of our hero, as being best calculated to interest the reader.

Captain Milford, then, on separating from his companions, turned off to the right, and ran across an open plot of ground, which, from having been soaked with the late rain, and only partially frozen, was still soft in many places, often clogged his feet, and, in a great degree, retarded his progress; but still he struggled forward manfully, and strove to console himself with the reflection, that it was as good for him as for his pursuers.

The latter were not more than twenty yards behind him; but though somewhat blown with hard running, Milford succeeded in preserving his distance, till he struck into a lane, intended for a street, and which, at this day has a compact row of houses on either side, and is a very busy thoroughfare of the great metropolis. This, like the other half-built street out of which he had turned to get here, led direct from Broadway to the river; and, as a matter of course, Milford took the latter direction. He was still some way below the point where he hoped to find the boat; to gain which, in advance of his pursuers, was, in his view, the only chance he had of saving his life—for if taken, he felt certain the fate of poor Andre would be his. The execution of that unfortunate young man, right in the face of all protestation and remonstrance on the part of his influential friends, he keenly felt would utterly close the door of mercy against himself, even did not the stern policy of war demand his life as a sacrificial warning to such as might think of venturing upon a scheme as rash as his own.

As Milford turned down the lane already mentioned, he heard the shouts of others than those whom he had been led to hope were his only pursuers; and glanced back over his shoulder, he caught a glimpse of three figures, between him and Broadway, coming toward him with a speed that seemed to lessen the distance between himself and them at every step. He now indeed felt that all was lost; for though naturally a fleet runner, he had so fatigued himself in struggling through the mud, that he despaired of being a match for men apparently fresh in the race. But he was not one to tamely yield while there was even a bare hope of escape; and consequently he renewed his exertions, and fled faster than ever. He was now rapidly descending a slight declivity, to a hollow or a level, the darkness not permitting him to tell which; and as the earth under his feet was less miry than that he had so recently passed over, he began to grow more confident of ultimately baffling his pursuers.

But, alas for human calculation! or perhaps we should rather say, alas for the dawning hopes of our hero! When he reached the bottom of the declivity, he was at least a dozen yards in advance of his nearest pursuer; and could he have gained the bank of the stream, which was now only a few rods distant, he would doubtless have succeeded in eluding them, even though it had been effected by jumping into the river, and striking out boldly for the opposite shore. But fate had decreed otherwise; for at the third step, he fell into a slough, and sunk almost to his arm-pits. He made two or three ineffectual struggles to extricate himself, and then gave up in despair, remaining a helpless prisoner, entirely at the mercy of the soldiers, who, hearing the plunge, and divining the cause, took good care to guard themselves against a like catastrophe.

CHAPTER XXI.

THE TRIAL AND SENTENCE.

"Well, old fellow, so you're caught at last, are you?" said the foremost of Captain Milford's pursuers, panting for breath. "By St. Dennis! you've nearly knocked the wind out of me; but if you are in that delectable place, I forgive you."

A loud laugh from the others, as they came up, denoted that they viewed the affair in a rather ridiculous light. Milford made no reply to the first speaker; and as it was too dark to distinguish objects ten feet from the eye: and as he remained perfectly quiet, two thinus buried in the mud; it became a matter of some doubt with the soldiers, whether he had escaped, been drowned in the slough, or whether he was fast, and in a condition to answer their questions.

"Get a pole off the fence there, to the left, push it into the hole, and ascertain if he is in there—and if so, whether he is alive or dead," said another voice, in the tone of one who, *ex-officio*, had authority to command the others.

As one of the men immediately went for the pole, Captain Milford, who now felt satisfied there was no chance of escape, said:

"Gentlemen, I must beg of you to assist me out of this."

"Ha! the scoundrel is not dead, and he has found his tongue at last," pursued the man in authority. "But get the pole, Carbon, for we shall need it. There! methinks I see him now," continued the speaker, drawing nearer to Milford, and striving to peer into the darkness, but taking good care to try the earth under him at every step. "Who are you," he demanded, in a rough tone, "that has caused so much commotion and alarm in the city?"

"I am your prisoner, sir," replied the Captain, drily.

"Yes, and by ——! you will have to pay dearly for this night's work, or I'm no judge of military matters. We are not to be raised in the middle of the night, out of our warm beds, to run a foot-race after such scapegraces as you and your companions, and then let you off with a slight reprimand, I can assure you. Who are you? and what have you been about, sirrah?"

"I will answer these questions only to your superiors," returned Milford, firmly. "At present it is enough for you to know I am your prisoner; and the sooner you do your duty, and set me before your commanding officer, the sooner you will know my secret—that is to say, if you ever know it."

"You are an insolent dog, at all events!" rejoined the other, harshly. "Quick, Carbon, with that pole, and let us have out this mud-diver."

"He speaks like a feller that knows a thing or two of military affairs," said one of the others. "Now I wouldn't wonder if he turned out to be some rascally spy, after all."

"I hope so," returned the chief of the party; "for then we'll have some satisfaction for our foot-race, in the pleasure of seeing him dangle at a rope's end."

The pole was by this time plunged into the slough, where Milford could reach it, and in a short time he was safely on the more solid earth, but completely covered with mud and slime, which made him a very repulsive object.

"Come, you vagabond, you shall soon have the desired interview with our commander," said the leader of the party. "Fall in, men—fall in; for though you don't all belong to my corps, I suppose you'll not refuse to serve as an escort to this mud-beauty."

"Certainly not," was the reply.

"Well, Smith and I will lead, Carbon will bring up the rear, and you two gentlemen will flank the prisoner on the right and left. Ready all—march!" and at the word, the whole party moved off, with military precision, shaping their course up the lane to Broadway.

Ere they reached the latter thoroughfare, however, the party was joined by another night-guard, consisting of half a dozen privates, commanded by a corporal. A halt was ordered, questions asked, and explanations given; and just as the two parties were about to separate, an officer of the staff rode up, and demanded to know the cause of the tumult and alarm.

"Our prisoner here can best give that explanation," replied the officer who had the Captain in charge; and he hurriedly related how and where he had been taken; but declared that he was ignorant of his crime, as he had refused to answer his questions.

"Let him be conducted at once to the presence of his excellency, Sir Henry Clinton."

"To-night, your honor?" queried the other, in a tone of surprise.

"I said at once, sir," rejoined the officer of the staff; and putting spurs to his horse, he rode swiftly away.

"Well, it will be short work with you, I'm thinking," growled the Corporal to Milford.

The latter made no reply; and the word being given to march, the party with the prisoner again set forward, at a quick step, shaping their course to the residence of the commander-in-chief. Broadway was astir with the alarm; and on his way to the mansion of Sir Henry, our hero met more than one party of patrols, and saw horsemen riding to and fro, with as much haste and apparent excitement as if the city were already in a state of siege. In fact, he saw enough to convince him that the alarm was general, and that on him must fall the heaviest punishment of military law, death on the gibbet.

"All is lost," he said, mentally; "but I must nerve myself to die as becomes a true soldier. Poor Andre! our fates are much alike; and we shall soon meet, perhaps, in another world."

The Captain thought of Rosalie; and for the first time his heart sunk, and a tear dimmed his eye.

There was a small guard of soldiers drawn up before Sir Henry's mansion; and the front door being open, Milford perceived several officers of high rank moving about in the brilliantly lighted hall. The Corporal reported himself and his business, and the prisoner was immediately conducted into the presence of the commander-in-chief. The latter was seated at a table, in the same apartment where we first introduced him to the reader in the "Female Spy." The room was lighted with a large chandelier of wax candles, suspended from the ceiling; and around the table sat several officers, in full dress, while others were standing back, more in the shade, their bright scarlet uniforms, gold epaulets, rich sashes, and sparkling ornaments, making a splendid and imposing display. To account for so many of high rank being present, we need only say, that they had been summoned hither to attend a council-of-war, which had not broken up when the alarm was sounded.

There was a dead silence as Milford entered, escorted by two of the soldiers, who fell back the moment he had crossed the threshold of the audience-room. All eyes were of course fixed upon him, with stern curiosity; and as he confronted the assemblage, covered with mud from head to foot, and full in the blaze of light, which flashed upon him so suddenly as to dazzle his sight—and remembered, too, for what purpose he was there, and how much like a guilty wretch he must appear to all present—it is no wonder that for the moment he should feel overcome, feel his brain reel, and stagger against the wall for support. But his weakness, or emotion, was only momentary; his natural firmness and lofty courage soon returned; and he stood up boldly, calmly, and looked his enemies full in the face, without the quiver of a single muscle of his noble countenance. He knew his fate, and had resolved to meet it without a murmur. Concealment, or prevarication, he fancied would be useless, and he had resolved to disclose all.

"Who are you, sir?" sternly demanded Sir Henry, with an angry frown.

"One not altogether unknown to your excellency," replied our hero, in a firm, calm, even tone of voice. "My name is Edgar Milford, and I hold the commission of Captain in the American army."

"Ha! Captain Milford?" exclaimed Sir Henry, in a tone of surprise. "Yes, methinks I recognize your features now, as the person with whom I had an interview a few days since. But how comes it, sir, that you are brought hither under guard, in this plight, at this time of night?"

"Your excellency and gentlemen, (bowing respectfully to the company,) I will be frank, and speak the truth; for prevarication I now deem useless, and unworthy of one who prides himself on being a man of honor and a soldier. I first appeared before your excellency as a deserter from the American camp; but, sir, I never did desert my country, I never did desert the cause of liberty, and, I hardly need add now, your excellency, I never shall prove myself a recreant and a renegade."

"Ha! then, sir, we see before us a spy?" cried the other, sharply, quickly, and with a dark frown gathering on his brow.

"Term me what you please, your excellency, it will alter nothing now. I came hither, sir, for the express purpose of seizing the traitor, Benedict Arnold. I have failed in my object · and I await the penalty of my temerity with a stout heart, and an unflinching faith in the mercy of Almighty God."

The firm, lofty, solemn tone in which Milford spoke—the frank, manly manner in which he avowed his object in coming to the city—together with the exciting, not to say startling nature of that object itself, caused a powerful sensation among the officers who heard him. Even Sir Henry himself seemed astonished to silence; and it was not till a buzz of admiration, for such dauntless, self-sacrificing heroism, began to run around the room, that he recollected himself, and again spoke. Milford, without appearing to do so, noted even the slightest indication of the feeling in which his confession was received; and we must do him the justice to say, that friendless, unprotected, ay, already doomed, as he felt himself to be, it was the proudest moment of his life.

"You have made this acknowledgment, young man, with the sad fate of poor Major Andre fresh in your memory," resumed Sir Henry, softening at the recollection of one so dear to him.

"I have, your excellency," replied the prisoner; "and were I assured I could die as much regretted, by friends and foes, as was that noble, high-minded, generous, confiding, and accomplished officer, I could meet my death wih a welcome seldom bestowed upon the grim king of terrors."

Sir Henry was moved at this tribute of respect to the memory of one he loved as a son; but he strove to conceal it, and rejoined:

"Will you favor us with the plan you had arranged for kidnapping Arnold?"

"Pardon me, your excellency! but I can not betray the secrets of others," was the lofty reply. "I have acknowledged to my own individual intentions—that must suffice."

"You had confederates, of course?"

"If I had, your excellency, you never will learn who they were from me."

"You are right sir; and in the memorable language of Greene, when a like question was put to the lamented Major Andre, who replied in a manner similar to yourself, 'We have no right to demand this of you.' But do you object to stating how it chanced you caused this alarm to-night? and how it happened you were captured?"

"Without wishing to appear obstinate, your excellency," said Milford, after a pause, for the first time exhibiting a slight embarrassment, "I would rather decline answering the former question: as to the latter, that is soon explained: I was endeavouring to escape from some soldiers, in hot pursuit of me, when I accidentally plunged into a slough, made I presume by the late rain, and was thus rendered helpless."

Sir Henry now turned to a gray-headed officer who sat near him, and the two held a short conversation in whispers. He then said aloud:

"Gentlemen, I must beg of you to withdraw for a few minutes, while these three Generals (naming the parties who sat at the table) and myself, hold a secret consultation. Colonel Dundas, you will call in the guard, and take charge of the prisoner. If you choose, you may conduct him into the library —but we shall not be long."

The apartment was soon cleared of all but the four Generals. Milford had scarcely taken a seat in the library, when Colonel Dundas received an order to reconduct the prisoner to the presence of the commander-in-chief. When Milford again entered the audience room, he found the same officers present as at his introduction. There was something ominous in the solemn silence which prevailed; but his mind was fully prepared for the worst, and he exhibited no emotion.

"Captain Milford," began Sir Henry Clinton, speaking in a slow, distinct, impressive tone, "as you are a soldier of no common intelligence, you of course are not ignorant of the laws of nations in regard to that class of individuals who come under the denomination of spies. That you are one of this class, we have your own voluntary admission; and therefore have deemed it useless to call in other evidence. The penalty of this crime, as you well know, is death by the hangman; and no matter what our own feelings may be in the matter, we are bound, by the policy of war, to see the law carried into effect. From my heart, young man, I sincerely pity you;

but pity must be sacrificed to duty; and therefore it only remains for me, as an instrument of the law, to pronounce your sentence. It is the unanimous verdict of this tribunal before which you have been arraigned, that, by your own admission, you are guilty as a spy, and ought to suffer death; and it is furthermore decreed, that at the hour of sunrise to-morrow, in the yard of the city prison, you be hung by the neck till you are dead. I will merely add, may God Almighty have mercy on your soul!"

There was a breathless silence in the audience-room, when this awful sentence was pronounced, and every eye was fixed upon the prisoner, with a look of sympathy. The latter listened to his doom with perfect composure, and, save a slight paleness, which overspread his features, there was no visible change in his appearance. There was no sinking of his calm, bright eye—no contraction of the muscles of his countenance—no quivering of his lips—and no one could say he was more affected than those who looked on as spectators. After the lapse of a few moments, he replied, in a clear, firm, manly tone:

"Your excellency and gentlemen, I beg leave to say a few words, ere we part forever, or at least to meet no more on earth. In the first place, I would thank you, from my heart, for the respectful manner in which I have been treated since I came into your presence, and for the sympathy which it is apparent you have bestowed upon a stranger and an enemy. I am still young, gentlemen, and will not deny that there is much to make life dear to me; but I have ever strove to act honorably, to do my duty to my country, and this reflection will console me in my last moments. I am a soldier, I trust in God a Christian, and fear not death. When I engaged in the hazardous undertaking which has resulted in failure and so fatally to me, I did it with full consciousness of its perils, and of the awful consequences that would ensue if taken. I was therefore fully prepared for what has taken place; and so far from regretting what I did, I here candidly avow, that with all my knowledge of the past, were I again at liberty, and the same chances of success or failure were to present themselves, I would re-enact the same part. To seize a vile miscreant—a traitor to his country—a villain of the darkest die—who honors no obligation to God or man—and bring him to justice—to the punishment he so deservedly merits—I conceived to be both a justifiable and a worthy act; and with death now staring me in the face, I find, gentlemen, my sentiments in this respect do not undergo any change. But your excellency and gentlemen, I will not tire your patience by longer occupying your valuable time. Once more thanking you for your kind attention, respectful demeanor, and true sympathy, I humbly bow to your decree."

When Milford had done speaking, Sir Henry took up a pen, and hastily wrote a few lines, while each of the officers conversed in low tones with one another. Sir Henry then made a sign for Colonel Dundas to approach; and folding the paper, he placed it in his hands, saying, in a low tone:

"Sir, you will take charge of the prisoner. Let him be conveyed to the prison, and see that, unlike the one we recently had there in durance, he does not escape. This paper is the order for his execution: see it carried into effect."

The guard was now summoned, and the prisoner removed. As Milford was descending the marble steps of the mansion, a lady, on horseback, rode up on a keen run, and, scarcely reining in her furious beast, wildly threw herself from his back. Milford turned his head a little to observe her, and the bright light of the hall flashed full upon his own features and hers at the same moment. The eyes of both met at once; and uttering a piercing scream of despair, the lady sank down in a swoon.

It was Rosalie Du Pont.

"Merciful God!" exclaimed Milford, covering his eyes and shuddering: "I had hoped to be spared this heart-rending scene. On! guard—on! for the love of Heaven! and take me from her sight."

The guard quickened their pace, Milford did not look back, and in a few moments the angle of a street shut her from his view, whom, of all others, he loved best on earth.

CHAPTER XXII.

THE TALISMAN.

It was about half an hour after the scene witnessed in the foregoing chapter, that Rosalie Du Pont was closeted with Sir Henry Clinton. She had been conveyed into the mansion, in a state of insensibility, and female domestics had been summoned to attend upon her. Her swoon—to which kind of disease, or debility, she was constitutionally subject, when laboring under violent excitement—soon passed away, and she gradually recovered all her faculties; and with them that self-control, and great presence of mind, which, paradoxical as it may seem, was also another of her several peculiarities.

On regaining her senses, therefore, she exhibited no more paroxysms of excitement, and the name of him she loved did not pass her lips. She calmly inquired if Sir Henry Clinton were at home; and being answered in the affirmative, she requested to have a private interview with him, on very important and urgent business. This message being conveyed to the General, a polite answer was returned, that his excellency was at present engaged with some gentlemen, but in a few minutes he would have the pleasure of waiting upon her.

The council with which, as the reader knows, Sir Henry was engaged, soon broke up, when, with true gallantry, he immediately repaired to a private parlor, where his fair guest was awaiting him, with that anxious and painful suspense which barely divides hope and despair, happiness and misery.

The greeting of Sir Henry Clinton was courteous, but bore a marked air of coldness and restraint, which Rosalie had never before perceived, and which made the heart of the poor maiden sink with a certain degree of fear and shame. The first salutations over, for a few moments she remained embarrassed and silent; but remembering the important mission which had brought her hither, and that it was absolutely necessary for her to state her business, she rallied a little, assumed a courage she did not feel, and in a tolerably even, but low tone of voice, said:

"Sir Henry Clinton, I am here to ask a favor."

"Say on, madam," replied the other. "What you seek is doubtless no trifling matter, or you would not have come in such hot haste, at so late an hour of the night."

"Your excellency is right," returned Rosalie, who began to gather courage as she proceeded; "it is no trifling matter; it is the life of a fellow being."

"I anticipated as much," was the cold response. "To come directly to the point—I suppose you are here to ask the pardon and release of one who has just been condemned as a spy?"

"Is Captain Milford already condemned, then?" cried Rosalie, in great agitation.

"He is, madam."

"But—but—he—he is—not—yet executed?" gasped the other, clinging to her chair for support.

"He is still alive, madam, but his hour is near. He dies at sunrise."

"Oh! no! no! no!" cried Rosalie, wildly, losing all self-possession, as the horrible picture of him she loved, dangling at a rope's end, rose up vividly in her imagination. "Oh! no! no! this must not—must not—shall not be! Oh! Sir Henry, unsay those cruel words, and on my knees I will bless you!"

"Calm yourself, madam," replied the other, "calm yourself; you are excited, and know not what you say."

"I tell you, Sir Henry Clinton, he must not, shall not die!" cried Rosalie again, with a wild, haggard look. "Sir Henry, it is in your power to save him; and oh! sir, that power must be exercised, at all hazards!"

"I pray you, madam, be calm, and let sober reason resume her sway. You permit your feelings to get the better of your judgment, and do not rationally consider what you ask. Remember your position, madam; that you, a maiden, are sueing for the life of a condemned spy—condemned by a military tribunal, and by his own voluntary admission. Were you even the wife of this man, you could not exhibit more passionate, riotous, maniacal, hysterical emotion."

"And I am his wife," said Rosalie, solemnly; "his wife in the sight of that God before whom we must all appear in judgment. The worldly forms that would make him legally mine, have not been gone through with, it is true; but I have a right to plead for him which is as just, and holy, as the sacred ceremony of chaplain or Church could give me."

"Well, madam, even admitting that, you surely can not expect me to so far swerve from my duty, as to set at liberty a rebel spy. And you, Miss Du Pont—you, who are, or *profess* to be, so *loyal* (and there was a cutting emphasis on the italicised words)—I am astonished that *you*, madam, should so earnestly plead for an enemy of your sovereign. I am loth, Miss Du Pont, to bring home to you certain little matters—but present circumstances justify me in speaking plainer than I otherwise should. I can not forget, madam, that this man was once a prisoner-of-war, and that, through your intercession in his behalf, I connived at his escape. He was not regularly exchanged, as is the custom of war, nor did I exact of him a parole that he would not again serve the enemies of his king. Well, he went back to the rebel camp, and took up arms against our cause; and while acting in this capacity, you, madam, as I have it from his own lips, corresponded with him. Next he assists at the execution of the unfortunate Andre; and then, pretending to desert the rebels, comes to me with a lie in his mouth—pardon me! but I am in no humor for being fastidious in the selection of terms—comes to me with a lie in his mouth, I say, and, in order to blind me to his true purpose, acknowledges what I have just set forth, endeavors to prove he had long been loyal, and that you had obtained much of your information regarding the enemy's movements and plans through him. This seemed all straight-forward, so long as I believed him a true deserter; and I acknowledge I was for the time being his dupe; for in you I had unlimited confidence; and in using your name, he rendered the deception complete; but now, since I *know* him in his true character—since he has boldly denied he was ever a deserter; and has as boldly stated, that, were he free, and the same opportunities were again to present; he would do the same thing over again,—since all these matters have come to my knowledge, I say, you must pardon me, madam; if I err in attaching even to yourself a suspicion of double dealing."

Rosalie was confounded. This strong array of facts, set forth in so straight-forward a manner, came home to her with terrible force; and completely overcome by her feelings, she covered her face with her handkerchief, and burst into tears. Sir Henry gazed upon her in stern silence for a few moments; and then, seeing she was not inclined to speak, even in her own defense, he resumed:

"Your silence, madam, on the point of my implied accusation, leads me, I grieve to say, to a serious conclusion—I grieve to say it, because it is very painful to find ourselves deceived in those we have regarded as our true friends; and because a breach of confidence tends to make us suspicious of all we meet, hardens us against the world, sours our temper, closes our hearts to sympathy, and, in short, renders us very unhappy. But, madam, though never so guilty, you have nothing to fear from me; your sex protects you; we do not war against women, and you are at liberty to depart; but if you would have me keep my temper, and separate from you with a show of friendship, ask nothing for the prisoner."

As Sir Henry said this, he rose to take his leave; and this action, together with his last words, produced an immediate and marked change in the humbled maiden.

There was no more weeping—no more of that wildness and agitation which she had exhibited during much of the interview. She lifted her head, proudly, loftily, haughtily; and there was more of command, than entreaty, in her voice, as she said:

"Pray, sit down, your excellency—we must not part thus."

"It is late, madam, and I—" hesitated the other; but he was interrupted by Rosalie, in an imperious tone, that would have done credit to the proudest queen; while her eyes, which so lately were dim with tears, now flashed and sparkled with lofty indignation.

"Sir Henry Clinton," she said, "sit down

and listen to what I have to say—unless you have resolved to arrogate to yourself the triple province of accuser, judge, and executioner!"

"Madam, I listen," replied the General, biting his lips, as he resumed his seat.

"In the first place," said Rosalie, speaking in a calm, firm, almost haughty tone, "I am going to admit that I am guilty of all you accuse me, and doubtless of all you suspect me; and in the second place, I shall proceed to state such matters as I think proper for my own justification, trusting your excellency is too much of a gentleman to refuse to listen to my defense. To do this, it is necessary that I touch briefly upon my own history, as well as some things pertaining to this war.

"To begin, I must set your excellency right on one point, by telling you—what you appear to have overlooked, forgotten, or are ignorant of—that I was born and educated in France; and that when you speak of *my* sovereign, and allude to George the Third of England, you commit a great error. The rank and name of my father—who is at present, I am proud to say, a distinguished officer in the allied forces of the Americans—I do not deem proper now to mention; nor shall I trouble your excellency with any more of my history than pertains directly to my defense. Suffice it, therefore, to say, that when the colonies here, by reason of unjust legislation, revolted against the Mother Country, as England is termed, I was a mere girl, in my teens; but, sir, I was old enough to think, and feel, and sympathise with the oppressed; and when I had read both sides of the question, with which the French journals teemed, I said the Americans were right; I even gloried in the bold, manly, noble stand they had taken; and I sometimes regretted I was not American born, that I might do something toward assisting them in their unequal struggle.

"From my earliest recollection, your excellency—though nobly born myself, and mingling among the great, the titled, the proudest of the realm—one idea, which I must think inherent in my nature, ever held full sway in my mind, namely: that kings, princes, and all hereditary nobilities, were wrong; and that if all such distinctions were swept from the face of the earth, the great mass of mankind would be the gainers. Why, I reasoned, should one man be better born than another, and usurp the scanty pittance of his fellow man—roll in wealth, ease, luxury, dissipation—and leave his brother to starve, or grind out a life of misery worse than death? Surely, the same God made all, would judge all, and before his awful and searching eye the meanest beggar must stand on an equality with the proudest king. Death, too, the great human leveler, would know no distinction; and the man that feasted, and the man that starved, the prince and the peasant, would alike crumble to dust in the great tomb of earth.

"With these sentiments, your excellency, unalterably impressed upon my mind, it will not surprise you if I say, that when first I read the declaration of independence of these colonies, I exclaimed, 'There is a people after my own heart, who boldly assert the true principles of right; and the good God, whose three great attributes are justice, love, and mercy, will sustain them. I longed to be with them, if I might in any way aid them; and though at the time I regarded my wish as hopeless, yet circumstances gave me an opportunity to accomplish my desire.

"But I will not weary your excellency with detail. Suffice it to say that my beloved mother, who was then living, soon after died; and as I felt inconsolable for her loss, my father advised me to travel. We went to England; and there, for the first time, I saw the sister of my poor deceased mother, the present wife of Graham Percy, who is, as your excellency knows, a distant kinsman of the Earl of the same name. She had resided many years in the colonies, chiefly in this city, and was here on the breaking out of the war. As her husband was a staunch royalist, he left New York during the time it was occupied by the American army, but returned soon after the British got possession. But why repeat what your excellency already knows?

"I questioned my aunt eagerly with regard to America and the Americans; but soon found her prejudices were all against the latter, and that her sympathies were altogether with the British. However, as she was about to return to this country, this did not prevent me soliciting, as a great favor, to be allowed to accompany her—for I was desirous of seeing and knowing the true character of a people that, in my view, had acted so nobly. My father at first objected to my coming, but finally consented, and we shortly after embarked. I took with me only one domestic, a dumb mulatto girl, whom I persuaded my aunt to allow me to dress as a youth. I also assumed the maiden name of my mother, by which I am known to your excellency, and made my kinswoman promise not to divulge my real name and rank.

"Your excellency is already acquainted with the circumstances which induced me to accompany you in your expedition against Charleston. While in that place, after its surrender, I accidentally became acquainted with Captain Milford; and my sympathies being altogether with the Americans, and a mutual liking springing up between us, it will not perhaps surprise your excellency, when I say we became intimate as friends. I subsequently interceded in his behalf, and, thanks to your excellency's noble generosity and kindness, procured his release.

"That there was an understanding between Captain Milford and myself, with regard to keeping up a correspondence, I do not deny; but to the best of my recollection, I made no promise to him that I would communicate any thing beyond personal matters; if I did more, it was voluntary, and unsolicited. When he told your excellency that much of the information I had imparted to you had been obtained through him, he told you, sir, no falsehood; but if your excellency will recollect a moment, the truth will flash upon your mind, that I never gave you any intelligence concerning the Americans, but such as your excellency had already obtained, or such as was of little or no importance.

"That I am personally known to the noble Marquis de Lafayette; and that I have once looked upon the mild, majestic, sublime face of the great champion of freedom, the immortal George Washington, is equally true; and to those two great generals, have I generally forwarded such communications as I had to make.

"Your excellency has alluded, in a rather unpleasant manner, to a breach of confidence on my part. Sir, I am not aware that your excellency ever made a *private* communication to me, that I ever imparted to a living soul; nor would I have done so, had your excellency confided to me a secret that jeopardised a nation whose cause I have espoused. No, sir, base as I may seem in your eyes, I feel myself incapable of such an act, which would in truth be a breach of confidence: that, sir, is a double-dealing foreign to my nature. The most I have done, is in having sent off such intelligence as I chanced to gather casually; and in doing this, I pledge you my word, I have often and often regretted that I was personally acquainted with your excellency; for I looked upon you as a true gentleman, an honorable man—high-minded, generous, benevolent, and humane—an ornament to society and your distinguished position—and I have had for you that veneration, esteem—ay, sir, even affection—which a daughter may have for a parent. I say this, sir, candidly—not as flattery, to cause you to swerve from what you regard as a duty—but as a sacred truth, which is only just and proper your excellency should know.

"Your excellency is aware, there is an old maxim, much in use, to the effect, that all stratagems are fair in war; and on this principle I have acted. I have never warred—if I may give to my humble doings so strong an appellation—against persons, but principles; and for the little I have done toward assisting a wronged and oppressed people in their manly efforts to establish a glorious independence, my conscience gives me full justification. And if your excellency will regard my acts in their proper light, taking all the circumstances into consideration, I think your excellency will be forced to admit, that I could not have done otherwise and been true to myself.

"And, now, your excellency, not to detain you too long, I will, in conclusion, state a few brief facts. As your excellency has been plain with me, you must pardon me if I am so with your excellency. A man, holding a high and distinguished position in the American army, and possessing in a great degree the confidence of his chieftain, makes known to your excellency a desire to betray his trust —to put your excellency in possession of that wherewith you can crush the hopes of a struggling nation, as it were, by a single blow. And for this base action, prompted by the vilest of motives, what does he exact in return? Gold, and a position as high in the British army as the one he would vacate in that of your noble foemen. Does your excellency scruple to treat, to bargain, with this vile traitor—to pay him his price for his dishonesty—to reward him unjustly for chaining himself to infamy here, and in all probability hereafter? No, your excellency exhibits no scruples on this point, because your excellency fancies you can shield yourself and your motives behind a rampart of pseudo policy. But your excellency does more. Instead of letting this miscreant come to you, to sell his honor and his soul, you select one who stands as far above him as angels of light above demons of darkness, and send to him—send, too, without the pale of your jurisdiction, and within that of a people you are heavily wronging by his very mission—thus, in actual deed, sanctioning and approving what your excellency has seen proper to so bitterly condemn in others. Well, sir, what are the consequences? By that dimmed eye, that quivering lip, that averted face, I perceive your excellency full well and painfully remembers them. And now, sir, when one comes, armed with right, to seize the traitor, and drag him to the doom he so richly merits, you are possessed with a holy horror of his mission, and are pleased to hurl upon his devoted head the last and greatest penalty you can inflict; and when another ventures to intercede for him, you grow indignant that any one should have the temerity to ask such a boon. On reconsideration, sir, perhaps your excellency is right; for the miscreant that has been purchased by a royal commission, ten thousand pounds from the royal treasury, and the life of one of the bravest, noblest, most accomplished and devoted of the King's subjects, should be preserved at all hazards, as a priceless gem; and the gibbet is only too light a punishment for him who dares to think of molesting so expensive a treasure. And now, sir, I have done with my defense. If, when your excellency shall have calmly considered all I have said, your excellency sees no extenuation, no justification, of my motives and deeds, I must suffer myself to be visited with your excellency's displeasure in an unequivocal denial of the boon I crave."

For some time after Rosalie ceased speaking, Sir Henry Clinton remained silent and thoughtful. He had listened attentively, to what she termed her defense, with varied feelings; and toward the last, as one who was struck with the force of the statement she put forth. His silence was an awful suspense to Rosalie, who secretly trembled in anticipation of his reply, though she strove to appear calm and composed. At length he spoke, in a tone that denoted his feelings had undergone a material change.

"Miss Du Pont," he said, "you are a remarkable lady, and possess talents of no common order. It would certainly be impolitic in me to acknowledge any weight to your statement, beyond personal feeling; but I will admit you have made out a better case than I thought possible; and if it will be any satisfaction to you to know it, I will frankly admit, also, that though I now know you as an avowed enemy of the royal cause, I entertain for you feelings of deep respect; and though in my humble opinion you have greatly erred in espousing what you term the cause of liberty—but which, if successful, would only prove to be another name for anarchy in the aggregate, misrule and confusion—yet I believe you have acted conscientiously in the main, and that your error belongs rather to the head than the heart."

"I humbly thank your excellency for this admission," replied Rosalie, "and rejoice to say, that though enemies in principle, we may still be friends in person."

"That will, perhaps, depend somewhat on circumstances," rejoined the other, warily; "but I trust we may yet be friends in both. I shall seek an early opportunity to confer with you privately; and I hope to be able to make a true convert of one as intelligent and clear-minded as yourself."

"That your excellency could never do, even should your excellency have an opportunity for the trial," replied Rosalie, firmly; "but I feel constrained to say, that this will probably be our last meeting."

"You intend to leave the city?"

"Immediately, sir, with your excellency's permission."

"Well, then, Miss Du Pont, all things considered, I must own I think the course proposed the wisest you could adopt."

"But the prisoner, your excellency!"

"Madam, I must repeat, that you ask nothing for him," answered General Clinton, the frown again gathering on his brow. "Be satisfied that I let you off thus easily; but do not add insult to injury, by asking me to violate my duty—to forget the respect due to the laws of my sovereign."

"But, sir, your excellency is likewise bound to respect yourself; and as a man of honor, sir, you can not violate your plighted word. Know you this ring, sir?" and Rosalie disengaged one from her finger, and handed it to the other, who, on receiving it, looked perplexed and troubled. "That, sir, was a present from your excellency to my humble self, through the hands of the lamented Major Andre—whom you loved, and who I trust is now in heaven—and was accompanied by the pledge of your excellency, that whosoever should return it to you, and ask a favor within your power to grant, should not ask in vain. I now return it, sir; and by the soul of Andre, and the honor of Sir Henry Clinton, *demand* the instant release of Captain Milford."

"You are cruel, Miss Du Pont," replied the General, with considerable embarrassment.

"No, your excellency, I am only just. I did not exact the pledge—it was voluntary on your part—I only exact that it shall be redeemed; and, sir, your excellency is bound in honor to redeem it. And besides, what is the life of this man to you or your cause? One great attribute of heaven is mercy; and they who show it here, will never regret it hereafter. Your excellency perceives I am now calm, but firm. I no longer sue for a favor, but demand it as my right."

"And you *demand* that I set free a spy, and thus add another enemy to the crown," rejoined Sir Henry, bitterly.

"Sir, I will pledge you my honor, as a lady, that if your excellency will liberate Captain Milford, he shall not serve again in this war of the Revolution."

'Madam," returned the other, somewhat haughtily, "the honor of a Clinton is sacred—the pledge of a Clinton shall be redeemed—your suit is granted."

"O, thanks! ten thousand, thousand thanks!" cried Rosalie, sinking on her knees at the feet of the other, and bursting into tears, so overcome was she with joy and gratitude.

"Rise, Miss Du Pont," returned Sir Henry, coldly. "You owe me no thanks for keeping my plighted word; that which is accorded to your demand, backed by my honor, would certainly have been denied to your pleadings."

There was some further conversation between Rosalie and Sir Henry, maintained on his part with studied coldness. He then wrote a few words on a couple of slips of paper, which he handed her, saying:

"And now, madam?"

"It only remains for me to bid you farewell," replied the warm-hearted girl, taking his unresisting but not proffered hand, and pressing it with a feeling of gratitude. "I am sorry your excellency sees proper to part from me with this reserve, for it is not likely we shall ever meet again. But I will not complain. Whatever you may think of me, the name of Sir Henry Clinton shall be ever in my prayers. May you live long, and enjoy the blessings of heaven! Farewell!"

"Farewell!" returned Sir Henry, in a softened tone, moved in spite of himself.

A moment more and he was alone. He and Rosalie had parted for the last time.

CHAPTER XXIV.

CONCLUSION.

Captain Milford sat alone in his cell heavily ironed, ruminating upon the past and its associations, the present with its terrible realities, and endeavoring to prepare himself for the last great change that awaits us all. He heard, with painful distinctness, the busy sounds of the workmen preparing the gibbet, from which, as he believed, he would soon be launched into eternity. Had there been light in his cell, it would have exhibited features pale, but firm and composed, as one who is fully resolved to meet his fate in a manner becoming a brave man and a true soldier. He had no hope of pardon or reprieve; and he looked upon himself as one already done with the things of earth, and standing within the very portals of the invisible world. And yet he was still mortal; and there were moments, when he pictured to himself the inconsolable grief of her he loved, that he felt his heart quail, and that his doom was indeed terrible. Death, abstractly considered, had no terrors for him; it was only as regarded the living that he trembled.

"Poor Rosalie!" he murmured—"it will break thy fond heart, and thou wilt sink to a premature grave! But then," he added, in a more cheerful mood, "we shall the sooner meet again, to roam forever through the blissful fields of paradise. Oh! but for thee, dearest, and my country, I could die content—but God's will be done."

As Milford said this, half aloud, he heard footsteps in the corridor that ran past his cell. The next moment he heard a key applied to the lock of his door, and the rattling of bolts and chains, and as the door was thrown open, he beheld the under turnkey, with a light in his hand, and just behind him, somewhat in the shade, the martial figure of Colonel Dundas.

"Ah!" said Milford—"so my hour has come. Well, I am prepared; though if it be now sunrise, time has flown more swiftly than I thought."

To this there was no answer. The turnkey entered and took off his irons; and the moment he stood unshackled, Colonel Dundas said:

"Captain Milford, you will please to follow me."

On entering the corridor, Milford was surprised to see no guard in attendance. He made no comment, however, asked no questions, but followed his military guide in silence. He was still more surprised when he found himself conducted to the street, instead of to the yard of the prison, and perceived that darkness still enshrouded the earth. A carriage stood in front of the prison; and between it and the steps, which he now descended, a solitary sentinel was slowly pacing. The latter halted, on perceiving Colonel Dundas, and lowered his musket, in military deference to his superior. The Colonel took no notice of the man, but moved direct to the carriage, the door of which was opened by a small lad, who stood in waiting. Motioning Milford to enter, Dundas sprang in after him, the door was closed, the boy mounted the rumble, the driver cracked his whip, the horses sprang forward, and the carriage rolled away with great velocity, bearing our hero he knew not whither.

Milford was all amazement and perplexity; but he asked no questions, and his military conductor vouchsafed no explanation. On entering the carriage, he fancied he caught a glimpse of a figure on the forward seat; but he was not certain; and the moment the door closed, it was too dark within to distinguish any object. Not a word was spoken during the ride; and when the carriage stopped, the door was again opened by the boy. Colonel Dundas was the first to alight, Milford followed next, and then, to his surprise, was in turn followed by a female, so closely muffled in hood and cloak that neither her figure nor features could be seen, even had there been light enough for the purpose. But what surprised the Captain still more than all, was the fact, that he had been conveyed to the bank of the Hudson, which he could faintly perceive flowing along before him, and at a point of the town where there were no houses.

The whole party, as by pre-arrangement, now moved to the edge of the water in silence; where a boat was discovered, half hidden among a cluster of bushes, and tied to a sapling.

"There," said Colonel Dundas, pointing to it, "my business ends here;" and without another word, he hastily retraced his steps to the carriage, which was soon whirling away and lost in the darkness.

Milford, as may be readily conjectured, was stupified with amazement; and he rubbed his eyes, to assure himself it was not all a dream. Suddenly the whole truth flashed upon him; and advancing to the female, who seemed to tremble at his approach, he exclaimed:

"Rosalie!"

There was a thrilling cry; and the next moment his neck was encircled by the arms of her he loved, her head was pillowed on his manly breast, and tears and sobs alone attested how deep were her emotions of joy.

"And have you then resolved to fly with me, dearest?" he tenderly inquired, when the first transports on the part of both had begun to give way to calmer, but not less happy feelings.

"Yes, dear Edgar, yes," she murmured; "I will fly with you even to the end of the earth: we must part no more."

"Bless you, fairest and best of mortals! my own loved one, bless you! and as I deal with you, so may Heaven with me. Oh! this happiness is too great for me to bear; and to you, my own, sweet Rosalie, I owe it all—ay, even my life and freedom—and to you, from this moment, that life shall be devoted; and I will guard and cherish you as a tender flower, on which even the winds of Heaven might blow too roughly."

The party, the third one of which was Munee, now entered the boat; and as Milford rowed slowly across the stream, Rosalie gave him a brief account of her interview with Sir Henry Clinton.

"But how did you first learn of my arrest?" he inquired.

"You remember Henry, Edgar?"

"Ah, yes; and so the poor lad escaped?"

"He fell behind your party in running; and finding his pursuers gaining on him, fortunately secreted himself till they had passed, and afterward saw you in custody. He then hurried home, changed his habiliments, and now appears before you in *propria persona.*"

"I do not understand you."

"Ah, Edgar," said Rosalie, laughing, "I fear you will think me a strange creature, and unworthy of your high encomiums. You little dream how often I have been your companion, when you thought me far away. But I have no longer a reason for concealment, and you must know all. In a word, then, Henry Pierpot and Rosalie Du Pont are one and the same person."

"Good heavens!" cried Milford, dropping his oars in astounding amazement, and for some moments sitting as one stupified. "Yes, yes," he said at length, "I see it all now. O, Rosalie, Rosalie—fool, fool that I was to mistake thee for a mulatto youth! Yes, I see it all; and now I understand why that impertinent lad called me Edgar in the country."

Rosalie indulged her mirth freely, and Milford soon joined her; though he felt chagrined at what he considered his want of penetration; but when she assured him that others, even Carlini, had failed to recognize her till she had made herself known, he became better satisfied with himself, and replied:

"After all, dear Rosalie, you looked and played your part so well, that, in giving you great credit, I hope to escape being thought a simpleton."

"But you will forgive me, dear Edgar?"

"Forgive you? Come, come, that is too much. I shall be happy to *exchange* pardons, and still remain your debtor."

Reader, our story has run its course, and there is little more to be said. On reaching the west bank of the Hudson, Milford was soon fortunate in finding his friends, and great was the rejoicing of all parties. Carlini, Josh, and Dame Hagold, had all succeeded in making their escape. They had waited in their boat, near the city, for more than an hour, hoping to be joined by Milford; but as he came not, they finally gave him up for lost: and rowing across the stream, reported to Lee their failure. The latter was greatly disappointed, for he had indulged the hope of soon having the traitor in his possession; but he was in a measure prepared for the news, having heard the alarm that had been so uproariously sounded. He thought it not impossible, though improbable, that Milford might yet escape; and had resolved to wait till daylight, before abandoning him to his fate

Our friends now prepared to set out for the American camp; and just as the morning guns resounded from the different forts, batteries, and shipping in the harbour, and the first streak of day shot up in the east, the cavalcade ascended a slight eminence, whence the city of New York could be faintly seen in the distance. An angle of the hill soon shut it from the view of all, more than one of whom had beheld it for the last time.

On reaching Tappan, Major Lee, Captain Milford, and Rosalie, at once repaired to head-quarters, where they had an interview with the commander-in-chief, which lasted more than an hour. When they were about to depart, General Washington arose, and taking the hand of our hero, said:

"Captain Milford, I sincerely regret that the circumstances you have named will deprive us of so valuable an officer; but as a man of honor, you can not serve again during our struggle for independence. That you have failed in your gallant attempt to seize the traitor, I am convinced was more your misfortune than your fault. You deserve well of your country; and, as the military executive of the nation, I thank you for your zeal. It was my intention, at the first suitable opportunity, to have recommended you to Congress for promotion; and had you volunteered less in the great cause of liberty, perhaps your military reward would have been greater; though I trust that your conscience, and the happiness I see in store for you, will be ample compensation for what you have lost. Retire to peaceful and domestic life, and may the blessings of Heaven attend you! In my view, your lot is enviable; for deeply do I long for that time when I may be permitted to enjoy the same quiet retirement."

Milford was too much overcome with emotion, to make any reply, and he pressed the hand of the great American chieftain in silence. Turning to Rosalie, Washington now took her hand, and continued:

"And from you, Rosalie, Arminé Countess d'Auvergne, daughter of one of our distinguished allies, I can not part, without returning you my humble thanks, in behalf of that oppressed and struggling people you have so long and faithfully served, at so much noble, heroic self-sacrifice. Your ladyship's history is not unknown to me; I have long since heard all, from your gallant friend, the noble Marquis de Lafayette; and I, at least, can appreciate your generous efforts, in behalf of the cause of liberty, as they deserve. Nobly born, surrounded by affluence, with a lofty title and unspotted lineage, you might have passed your days in ease, and luxury, and sat down an equal with the greatest and proudest of the earthly titled. Without ambition, because unneeded, and because it could add nothing to the lustre of your ladyship's name, it required naught but the pure and generous promptings of your heart, to induce you to boldly venture thousands of miles, among strangers, and espouse a cause, which many, in your ladyship's station, deem disgraceful, and which is diametrically opposed to the system of monarchy under which your ladyship was born and bred. In consideration of all I have named, I feel that my poor thanks is a miserable reward for your many sacrifices; but, Countess d'Auvergne, it is all I have to offer. May you live to see liberty triumphant, and in a happy and contented heart find heaven's greatest boon, without which all earthly treasures, titles, and distinctions, are to be counted as dross."

Rosalie was deeply affected, and it was some moments ere she ventured to trust her voice in reply. At length she articulated, in a scarcely audible tone:

"Your excellency has been pleased to overrate my poor abilities, my humble endeavors, and to flatter me far beyond my deserts; and had I been ambitious of reward, the present would a hundred fold repay me for the little I have done. I will only say, in conclusion, that I, who have associated with kings, princes, and the noble of the realm, now look upon this moment as the proudest and happiest of my life; and had I a single claim to prefer, I would only ask, that I may ever enjoy the regard and esteem of your excellency."

* * * * * * * *

A short time subsequent to the foregoing events, the solemn, sacred ceremony, which united in a tie indissoluble the fortunes of Edgar and Rosalie, was performed by the chaplain of the army, in the presence of General Washington, the Marquis de Lafayette, Count d'Auvergne, and many other noble and distinguished officers of the allied armies.

Captain Milford settled in the interior of Massachusetts, and, with his lovely wife, long lived to enjoy the blessings of that liberty which both so dearly prized, and to assist in gaining which both had undergone so many perils and privations. Rosalie received a large fortune from her father, who, at the close of the war, went back to his native land, settled up his affairs, and returned to the country of his adoption, where he lived to an advanced age, enjoying a quiet happiness, in being surrounded with numerous descendants, all of whom venerated and loved him.

Munee followed the fortunes of her mistress.

Josh took up his abode with Captain Milford, and died a confirmed old bachelor; declaring to the last, that "he never seen a gal he cared a cent abeout, without 'twas Sally Stacy; and as she'd kind 'o gin him the mitten, he wasn't so darned particular abeout her; and he guessed he'd have his revenge, by letting all the tarnel coquette critters alone, the rest o' his born days, and content himself with being Captain Milford's hired man."

George Nugent enlisted in the army, and so distinguished himself, that, before the close of the war, he received the commission of Lieutenant; and, afterward, by energy and perseverance, accumulated a fortune, which he long lived to enjoy, under the benign reign of peace, in the land of liberty.

Carlini found means to secretly return to New York, where he remained, during the war, in the triple capacity of astrologer, magnetizer, and spy. After the war, he took up his abode with George Nugent, with whom he lived till appointed to a foreign office under the administration of Washington. He died abroad. His early history was never known beyond his most intimate friends, with whom the secret perished.

Dame Hagold, we regret to say, died of grief for the loss of her unworthy son, who was executed by the British shortly subsequently to the events narrated.

Paulding, Williams, and Van Wert, the captors of Andre, were rewarded by a public vote of thanks from Congress, an annual pension of two hundred dollars each for life, and a silver medal each, from the same source, bearing on one side the inscription, "*Fidelity*," and on the other, "*Vincit Amor Patriæ:*" "*The Love of Country Conquers.*"

Smith was ruined by the part he took in the schemes of the traitor—whether innocently or not, we have no positive means of knowing. He was tried by a military tribunal; but not being convicted, was handed over to the civil authorities; from whom, after great mental and bodily suffering, he eventually escaped, by breaking out of prison; and subsequently fled to England, where he published a book, containing his adventures and defense, in which he bitterly reflected upon the Americans and their commander-in-chief. His wife had previously died of bodily disease, assisted by family affliction.

On the night when the last trial of our gallant spies was made to seize Arnold, Sergeant Champe was safely aboard one of the British transports in the harbor, whither he had been removed during the day, together with the whole of the American Legion, preparatory to an expedition against Virginia, to be conducted by the traitor himself. This explanation accounts for the absence of both Champe and Arnold on that eventful night. The former finally made his escape from his enemies, in Virginia, and returned to his friends. He afterward had an interview with Washington, "who," in the language of a biographer, "munificently anticipated every desire of the Sergeant, and presented him with a discharge from further service, lest he might, in the vicissitudes of war, fall into the hands of the enemy, when, if recognized, he was sure to die on a gibbet." The close of his life was spent in Kentucky.

Of Arnold the traitor, we will only say in conclusion, that, at the close of the war, he sailed with his family for England; where as a general thing, he was treated with that neglect and contumely his base conduct merited

Men of high standing did not scruple to openly despise and insult him; and if he ventured to demand satisfaction, by the code of honor, the insult was doubled and thrown back in his teeth, by the reply, "*that no gentleman could stoop to fight a traitor.*" He finally died in obscurity, without a single friend to mourn his loss. Surely his fate was not an enviable one.

Of the other characters introduced in the foregoing pages, it is unnecessary to speak—their names and deeds are already recorded on the living pages of history.

Thus we close an important episode of the American Revolution. If we have succeeded in pleasing you, reader—in beguiling a few hours that you will not look upon as misspent—if we have succeeded in presenting to your imagination one striking picture of "the times that tried men's souls," and arousing in your breast one patriotic feeling for our beloved country—one single desire to see that Union preserved which cost our fathers so much to establish—then is our end gained, and we shall rest satisfied: otherwise, our labor has been in vain. In either case, Adieu!

THE END.

MISS ELIZA A. DUPUY'S NOVELS.

Emma Walton; or, Trials and Triumph. 8vo, paper cover. **Price 50 cents.**

Annie Seldon; or, The Concealed Treasure. 8vo, paper cover. **Price 25 cents.**

Miss Dupuy's name is familiar to the readers of fiction throughout the Union, and deservedly so; for in addition to a fluent and natural style, by which she is at once at home with her readers, a happy faculty of delineation and description, and just conception of the probable and the possible, eschewing humdrum improbabilities, ever avoiding vulgarity of sentiment or expression, her writings tend to the inculcation of virtue and morality.

SIR E. L. BULWER'S BEST NOVELS.

The Last Days of Pompeii. 8vo, paper cover. **Price 50 cents.**

Eugene Aram. 8vo, paper cover. **Price 50 cents.**

Pelham; or, the Adventures of a Gentleman. 8vo, paper cover. **Price 50 cents.**

Ernest Maltravers. 8vo, paper cover. **Price 50 cents.**

Alice; or, The Mysteries: a Sequel to Ernest Maltravers. 8vo, paper cover. **Price 50 cents.**

The Lady of Lyons; or, Love and Pride: a Play in Five Acts. Paper cover. **Price 15 cents.**

Zanoni, a Romance of Italy. 8vo, paper cover. **Price 50 cents.**

Godolphin. 8vo, paper cover. **Price 50 cents.**

ALEX. DUMAS'S NOVELS.

The Convert of Saint Paul, a tale of Greece and Rome; translated by Henry W. Herbert, Esq. 8vo, paper cover. **Price 25 cents.**

Louisa; or, Adventures of a French Milliner; translated by J. Griswold. 8vo, paper cover. **Price 50 cents.**

HENRY COCKTON'S NOVELS.

[AUTHOR OF VALENTINE VOX, ETC.]

The Love Match, designed to illustrate the various conflicting influences which sprang from the union of Mr. and Mrs. Tom Todd. 8vo, paper cover. **Price 50 cents.**

The Prince; or, George St. George Julian. 8vo, paper cover. **Price 75 cents.**

EDWIN F. ROBERT'S NOVELS.

The Twin Brothers; or, The Victims of the Press-Gang, a Romance of the Land and Sea. 8vo, paper cover. **Price 25 cents.**

The Road to Ruin; or, The Dangers of the Town, a Career of Crime. 8vo, paper cover. **Price 25 cents.**

G. P. R. JAMES'S BEST NOVELS.

One in a Thousand; or, The Days of Henry IV. 8vo, paper cover. **Price 50 cents.**

Richelieu, a tale of France. 8vo, paper cover. **Price 50 cents.**

The Robber. 8vo, paper cover. **Price 50 cents.**

Philip Augustus; or, The Brothers in Arms. 8vo, paper cover. **Price 50 cents.**

The Gipsy. 8vo, paper cover. **Price 50 cents.**

The Ancient Regime; or, Annette de St. Morin. 8vo, paper cover. **Price 50 cents.**

The Gentleman of the Old School. 8vo, paper cover. **Price 50 cents.**

"Richelieu is one of the most spirited, amusing, and interesting romances I ever read."—*Prof. Wilson.*

"His romances are almost entirely founded on historical facts, and the subjects drawn from every age and clime."

EUGENE SUE'S BEST NOVELS.

Latreaumont; or, The Conspiracy: a Historical Romance of the days of Louis XIV; translated from the French. 8vo, paper cover. **Price 50 cents.**

The Temptation; or, The Duchess of Almeda: a Romantic Tale; translated from the French. 8vo, paper cover. **Price 25 cents.**

The Princess of Hansfeld, a Story of Love and Intrigue; translated from the French. 8vo, paper cover. **Price 25 cents.**

The Commander of Malta, with illustrations. 8vo, paper cover. **Price 25 cents.**

GOOD BOOKS, BY VARIOUS AUTHORS.

A Man Made of Money, by DOUGLAS JERROLD, editor of "Punch," "Mrs. Caudle's Lectures," etc. 8vo, paper cover. **Price 25 cents.**

Abednego, the Money-Lender: a Romance; by MRS. GORE. 8vo, paper cover. **Price 25 cents.**

"Antonio and old Shylock, both stand forth." —*Shakspeare.*

Adventures of Caleb Williams; or, Things as They Are. By WILLIAM GODWIN. 8vo, paper cover. **Price 50 cents.**

"It is a book which takes rank among the classics of English literature. It is one of the most vigorous, masterly, and philosophic fictions in the language, or in any other."—*Daily Globe.*

"For fifty years it has been considered an extraordinary work, and amid all the changes of taste and circumstances which have been in the literary world since its publication, has kept a position as a classic."

"If the power of William Godwin can be relished now, there is still some hope of a manly literature."—*Cincinnati Daily Gazette.*

"The story is intensely interesting, and the characters admirably delineated; * * * its execution bears the mark of the highest order of intellect."—*Logan Gazette.*

Alonzo and Melissa; or, The Unfeeling Father. An American tale. By DANIEL JACKSON, Jr. 8vo. **Price 25 cents.**

Adventures of Mr. and Mrs. Sandboys. By HENRY MAYHEW. 8vo, paper cover. **Price 50 cents.**

Blue Laws of Connecticut. The Code of 1650. Being a Compilation of the Earliest Laws and Orders of the General Court of Connecticut. Also, The Constitution, or Civil Compact entered into and adopted by the towns of Windsor, Hartford, and Wethersfield, in 1638–9. To which are added some extracts from the Laws and Judicial Proceedings of New Haven Colony, commonly called BLUE LAWS. Paper cover. **Price 50 cents.**

A curious record of the early days of our country.

Caudle, Mrs., Curtain Lectures, by PUNCH, (Douglas Jerrold.) Paper cover. **Price 25 cents.**

"Rich Humor and Fun in this book."

Christopher Tadpole, The Struggles and Adventures of, by ALBERT SMITH. 8vo, paper cover. **Price 75 cents.**

Charlotte Temple, a tale of Truth, by MRS. ROWSON. Paper cover. **Price 20 cents.**

More copies of this highly interesting and celebrated work have probably been printed, and worn out in reading, than any other book of the class in the English language, and the demand and interest continue unabated.

Clay, Henry, his Principal Speeches, and Sketch of his life. Compiled from the latest and best authorities. 8vo, paper cover. **Price 25 cents.**

Count Monte Leone; or, The Spy in Society: a legend of the Carbonari of France and Italy; translated from the French of H. de St. Georges. 8vo, paper cover. **Price 50 cents.**

Collegians, The, a novel, by GERALD GRIFFIN, Esq., the author of "Tales of the Five Senses," etc. 8vo, paper cover. **Price 50 cents.**

"We regard it quite an era in a reading life to peruse *The Collegians.*"—*Wm. Howitt.*

Doniphan's Expedition, containing an account of the Conquest of New Mexico; Gen. Kearney's Overland Expedition to California; Doniphan's Campaign against the Navajos; his Unparalleled March upon Chihuahua and Durango; and the operations of General Price at Santa Fe; with a sketch of the life of Colonel Doniphan; by JOHN T. HUGHES, of the 1st Regiment of Missouri Cavalry. Illustrated with plans of battle-fields and fine engravings. 8vo, paper cover. **Price 50 cents.**

Ellena, a Romance, by MRS. RADCLIFFE, author of "Romance of the Forest," "Mysteries of Udolpho," etc. Octavo, paper cover. **Price 50 cents.**

This is a thrilling work by a well-known and talented authoress.

Empress of the Isles; or, The Lake Bravo: a Romance of the Canadian Struggle in 1837. By CHARLEY CLEMLINE. 8vo, paper cover. **Price 25 cents.**

Eveline Mandeville, by ALVIN ADDISON, author of "The Rival Hunters." 8vo, paper cover. **Price 25 cents.**

Grace Willoughby, a Tale of the Wars of King James. By W. H. MAXWELL, Esq., author of "Brian O'Linn," etc., etc. 8vo, paper cover. **Price 50 cents.**

Glanmore; or, The Bandits of Saratoga: a Romance of the Revolution. By PARK CLINTON. 8vo, paper cover. **Price 25 cents.**

Heroic Women of France, comprising examples of the Noble Conduct of Women during the French Revolution. From the French of M. Du Broca. Paper cover. **Price 25 cents.**

Ike McCandliss, and other Stories; or, Incidents in the Life of a Soldier. Illustrated. By GEORGE C. FURBER, author of "Twelve Months' Volunteer." 8vo, paper cover. **Price 25 cents.**

A truly entertaining and mirth-provoking book.

Jeremiah Saddlebag's Journey to the Gold Diggings. Illustrated with **113** engravings. 8vo, paper cover. **Price 25 cents.**

James Wellard, companion of John A. Murel. Illustrated. 8vo, paper cover. **Price 25 cents.**

www.ingramcontent.com/pod-product-compliance
Lightning Source LLC
LaVergne TN
LVHW021425110826
845150LV00007B/2095

* 9 7 8 1 4 2 5 5 0 8 0 2 9 *